Welcome to Our Conglomerate— You're Fired!

Also by the Same Author

The Self-Made Man

Welcome to Our Conglomerate— You're Fired!

ISADORE BARMASH

 Delacorte Press, New York

**To My Mother,
Who Always Believed**

Contents

Preface

Nothing is more visceral in the human animal than the acquisitive instinct. Whether a man collects objects, money or businesses, it is usually marked by a headlong rush to outdo others. Why? First, to achieve security; second, affluence; third, power. Anything that he might also pick up on the way is not to be discarded, either. Individuals behave this way as individuals; businessmen, through businesses.

The fervor of individuals acting as businessmen has made the merger and acquisition trend the most significant characteristic in the American business scene in the last 20 years. Its grasp and effect on people—propelling them into a form of ego-money-merger mania—built a subculture of social and luncheon table talk around the subject, made the "urge to merge" and its variations part of the American idiom and led to the devising of new expressions, greetings and catchwords that combined the trend and the time.

An astrologically inclined chairman of a meeting on mergers

xi

greeted his audience with, "Welcome to the Age of Acquireus." *The New York Times* wondered what happens when a company is taken over by a conglomerate, noting that one executive said: "I don't know about the others but we got the mushroom treatment. Right after the acquisition we were kept in the dark. Then they covered us with manure. Then they cultivated us. After that, they let us stew awhile. And, finally, they canned us."

Coyness became the subterfuge of those who yearned to be acquired. Declared a determined go-it-alone company founder, "I am not for sale. I do not want to get married. I do not want to merge. I do not want to be wooed. I do not want to be pursued. Except, of course, if the price is right. If that's the case, I'll meet you anytime and anywhere you say."

Of course, it soon became apparent that the gleam in the eye of men locked in merger deals was genuinely avaricious. One merger expert quoted herein observed that mergers bring out men's different qualities, especially their greed, avarice, frustration and hangups. Very rarely have mergers brought out the qualities of altruism, heroism, charity and love. He cited the man in partnership with his brother who said, "I'll sell on one condition only. That you give me $50 a share, but my brother should only get $25."

The period couldn't help but also lead to the "finder's" syndrome. "Let's find a company that wants to sell and a company that wants to buy and we'll share the finder's fee" was not an infrequent suggestion heard in many walks of life. It was certainly as rewarding, probably less frustrating and maybe less costly than betting on horses.

I have tried in this book to tell the inside story of business takeovers and of the circus that functions in the merger field; to spell out some of the human drama, to relate the people to the actions, the economic, financial and political forces; and to pinpoint some of the intrigue, "unethica" and conflict of interest that emanates from that five-ring circus. As a financial writer for *The New York Times*, I have acquired what I hope may be termed a modest knowledge of those rings.

For those unfamiliar with financial terms a glossary is appended. Every incident and story told in this book is true and accurate, but I have been compelled by the libel laws in a number of them not to use actual names. I find myself reluctant to spend my hard-earned royalties in court.

ISADORE BARMASH

Welcome to Our Conglomerate— You're Fired!

An Early Note on
a Late-Hour Concept

Business mergers, like babies, are mostly made at night.

Are you the seller? The morning comes to you with an instant recall of the night's deed. Along with that shock, you become aware of a cold overcast outside your window. You have an immediate feeling of dour reality, then a rumbling in the stomach and the first hint of bile in the mouth. You begin to feel your eyes bulging in disbelief at the enormity of it. You have given it all away for a pittance, married off your business, so that in the morning it is no longer all yours, as it has been almost, it seems, forever.

You're the buyer? Then the morning after has an altogether different hue. It is rosy—with orange—the color of hope tinting its edges. You have bought yourself instant success, or so you think. Your eyes, too, enlarge. With money that you probably don't own and with a gambler's instinct that you probably shouldn't have, you have bought someone else's hopes and years of struggle and success.

1

I can't fault you if you doubt that mergers are mostly made at night. It would seem to be something that should be left to the fresh clarity of the morning, but more often it isn't. Emotions in deals charge up slowly during the day. Then, suddenly, in the very late hours, there comes a release as you lose your head, so onerous are the fatigue, dismay and confusion. The signatures are affixed, the opposing lawyers smile wearily at one another in joint triumph and—

I know, because I was there, not long ago, as an outsider on the inside. One night, as I was preparing to leave work, the telephone rang and soon I knew that I could not leave for the pleasures of the subway. It was the secretary in a law firm calling for the president and founder of a company that had recently announced that it was holding "exploratory discussions" on a merger with another company. The talks had progressed and it was well known that the boards of the two firms would soon meet to consummate an agreement.

That night, in fact, just at that hour, said the secretary blithely but with a tremulous undertone, the boards were holding that meeting. Could I "sit tight" for a little while? she wanted to know, tensely.

I would remain, I said, but I refused to "sit tight." There was a reproachful silence, then she managed a brittle, "Thank you, I'll call you right back."

I slumped into my chair, feeling a little sorry for myself and ruminating on why businessmen can't be reasonable. An hour was to pass this way, during which I decided to ring up on another phone my friend Harold Harolds (a fictitious name, of course, as are all the names in this chapter), who was a company finder with a curiously psychological bent of mind.

He was in his office, as I expected, having his usual nightly chicken salad on white and black coffee. As a late worker who never went home to his family in Larchmont until 10:00 or 11:00 P.M., he similarly paid little attention to his food. "I hate to interrupt your repast," I told him, "but I was just curious. Here I am hanging around the office for a late story on an important merger. Why can't deals be worked out during normal business hours, anyway?"

I heard Harold's teeth working through the chicken salad, but he replied quickly with clear diction if somewhat moot logic:

> I could give you lots of obvious reasons, like emotions reaching a boiling point after many hours of discussion—don't forget, giving away your business is nothing as superficial as giving away your daughter—but I seriously suspect it is something else entirely. People who give up their businesses merely for money and people who buy them for profits or power would hardly feel that it would be proper to arrange the matter during normal hours. Something as serious as a business merger or acquisition has to have the aura of group soul-searching, psychodrama and personal sacrifice. So it's done at night by common consent—the consent, you understand, doesn't even have to be articulated—to keep it all going into the wee hours and to sign on the dotted line about the time the milkman starts making his rounds.

I thanked him rather weakly and he hung up with evident self-satisfaction.

Almost an hour to the second the woman who had telephoned me rang up again to ask me to come right over to the forty-first floor of a building on upper Fifth Avenue.

It turned out to be the office of one of New York's most prestigious law firms. Even though it was almost 8:00 P.M., the lavish suite of offices was ablaze with light. All the secretarial and clerical help seemed to be on tap, too, and I was ushered in with all the welcoming fanfare of pleased stares, a thrilled "Oh, yes indeed," and the softest chair that they could find. Obviously I was to be in almost at the natal moment itself.

"What's happening?" I asked the secretary, who introduced herself as a Gladys Hamerman. Her eyebrows rose as she motioned to a room off to my left about 25 feet. "They're still hammering things out—we were so sure they would be finished by now, but it really shouldn't be too long."

Attempting to activate my antennae, I could well imagine what was going on inside the conference room, who its human ingredients were and what its content was. As I learned later, there were about 20 people there representing the two companies, with each side confronting the other across the table. Besides the principals of the two firms, there were lawyers, accountants, tax experts, a consulting psychologist, two secretaries and a stenotypist.

As I sat there fidgeting through 15 minutes and then a half hour, it all came to me. I had been summoned not merely to be in a good position to report the event accurately and from near firsthand observation, but also to become part of the drama itself. Not that I didn't appreciate the advantage of being the only reporter to be present at the tieing of the bow at one of the year's most important business mergers. Yet I realized rather uncomfortably that, while I was being given an opportunity, I was also being used.

About 40 minutes after my arrival I got up and said to Gladys, "You know, I think—" But the rest of my intended sentence, "I'll have to follow this up by telephone from home," could not be uttered, because a young man in a dark blue suit, a flashy red tie and a soft white shirt suddenly emerged from the labor room, saw me, stopped short and exclaimed, with not just idle curiosity: "What the hell is he doing here?"

Gladys and the surprised young man, obviously a partner in the law firm, then had a whispered conversation during which he gesticulated dramatically at the room and at me and then spun off down the hall. Red-faced, evidently mortified, Gladys came over and said, "I'm terribly sorry. That was Mr. Garrison. He said that under the circumstances, with everything being so confidential, would you mind waiting in his office until they're ready for you?"

I told her that it was time for me to leave anyway, a statement which seemed to horrify her. She pleaded, "But Mr. Morton insisted that we have you here. Please don't leave, not until I get word to him in the conference room that you plan to leave. Please."

Her eyes suddenly filled with tears. I let her escort me to a hallway more removed from the battle area and into a lush lawyer's cove that turned out to be that of the surprised young man with the blue suit and red tie, judging by the law degree and the photographs on his wall. I was angry, tired, and felt completely useless. I had figured that it was Morton who had issued the invitation for me to come over, but this was getting silly. Then the door opened and Morton came in. He was in his midfifties, dapper and saturnine, a tycoon with boom-

ing voice and a histrionic flair for making money and letting the world hear of it. I had known him for years and had never quite made up my mind whether I liked him more than I disliked him. He wasn't exactly a phony, because he certainly produced: he had come from a really poor background and was really a great philanthropist. But for years I had been irritated by his unflagging attempts to control everything, everyone and every situation, just as he had been trying to make the merger with an even larger company, whose founder was less dynamic and self-aggrandizing but more brilliant.

"These goddam lawyers," Morton said. "One of them got nervous because you were sitting so close to the action. Nervous little bastard, always worried about the SEC, FTC, maybe even the CIA. Look—come out. I'll make you more comfortable."

"No, I've really got to go. Just give me a number where I can call you and—"

Morton had taken my arm and was moving me along. "I want you to stay. It can't be more than another 15 minutes. Let me take you into a more comfortable office. It will be worthwhile for you, I guarantee it. You will be the only one with the inside story."

A minute later I was ensconced in an even more lavish office. I had lost any sense of direction now, not knowing if I was closer or further from the conference room, where Morton was now holding forth and was probably wielding his verbal meat cleaver. But, practically immediately Gladys came in with a tray of Cutty Sark, a glass, a container of shelled peanuts and a tray with two expensive cigars. "Please make yourself comfortable," she said, her eyes swimming with gratitude. "Mr. Morton was so distressed."

An hour later I was still there, standing at the window, looking down some 40 floors to Fifth Avenue, which was awash in moonlight reflected through a slight drizzle and the haze of polluted air.

Below, people walked like meandering ants, traffic struggled in a sluggish game, the store windows were lit up garishly. All of it was framed in the artificial backdrop of lights strung across the Manhattan or Brooklyn or Queens bridges that I could make out and the lights of the streets heading north and east and south. The immensity of the big city lay before me, static, glistening, wet, and it was seemingly immortal, or (such was my mood) until the bomb.

Yet almost at my elbow something of very immediate drama was in the making, within which a human comedy was being played. Two big companies employing about 50,000 people were about to join forces, climaxing dreams or creating nightmares for some and unfolding new opportunities and disappointments for many more. Millions of dollars—somewhere around $100 million, I figured—would be laid out in cash and stock as a dowry. Both companies were well known across the country. The announcement of their "exploratory talks" had sharply affected their stocks on the big board. The news had been carried in hundreds of newspapers, magazines and other publications, on radio and television.

I opened the window, with some difficulty, thinking for a moment of shouting down at those aimlessly walking along Fifth Avenue, "Hey, you'd never guess what in hell is going on up here. That big merger you read or heard about, it's all taking place right now at this moment in a smoke-filled room on the forty-first floor of this building!" Then, of course, I realized how silly that was. I was simply getting rocky.

As I closed the window, hoping that no one below had seen me and thought he might have caught a potential jumper, I found Gladys at my side. "Come," she whispered. "They're ready for you."

Outside, at my original station, I found half a dozen people waiting. Morton, his face shining with victory, introduced me to his top team, some of whom I already knew. The same glow of elation made their faces round, joyous, proud. But no face was more round, joyous and proud than Morton's.

"What were you doing while you were waiting?" he asked, his arm around my shoulder. "I bet you could hardly wait."

I looked him in the eye and said, "I was watching the people walking along Fifth Avenue. I was wondering how many thousands of them would have liked to come up here and wait almost two hours if they had known what was going on."

Morton grinned and slammed me on the back. "What a goddam sense of humor! That's one thing that I always liked about you." He turned to his people and repeated it. But the way he told it to them, I knew he meant just the opposite.

"Now," he intoned, his heavy black eyebrows dancing, "to fulfill my promise. I want you to talk to someone. And then we'll go out to dinner, the three of us, and you can ask us anything you want. And every goddam word will be all on the record!"

I replied that I would have swooned from sheer delight, only my weak physical condition probably would have made me fall in the other direction. But I don't think he heard me.

He went into the conference room. I knew, of course, whom he would bring out. It had to be Otto Freeman. He was the head of the other company, the one that would not be the survivor but was being merged into Morton's firm. Otto was just the opposite type, a lean, inwardly torn genius, an engineer who had developed a big electronics company but who hated personal confrontations of any kind, simply hated the media and feared all strangers. His only real problem, though, was that he hadn't Morton's drive and brass, and he knew that better than anyone else.

All of us waiting there couldn't help overhearing the conversation going on just inside the conference-room doorway. It went something like this:

"Come on, Otto, I told you I had invited him here. This is a history-making merger. It's only right that he should be here. Come out and at least say hello. This is for posterity."

"Screw posterity. You talk to him."

"Otto, what's wrong with you? You afraid of a newspaperman?"

"Hell, yes. I just don't want to have anything to do with that pain in the ass. You talk to him—I'll just go out the back."

"That's just like you, Otto. No wonder all those federal contracts slipped through your fingers. You yourself said that this merger is your lifeline, but you've got to come through, too. You got to face up to a tough situation and bull it through, goddamit. That's the way you've got to play this game."

They emerged. Morton had his arm around Otto, supporting him and encouraging him at the same time. The unwilling

Freeman, ten years younger than his new partner, looked at least 20 years older. In fact, to put it mildly, he looked like death itself. His face was pallid and his chops were drawn, his eyes were tortured and red and he seemed to have trouble drawing his breath.

Morton introduced us. I almost couldn't help quailing under Otto's hot glare. As we shook hands (his was like an expiring fish), he said, "You wrote some rough ones about me. Anything personal?"

How would you answer that? I foolishly resorted to desperate humor. "Sure. I'm jealous of that big dowry."

Morton came through. He guffawed and slapped us both on the back. "Goddamit" he said, snapping his finger at his executive vice-president, "this calls for a celebration. Who stole the booze?"

Otto revived a bit after a couple of drinks. The three of us then walked through the ranks of possibly 30 people in the law office on our way out to the elevator, like a triumphant procession after a hard-fought battle. I never saw so many obedient smiles, heard so much well-wishing from so many people. It should have been inspiring and might have been, if I hadn't been so pooped and hadn't felt guilty about Otto.

Down on Fifth Avenue we didn't mind the slight drizzle. The cool air and the spray on our faces were invigorating. I looked up and could just barely make out the windows of the law offices. Some lights were being extinguished as I watched, but others remained on. How long, I wondered, would they stay on into the night, picking up the pieces?

It was well past ten o'clock and we had a late dinner at one of the city's best Italian restaurants. Both men talked to me for hours, and it turned out to be worthwhile for me journalistically, if you will pardon that term. Otto said the night was both the greatest and the worst in his life. Morton said that the night has fulfilled his career dream of heading a $1-billion company. I said that the night would force me to file for overtime under the Newspaper Guild contract. This, oddly enough, seemed to break them both up.

When we parted, the two of them left together. Morton explained that, even though it was almost 2:00 A.M., they still had some things to talk over about their deal. Otto didn't say anything, not even good night. But I could just imagine his feelings. How far would he have to crawl?

Mergers, you see, *are* made at night.

2

Mergeritis: An Infection Accompanied by Chills, Hot Flashes and Paradoxes

Between 1960 and 1970 a fever of epidemic proportions gripped America. A virus named "mergeritis," which did not appear in any medical annals, swept the business scene. It leveled or swallowed thousands of companies, changed the lives of millions of people and carved new rills, waves and patterns on the course of the American economy.

But it gave everyone thrills and chills, often the same people. It revived yet another exciting dimension to add to the American dream in the latter twentieth century. This is, of course, to make it big and fast. But since mergers, in fact, helped to "make it" bigger and faster, what could be more irresistible?

Here's how the virus attacked and what its victim's behavior pattern was:

The organism entered the body by means of a recurring emotional condition which left the senses and the bodily orifices in a weakened, penetrable state. Almost immediately the system reeled under the trauma of the attack so that the normal anti-

11

bodies could not be rallied or deployed in time. So the state of siege of both body and mind was often short, one-sided and usually permanent.

But so effective was the virus that few victims sought a quick recovery. Most leaned back and accepted, even enjoyed the combination of malaise and promise that it brought. After all, few patients wanted to shake off quickly an indisposition that filled their pockets while it lightened their loads. When they got up occasionally, they felt heady, even nervous at the shadow that now and then flickered behind them, but the bright jingle in their pockets and the new feeling of relief acted as a sort of tranquilizer. That is, for a while, until some learned that the infection's aftereffects had illusory benefits.

These unfortunates found, in fact, that they had lost some of their most important bodily functions, such as mobility, energy, the ability to differentiate between existence and joy and, in the case of some of the most masculine, even some of their sexual virility. However, others, the majority, enjoyed the new state of euphoria because they either had always sought the jingle and the light pack—or had come to savor them as a condition of the illness itself.

The same insidious attack has marked at least three earlier periods of great American economic progress: 1898–1902, 1926–1930, and the post-World War II period.

Mergers and acquisitions somehow always seem to occur most often during periods of massive economic activity. When the thrust of business is sharp and deep, it appears the emotional level of business is at its highest pitch. The idea perhaps is to sow most quickly when the economy is obviously most fertile.

In the earliest period, about the turn of the century, the merger trend involved consolidation within certain industries that saw the emergence of some great dominant companies, the first big ones in our national history. These were giants that thrust their way through the immature economy by absorbing others in industries which had been highly fragmented. Such new, broad-based companies, whose merger efforts were geared to control or dominate a market, were Standard Oil of New Jersey, United Steel Corporation, General Electric and the American Can Company. Another big stimulus at the time was the widespread effort to capitalize on expanding natural resources.

In the 1920s, after the Sherman Anti-Trust Act had curbed some large-scale mergers and voided others, holding companies which took in an enlarged range of related products appeared as the main element of merger activity. American Cyanamid, National Dairy Products, Radio Corporation of America and General Foods were a few of the emerging firms of the time.

After World War II the widely divergent product companies known as "conglomerates" began sprouting. These were largely financially oriented combines, which sought consolidations not so much for zeal in product mixture as in earnings expansion. Often, however, the two were inseparable. Such early conglomerates were Textron, Inc., W. R. Grace and American Machine and Foundry.

In the 1960s, however, all the previous trends coalesced in a heady brew that produced a vast merger movement in the direction of both related product and nonrelated product orientation. The emphasis was more than ever on financial leverage, even where the products were complementary. It was the time of the maxi-conglomerate and the mini-conglomerate, the time of the holding company, the time of the diversified company within a broadly related product array, the time of the merger-masters and the merger-makers. It was for most of the way a time of great prosperity for bankers, Wall Street and many small investors. As the decade moved to constantly increasing rises in gross national product, the merger rate skipped annually to new heights in keeping pace with the galloping GNP.

What's the relationship between a big increase in mergers and periods of heightened business activity and expanded national economy, anyway?

The two are obviously interconnected. Mergers and acquisitions in most industries come with greater frequency when those industries are undergoing strong growth. Perhaps the main reason is that a business must change its product mixture and its approach to its market or else the force of competition and the rate of change will combine to curb its profits. This fact of business life has in itself stimulated industry growth.

Which is cause and which is effect? Take your choice.

But there was something peculiar about the merger trend of the 1960s. To me, it defied comparison with the previous consolidation for more than a few reasons. In fact, the strange combination of factors was so highly intriguing that I went to see a good friend on Wall Street. After he listened carefully for about a quarter of an hour, looking down at his ornate desk through a cone of his fingers as though it were some form of a crystal ball, he said dourly:

> It's only because I like you that I'm going to give it to you straight. Don't get yourself involved. Forget it, or you might wind up losing your professional confidence, maybe even your sanity. The whole goddam thing is too involved to be convincing to anybody. Leave it to the technicians. They'll tell it the way it is in their own complex, bloodless way and only those people who like complicated things told in a technical way will believe it.

He said a lot more, but you get the idea by now. "Listen to me now," he warned as an afterthought in all seriousness. He stared glumly down on the canyons of Wall Street from his twenty-fifth-floor suite and just shuddered.

He was referring, of course, to my plan to do a book, nontechnical and intended for the layman, on mergers and acquisitions. It would emphasize the events of the 1960s and have projections for the 1970s and beyond. As you can see, he didn't convince me. He was unquestionably older and wiser, but I didn't like his attitude, although I have to admit that he had a point. The whole matter is really quite unbelievable.

Imagine, for example, five separate forces fighting one another over a business practice. This made it not a three- but a five-ring circus.

Imagine thousands of mergers taking place during periods of excessive declines on Wall Street, such as in 1962 and 1969–1970, the consolidation trend showing a decline in percentage gain but nevertheless a sharp rise over some earlier years.

Imagine thousands of businessmen selling out their businesses when their bankers, lawyers, accountants, wives and friends warned them that it was at the time one of the most hazardous risks that they could undertake. Yet they went ahead. Were they just foolhardy, courageous or simply all played out?

Imagine the crust, *chutzpah*, and the great successes of the conglomerates that rose from a telephone and a battered desk in a back loft to building a great office tower on Park Avenue, Madison Avenue, Columbus Circle, Michigan Boulevard or Wilshire Boulevard in a scant decade, putting together companies that were about as divergent as sugar and building products, as motels and shipbuilding, as hosiery and teaching machines. All this in the face of some of the most widespread maligning of a particular form of business in years.

Imagine Wall Street backing those same conglomerates, then damning them and making dire predictions about the future of those diversiplexes. And bankers financing them as quietly as possible, then publicly condemning their practices.

Imagine the crunch on people, the insidious maneuvering and intrigues both on and off stage, the mergers that fell apart because the principals didn't like the way that their opposite numbers squinted or parted their hair, the shenanigans of the mergermasters themselves in indulging their egos while thousands of people might be affected by the simple signing of two signatures, and the thumbing of the nose at Washington.

Now you have some idea of what my Wall Street friend was driving at. Others I ran into felt the same way, cautioning me that I would be getting in over my head so much that it would be merely a fruitless exercise with frustration as its end result. They were mostly—but not quite all—of the mind that while it might be possible to tell the truth, the complexity, the enormity and the paradoxes involved would merely turn a recounting of it all into a sort of blue fantasy.

Fantasy it is, but only because it seems that way. Between 1960 and 1970, there were about 22,000 business mergers or acquisitions. Each was different from any other because of the peculiar combination of human, economic and financial characteristics. Perhaps therein lies the fantasy.

But they all had one thing in common. They were all subject to one or more of some of the wildest, most controversial developments in modern business history, paradoxical influences of a wide variety.

The surprising thing about many of these mergers and acquisitions was that they were either curiously self-defeating or destructively self-perpetuating; either economically unsound or a socioeconomic breakthrough; either doomed to failure because of the great opposition they aroused or due to succeed because they are necessarily changing the contemporary climate.

Generalities aside, what are some of those complex paradoxes, those night-day, day-night customs that seem to many to defy sense, logic and orderly enterprise in the form of growth through takeovers?

One, the federal government, which since 1968 has been conducting perhaps the most relentless campaign of antitrust action in many decades, is also the greatest proponent of business consolidation. Tax laws, for example, are driving more privately held companies into the arms of acquisition-minded suitors than any other single factor. The still loose laws involving corporate securities offer fruitful opportunities for many firms to go public which shouldn't. They have neither the growth potential nor the possible securities base to offer investors something for their money. And public ownership breeds mergers, too, because shareholders naturally push management to seek appreciation of earnings, which can most quickly be attained through acquisitions.

Of course, the government in no way has taken a directly adverse position toward mergers and acquisitions *per se.* But it, as well as several congressional committees, has taken the offensive against those consolidations which they contend have acted to lessen competition and to create monopolies. But let's face it squarely, mergers and acquisitions do tend to be synergistic, to build economic power and to move toward increasing market share. How can anyone be naïve about that?

Is the government's position to encourage business growth and progress, on one hand, and to fight the increasing power of consolidations, on the other hand, a contradictory one? Yes, it would seem so. Much more on this in later chapters.

Two, that five-ring circus I mentioned earlier—it's a battle royal consisting of Wall Street *vs.* the banks *vs.* the U.S. government *vs.* conglomerates *vs.* over 30 million investors.

Wall Street brokers and investment bankers are convinced that the commercial banks have subsidized far too many mergers which have not been either economically feasible or commercially pragmatic or sufficiently sound from a securities standpoint.

Commercial bankers feel that Wall Street and the investment community generally use their broad access to capital to underwrite or sponsor mergers or acquisitions that have no right to be born for much the same reasons that Wall Streeters claim bankers are foisting bad mergers on the American public. The big beef from the banks is that Wall Street pushes a stock based on the earnings per share of the company so that manipulation of earnings per share or undue concentration on pushing up the earnings per share becomes a way of life of merged companies.

The U.S. government, unleashing what is surely the biggest antitrust onslaught in years in the late 1960s, has curbed the incidence of conglomerate mergers. But it has also dampened the enthusiasm for giant-sized takeovers, for those in which reciprocal benefits are implicit, for those which create a larger market share in a particular geographical area and even for non-conglomerate but diversifying mergers in which more than a "foothold" is to be attained in another industry.

The upshot of all this is that many Wall Streeters, commercial bankers, corporate development or merger specialists and others on the fringes of the merger scene have been infuriated with what they are convinced is an extra heavy hand at the antitrust throttle.

I offer one untouched and unedited comment by a top executive of a leading investment bank–stock brokerage, who labeled it "The Danger of Giant Corporations *vs.* the Danger of Giant Government" (*sic*):

> I am much more concerned about the unrestrained power of Washington than I am about the power of Wall Street. The public corporation submits itself daily to the electorate, who cast their vote of confidence or no confidence through the stock market. This is real grass-roots democracy and traders comprise a really informed electorate.

Government bureaucrats can create untold havoc before enough information filters down to the public, who must then find a way to make
their voices heard. If Wall Street worked that way, Transitron would be
still be selling at 60.

Transitron, you may or may not know, wound up in 1969
at 6½.

In rebuttal to that stockbroker's comment, I offer you this,
not from government but from a senior official at one of the
country's best-known commercial banks:

Wall Streeters have a mobility of capital which they use to feed many
mergers like fuel on a fire, then they get out on the high side of stock
values. They play the game for their own benefit, too. The new-issue
market today is a sad thing, running rampant and uncontrolled.
Ultimately it will all have to come to the end of the rainbow, the
runaway mergers and the runaway new-issue market, but all that will
come gradually from the disenchantment of the investor. The government is simply unable to do this, in our free-enterprise system. I do not
blame Washington, unless we want a totalitarian system, which, of
course, we don't.

In defense of government, its agencies and the congressional
committees involved in antitrust investigation, let it be said
there is a widespread effort under way in Washington to imple-
ment the various statutes which came on the books starting
in the early years of the century and augmented in more recent
years. In recent years antitrust zealots, particularly in the Justice
Department, the Federal Trade Commission and in antitrust
committees of both the House and the Senate, have thrown a
strong element of fear into the financial community as well as
in business generally over actual and potential merger curbs.

Is that good or bad or somewhere in between?

My guess is that it has contributed more good than harm,
because it will compel many in the merger-making arena to take
stock of their policies, ethics and techniques.

Has the government antitrust push stunted the merger movement? Yes, it has, mainly those of the conglomerate type, giants
reaching to new areas of geographical or industry domination,
but the stock-market decline, particularly in late 1969 and most
of 1970, sharply cut the appeal of multiples reduced in leverage.

Has the antitrust push hurt the medium-sized or small-firm merger? Yes, but to a lesser extent, although the merger appeal continues to attract in substantial numbers as smaller companies find themselves looking to each other for marriages or toward the bigger companies which will be eschewing giant-size mergers for awhile.

Now, what about conglomerates, many of which have decided to stand pat for a bit to let the government noise subside? Some, such as the International Telephone and Telegraph Corporation and Ling-Temco-Vought, have elected to fight federal restrictions on their merger plans in the courts. But most have decided to consolidate their positions, which is probably a blessing in disguise, until they map new approaches to their empire-building quests.

And what about the more than 30 million investors, many of whom have been dismayed by the decline in the stock values of conglomerates? Their disaffection has not been widespread in terms of dumping conglomerate shares, as yet, that is, any more than other types of stocks. One big reason for this is probably the fact that 1969 and much of 1970 were especially bad times on the stock market, with even nonconglomerate blue chips bowing to the heavy wind that ripped along Wall Street.

But the big question in this five-ring circus may well be what the nation's small investors will eventually do with their stocks *vis à vis* conglomerate and all mergers. Since I have already risked a few guesses, I'll try one more: The investors will return to the market and generally continue to regard mergers of all kinds as a direct entrée to stock appreciation.

Three, and, with all that, or about the time that the Dow-Jones industrial average had fallen 60 points after reaching the 863 level early in November 1969, it had become evident that what had been evident all year long was coming true. The merger rate would be about 37 percent over 1968's.

And even the drop in the Dow-Jones below 700 in May 1970 did not have the disastrous effect, albeit it had an appreciably adverse one, on mergers *per se* that year. Estimates were that 1970's number of mergers would still be one of the highest in recent years.

You will agree, I trust, that it is rather singular—I won't belabor the point by calling it "paradoxical"—that mergers which are stimulated by managements and shareholders looking for stock appreciation had jumped 75 percent by the time the Dow-Jones had plummeted 60 points and more.

If that is the case, how come? What was the relationship between mergers and about ten months of almost continuous declines in the stock market? There can be only one answer to that and it is that mergers are not made because the numbers add up but because the people do. The emotions, the chemistry, the gut reaction of the protagonists are what binds the tie.

As a rather astute Wall Street banker put it to me in the midst of the combined thrust of the government antitrust push and the deepening trough in stock-market activity:

> Many people feel that the merger fever will cool as securities prices fall, as the Justice Department digs in its heels, and as the novelty wears off. They are right to the extent that super-mergers may become impossible, and that high-flyers will lose some of their buying power. However, a "down" market removes a lot of the glamour from small public companies which now find that their only growth window is merger. This brings a new crop of merger candidates into view. At the same time, with the flyers out of contention, a lot of solid companies can become acquirers at reasonable multiples, which makes for a sounder merger climate.

Four, why are so many businessmen continuing to sell out when their closest advisors, as well as their wives, sons, and yes, mistresses, are advising them not to, to hold on a bit longer, the time is not right, or to wait until they can go public?

"Whenever a man sells a business that he founded or took over or inherited, or he decides to go public," says a prominent New York psychiatrist, "he is expressing his belief that this business is either expendable or will eventually experience difficulty in maintaining a continuity of ownership."

What does that really amount to? For one thing, it means that the owner or founder fears he is getting old and should cash in his chips before the old man with the scythe comes along.

This, as the Manhattan analyst explained, is a deeply rooted anxiety which produces plenty of neuroses among businessmen.

Usually, when such a guy reaches fifty, he begins chewing his fingernails. As he advances in age, he begins biting down to the knuckles wondering what his best move is so that he can put his house in order for estate purposes. The inheritance-tax bite is a big one, especially if the company is a privately held one. The owner usually can't establish the kind of market value for the company that will keep the chips stacked in a sizable pile, unless its worth can be represented in a listed stock or other type of securities.

There is another problem, which often makes the man shush up his wife when she tells him he is still virile at his advanced age and shouldn't really think of selling his life's work for a "pile of paper." That is when he finds that their sons or sons-in-law, or what is commonly referred to as "the younger generation," couldn't be less interested in coming into the company and taking it over so there can be a continuation of the family line.

"I see it again and again and again," observes a company finder, feigning sadness, since this type of situation has already made him rich.

> The young men want to make it by themselves or, coming from a very comfortable home, couldn't care less about making it, because they have no motivation. Then, every so often you have the hippie son or daughter, and that kind of thing can make the old man run faster to a merger than anything else. To have no respect for the father's accomplishments and, in fact, to live in a style where the only accomplishment is no accomplishment, well, what can be more damaging to the ego and hopes of a father who ran all his life to build his business?

Five, the persistence and bounce of the maxi-conglomerates in late 1969 and early 1970, after a dual pounding in the stock market and in Washington, represented a surprise to many who thought that the conglomerates could not take the reverses. Like it or hate it, the conglomerate trend has been one of the most stimulating phases of the American enterprise system in decades. Yet many in all strata of business life were convinced that their day was over when the Nixon administration took off after them with a vengeance beginning in 1968.

But what happened? At first the conglomerates dug in. Gulf and Western, for example, which had put together 23 acquisitions in 1967 and 1968, made only four in 1969. Another big acquirer, 14 in 1967 and 1968, Monogram Industries also was engaged in only four acquisitions in 1969. "Our growth rate has to be slowed down, obviously," said Charles G. Bluhdorn, Gulf and Western's sparkplug. "But don't worry about our momentum. When we don't build internally, we'll build externally."

Since it was obvious that the government's antitrust broadsides on bigness, reciprocity, geographical dominance and monopoly—lacking a clear mandate from a fence-sitting Congress— created an environment in which conglomerators didn't know what the law is or isn't, it became obvious that the diversiplexes were digging in, consolidating.

But Loew's, Inc., one of the big conglomerates even though it doesn't like the designation, was trying to accumulate money and management potential in a plan to make a huge acquisition when opportune. Laurence Tisch, Loew's chairman, divulged that by the end of 1971 his company hoped to have some $500 million in cash for that very purpose.

And Meshulam Riklis, the Palestinian-born conglomerator who put together the $2-billion empire of the Rapid-American Corporation, the McCrory Corporation, and the Glen Alden Corporation, attempted an informal bid for General Host Corporation as a possible preliminary to taking over the big meat-packer, Armour and Company, in which General Host has a 57-percent interest. And then, in a characteristic light two-step, danced away from it. The timing wasn't right, but the feint showed that the conglomerates were still around.

Then both James J. Ling, the creator of Ling-Temco-Vought, and Harold S. Geneen, chairman of International Telephone and Telegraph, loudly declared their intention of fighting Justice Department suits against their pending large acquisitions of Jones and Laughlin and Hartford Insurance Company, respectively.

The administration's antitrust efforts then really began to flourish. Attorney General John Mitchell early in 1969 attacked "super-concentration" and promised to balk the nation's top 200 manufacturers in any monopolistic efforts. Then Assistant Attorney General Richard W. McLaren took up the cudgel directly against the big conglomerates. Strategically, the Federal Trade Commission unloosed a major blast of its own. An FTC staff report was released on the economic effects of conglomerates to question not only their performance but their overall desirability in the enterprise system.

This study, released in Washington with an appropriate publicity salvo, should normally have sent conglomerate stocks spinning to new lows. But this was not the case. The field held up well in comparison to the whole market and a few stocks actually moved up. One big reason for this was the Wall Street and general investor reaction to the conglomerates' coolness and confidence under fire and a belief that their stocks had bottomed out after taking a big shellacking.

The big hurdles facing conglomerates are whether they can truly and constructively grow from the inside (i.e., with what they already have) and whether their past and future acquisitions can withstand a possible further downturn in the national economy. The answers to those are not yet at hand. But one fact is: The conglomerate structure swayed, pitched this way and that, but did not fall in the big wind.

Six, why do Wall Street and the commercial banks seem to do one thing and then say something entirely different, not only on conglomerates, but on other matters as well? The question is essentially a very big one, since business's financial lifeline flows from these two sources, as well as from the big institutional lending market, such as insurance companies.

My own feeling is that the big guns in the financial world are faced with a most peculiar dilemma, one of almost schizophrenic proportions. On one hand, they must seek their growth from the money-lending, money-generating function—hence, loans, underwritings, general financing. On the other hand, they must try desperately to preserve an aura of judicious objectivity, so as not to appear to be pushing what may fall flat in the marketplace or trading arena.

Put another way, critics of the rampant merger trend of the 1960s can easily lay the fault at the doors of such financial backers as the big Wall Street investment bankers, the commercial banks and the giant insurance companies of the country. But advocates of the merger trend would not find it hard to place laurels at the same doors.

Paradoxical? That's the key symptom in the mergeritis fever of our time.

Seven, what about the future of mergers and acquisitions? If it is true that an estimated 22,000 new consolidations took place in the decade between 1960 and 1970, will the trend continue indefinitely? My unequivocal answer to that is—yes, yes, yes.

Let's examine the odds. How many businesses are there in the United States today? Somewhere between 4½ million and 5 million. How many new ones are started annually? It is estimated conservatively that in 1969 alone, despite all the burdens of higher taxes, government push on antitrust, tight money, lower consumer expenditures for products *vs.* more on services, something like 450,000 new companies opened their doors.

Of them Dun and Bradstreet said that only about 50 percent will last longer than 18 months and only 20 percent will survive a decade. But the drastic rate of change combined with the unparalleled prosperity of the country will produce no fewer than *several hundred thousand new business concerns* annually in the next decade or two.

Put that through your computer. And try this one, too: Using 1969 as a base year, the percentage of mergers of business extant was infinitesimal—less than two percent on the most conservative estimate possible.

With the stimuli mentioned earlier, I think it is a safe bet that the merger growth trend will continue to increase beyond present proportions despite all the dire predictions from the cynics.

But there is one further element of the next decade or two that may cause an even greater explosion in the merger frequency—the great underground swell among the country's emerging youth population to seek financial security and self-fulfillment via various forms of entrepreneurism.

What? An underground swell among today's kids to become eventual entrepreneurs when they seem to be spending so much time demonstrating, questioning every value we have, after all we've done, and spitting into the teeth of the Establishment?

Yes. The protesting young want security, but they want to make it on their own.

Another paradox?

So it seems.

3

Where Were You When They Got That Urge to Merge?

You're that Tom Smersh, I'll bet on it. I recognize you from our college yearbook, even now with your hat brim down over your eyes and your nose practically stirring your coffee at Schrafft's at only 10:30 in the morning. What's the idea, anyway, of an outside coffee break on a nasty winter day? Don't they serve good coffee anymore in the vending machines at Continental Transnation Corporation? Oh, not since the acquisition . . . reallocation of space . . . I see.

We renew our acquaintance in short order and soon I get the picture from good old Tom Smersh. It's happened before, many times, but the Tom Smershes of the world find it hard to adjust to, bitter, in fact.

This, friends, could be the story, the story of our time.

Tom has given Continental Transnation about ten of his 33 years and has made it to divisional marketing manager at a salary of about $25,000.

Or, if it brings it closer to home, he's an assistant sales manager, or controller, or manager of the accounting department. Or, female-wise, let's say that you're office manager, executive secretary, head of the typing pool or whatever.

In any case, Tom, or you out there, loves the company about as much as it is possible to love an impersonal being with a computer as its brain and a five-year plan as its heart. Suddenly, after a week-long vacuum of tension, comes the big announcement: A merger agreement has been reached between Continental Transnation and another company.

Now your duties are being changed as part of a restructuring of the combined company. Your specialty, your responsibility, your talent, you suddenly find, have come to mean less than the fact that you are not part of the company that came out on top in the merger. The outfit that you thought would always be on top, it seems, is now only a division of what in merger-acquisition lingo is known as the "surviving company."

But, in practical terms, this is what has happened to you:

Instead of being able to make a lot of your own decisions in your own category of marketing, or public relations, or advertising, or sales, or accounting, or whatever it is, you are now told that you must seek permission to do whatever you want to do from the appropriate department head in the "surviving company."

Now maybe, aside from the blow to your pride, that's not so bad. In a way, your responsibility is lessened. But also you feel that your creativeness, your drive, too, are being dulled.

That can't be good.

If it disturbs you, if you find, as many have, that within weeks of your company's being merged into another suddenly you are being inundated with directives from a department head in the larger company that betray an unfortunate lack of knowledge both of your own company and of its market, you are not going to be overjoyed. Moreover, you are quite abruptly the subject of a visit or, perhaps more often, summoned to visit some guy in the new corporate headquarters to discuss "joint objectives" or "necessary integration" or "management orientation" of the two companies. You come out of either, as often as not, at least with a permanent chill down your spine and a desire to run, not walk, to the nearest executive employment agency.

Or again, as an optimist, you decide from the directives and the confrontation that the future might be even better than the present. In any case, you, the Thomas Jefferson Smershes of the world, know that that world will no longer be as it was.

If you are shaken up by the new prospects, you might very likely decide to have a talk with your old boss, the head of the acquired company. In the very first hours of the merger, he has probably had a staff meeting and given everyone a pep talk painting a rosy picture of what's ahead. He has referred to the greater resources, the sophisticated information systems, the vigorous research and development program, the far-flung facilities of the other company and cited them as evidence of the bright future that lies ahead for "each and every one of you." And that may have been the last time you saw him, since he has been, you can be sure, very busy.

So now, you decide you have to talk to him. You walk in or you get an appointment and there you are. Weeks, maybe months have passed since the merger was consummated and this is your first recent close-up look at the man, who may well have been a father image for you for years.

He looks up at you from his desk and you see immediately that he has aged. The youthful, vigorous face has deteriorated. Shadows form dark blobs under his eyes and his cheekbones, so prominent and stern that he always had a sort of grand Uncle Sam look to him, albeit a young Uncle Sam, now threaten to break out of his face. His gauntness and extreme sensitivity to your presence, the influx of sunlight through the window, the loud, indifferent clatter of the secretary's electric typewriter, his bloodshot eyes and his somewhat unkempt hair, all these reach you. You begin to get some hint of what he's been through and at that moment you wish you could melt through the walls.

But, being you, courageous and determined, your purpose flows back into your veins and you tell him of your fears. In all probability you say something simple like:

"Mr. Harris, I just don't know where I stand around here anymore."

POW! You just couldn't have been any more direct and painful, because at the very split second that the last word comes out of your mouth, you just know that he is making that very observation to himself about himself.

At this point either one of two things happen. Let's take the most likely one first.

"Why, Tom? What makes you say that?" Harris asks, in a remarkable facsimile of his recent paternal manner. So then you tell him and he will then tell you that you are probably jumping to conclusions, that every "consolidation" (a fancy aphorism for takeover) requires a period of adjustment and that patience and faith are what are vitally needed. "I know," Harris says," that you have those qualities to a great degree and that you just need some reassurance. I think," he adds, "that once we are over the hump of adjustment, everything will fall into place." That place, you tell yourself ruefully, could be down and out, too, but his words might, as he hopes, reassure you.

Now for possibility number two.

"Yes," Harris says, "I know what you mean. I think that most of us feel that way. After all, what has happened has been probably the most significant change in this company since it was founded 55 years ago by my late father. Naturally, when ownership passes to another company, we don't know quite where we stand anymore, do we? But, ask yourself, Tom, why did they buy us out in the first place? Simply because they thought we were an attractive property. You know what the most important criteria are for acquiring companies? Management, the executive talent; and the company's ability to capitalize in a good market potential. Evidently we have both and that is a plus that they would not want to take away from us and now, incidentally, from themselves. Right?"

Try to knock down that viewpoint! You could, of course, remain and stubbornly try to compel him to clarify, even in that context, where you personally stand. But you would be a rare specimen indeed if you did that in the face of the calm wisdom he has just expressed.

Tom Smersh leaves the office, outwardly reassured but inwardly as confused and as unhappy as he was before, or maybe just a shade less. Now, let's stay with Harris as the door closes behind Tom.

You are about forty-five or fifty, maybe even a bit older. A few weeks or months ago you made your big decision and you really tried to think it through, with the help of your family, friends, your top executives and your board. Two phrases were dinned into your consciousness as valid reasons for an affirmative decision. As you heard them, you asked yourself with irritation why American business is so prone to settle for clumsy homilies and then to worship them. Those frightful phrases are:

> "To stand still is to fall behind."
> "Growth is the name of the game."

And, try as you would, you couldn't really argue with them. Perhaps the most telling thing that made you grin and bear it was the fact that your own father, whose memory is so dear to you and whose actions became your model, believed as much in those principles as he did in his own derby and blue-serge suit.

And he wore that derby and blue-serge suit, or identical equivalents of them, for a long, long time.

Dad worked long hours when he had first opened the business and even much later when he had many people working for him. He would leave the house about 6:30 in the morning and return precisely 12 hours later. He was stern but affectionate; greatly dedicated to his business but very conscious of his role as head of the family; devoted to the Protestant ethic and the American dream in about equal proportions. A man strictly out of *Life with Father* and lovable. A Theodore Roosevelt type who instead of saying, "Bully!" would greet you for years with, "How's my junior partner?"

There were some very late nights, too, when he came home, and you remembered one of them—it was actually one of your oldest memories—because you were only about seven years old at the time. You were half asleep in the warm bed with the great quilt that was really too bulky. You became aware suddenly of the big, square figure standing quietly in the doorway and you struggled to sit up in bed. He came over still wearing

that big square hat, his square shoes clomping into the room. "Dad," you said, sleepily. "Golly, you came home late."

"How's my junior partner?"

You nodded, trying to repress a yawn. "Dad, how come you're so busy all of a sudden—I missed you."

He sits down, causing a vast, dangerous upheaval on the bed, and takes you around. "Son, sometimes when you try to build something from the ground up, the hours just don't mean a thing. All you think about is that you are building something for your family, something that will last. That's what counts."

That's what counts, you repeat to yourself now, rather forlornly, some four decades or so later. And, as you swallow, your memory slides into another phase and you recall how much your father liked poets like Eugene Field or Henry Longfellow and the English ones like Edward Lear and liked to throw some of their tidbits at you, tiny, humorous stanzas that made you roar with laughter together. Like:

> I never lost a little fish—yes
> I am free to say
> It was always the biggest fish I
>   caught that got away.

Or:

> Joy and Temperance and Repose
> Slam the door on the doctor's nose.

Or:

> There was an Old Man with a beard
> Who said: "It is just as I feared!
>   Two Owls and a Hen
>   Four Larks and a Wren
> Have all built their nests
>   in my beard!"

You turn away from this flood of memories, hot and poignant as they are, and you try to assemble in your mind again what it was that caused you to stray so far from your father's convictions, to have let him down as you did. First it was Choate and then Yale and then a brief sabbatical in England and then sitting in Dad's office and learning the business for something like five years. Then, so suddenly that it stills hurts, you are back from his funeral and you are, as they called it in Dad's day, the "proprietor" of the business. And then you, too, find that "the hours just don't mean a thing."

You do quite well in the years that follow, building, adding, diversifying, and in time everyone tells you straight to your face that you are "your father's son." And then there is the recession of the 1950s and the downturn of the 1960s, and fear for the first time settles in under your heart. And the first planting of the seed that maybe, after all, times have changed and it is really passé for you to go it alone.

And then one day, the thought perhaps creating the deed, your telephone rings and it is a banker who tells you that a trustee has heard from a finder or a friend that another company is interested in yours.

The next days combine into an endless series of phone calls, meetings, phone calls.

Now your recollections are so vivid that you seem actually to hear a real phone call and it is and you answer with as much poise as you can muster under the circumstances. It is Henry Bruno, your new boss, president of the company that has acquired yours and personally put into your pockets something like more than $8 million, mostly in a pretty good stock.

"Harris, Helen and I wondered if you and your good wife would care to have dinner with us tomorrow night at the Four Seasons? It's been about two weeks since we've had that pleasure."

"Henry, we would be delighted but just to keep things peaceful at home, let me call June and tell her—ask her, I mean."

"'Course, Harris, and give her my best, will you?"

The connection is severed and, in his own office, Henry Bruno, a short, extremely alert, extroverted type with the confidence of a long financial background, walks thoughtfully over to a sofa in his office and sits down beside one of his visiting directors.

"They'll accept, all right," says Bruno, "and I'm grateful for your suggestion. I agree—Harris doesn't look well at all and I think it would be worthwhile for us to socialize a bit with him and his wife and try to find out what's wrong."

"Probably nothing but learning to live with you, Henry," the other man said. "You're not exactly a tiger, but you do roar, especially when there's a balance sheet in your hand."

In a few moments Bruno is alone. He is a bit disappointed in himself. He should have been a step ahead of the director and thought himself of getting the Harrises out again to dinner. The director will remember that. But, to be blunt about it, Bruno reassures himself, he was never quite certain of Harris anyway, despite his enviable reputation. It seemed to him that Harris was still given to the old ways, perhaps still living in the shadow of his father, the company founder, and maybe a bit too sensitive anyway to stand the gaff over a long pull. Bruno suspects that Harris had always been a father-dominated type. Otherwise, why not one instead of two portraits of the guy with the Teddy Roosevelt mustache in Harris's office?

After all, the firm has put out about $15 million for both Harris's interest and the shares of the other stockholders. That's a lot of moola, son, Bruno tells himself. Then he has an immediate, flashing vision of someone like Lewis D. Gilbert or Wilma Soss, the stalwart protectors of shareholders' rights, rising at the forthcoming annual meeting to demand: "Mr. Chairman, would you comment on rumors that the shareholders have heard that you are having some problems with the management of the new subsidiary for which our company has paid $15 million?"

A shudder passes convulsively through Bruno's short, compact form. He glares at his French telephone—should he call Harris now or wait until the bastard condescends to call him back?

At some later point we may return to those known as Smersh, Harris, and Bruno, if it seems appropriate. But, in the meantime, let us leave these men be with their merger-caused neuroses.

Sympathy is what they need. What are they but men shook up by a business mania running from a pile driver?

Who Built These Corporate Battlewagons? And the Pile Drivers That Drove Them

You know what pile drivers are, of course. Those fascinating machines use a vicious drop hammer to drive piles deep into the earth and build a foundation for the ironwork of buildings. They do their job with a horrible clang, raising a hell of a lot of dust, generating ozone, dismay and delight among sidewalk superintendents such as you. You are impressed with the engineering that can develop the great many tons of pressure to force the irresistible piles into the supposedly impenetrable bedrock. The reaction on your part is at least partially masochistic.

Now, the point I am trying to make is that there are pile drivers that are not exactly pile drivers but are forces with the effect of pile drivers. The trend of business mergers has had a platoon of them, some old and some new.

As mentioned earlier, the big consolidations of the late nineteenth and early twentieth centuries—such as Standard Oil Company of New Jersey, United States Steel, Bethlehem Steel, American Tobacco, International Harvester, General Electric,

American Can Company, etc.—came from a response by business to the discovery of expanding resources.

Who built those corporate battlewagons? A group of pretty ruthless but creative entrepreneurs who saw the development of large-scale companies as morally and economically justified in terms of shoving aside many smaller, old-established and less efficient producers.

So that, you might say, was *Pile Driver #1*—dynamic entreprencurism by men who were convinced that bigness by take-over was the only way of properly channeling the country's growing natural resources into a rapidly expanding market. It was an irresistible force, all right, sweeping away thousands of small businesses and enfolding many others into the new combinations.

Forget any altruism. The Rockefellers, Carnegies, Morgans, Fricks, Mellons, Harrimans, Goulds, Cookes, et al., might have given some random thought to what they were ultimately doing for the American society but what was uppermost on their minds was mergers that would control or dominate markets. And that would place them personally at the very top of the great big heap.

The outcry that marked the social reaction and the public opposition to the increasing domination became embodied in a stiff, colorless Midwesterner. John Sherman was three years the junior of his brother, General William Tecumseh Sherman, the Union Army's field commander whose march through Georgia helped end the Civil War. The younger Sherman, a tough, uncompromising man who might have been President if only he had known how to get along with other politicians, lent his name to the Sherman Anti-Trust Act, which was passed by the Congress in 1890.

Now, in pinpointing antitrust legislation as *Pile Driver #2*, let's examine Senator Sherman's famous gift to the practice of the legal profession. That statute came to be regarded as a sort of economic constitution of the United States, "guaranteeing" free enterprise as the Constitution sought to guarantee equal citizen's rights. Bowing to the demand for restrictive legislation that welled up in the 1880s, the act was based upon Congress's Constitutional power to regulate interstate commerce. It flatly declared illegal every contract, combination or conspiracy in restraint of interstate and foreign trade and which created monopoly. Its violation brought a maximum fine of $5,000 and imprisonment for one year. But in its first decade the act's effectiveness was watered down by wishy-washy Supreme Court decisions.

New vigor, however, was imparted to it by President Theodore Roosevelt's "trust-busting" campaigns. The court used the Sherman statute as the basis for dissolving the Northern Securities Company, a self-serving holding-company scheme by J. Pierpont Morgan to weld a transcontinental railroad. The act was used again as a cudgel by President William Howard Taft, in 1911, to dissolve original structures of both the Standard Oil Company of New Jersey and the American Tobacco Company.

But the Sherman Act, with its two-pronged thrust against conspiracies in restraint of trade and against monopoly, headed into real trouble that same year of 1911. The courts restricted the voiding of restrictive agreements to what were "unreasonable" restraints of trade. The burden was placed on the government to prove that a restrictive practice's detrimental effect on competition was greater than the business justifications—or economic values—of that practice.

This dilution of the statute's effectiveness was remedied in part in 1914 by Congress during the Wilson administration with the passage of the Clayton Anti-Trust Act. This supplement to the Sherman law applied more stringent standards to such specific restrictive practices as exclusive dealing contracts, contracts tying the sale of one product to another and discriminatory pricing. That same year the Federal Trade Commission was established by Congress as a policing agency to ferret out unfair competitive practices.

During the 1920s antitrust action declined sharply. However, during the administration of President Franklin Roosevelt, a third antitrust law was passed, the Robinson-Patman Act. It took a slightly more pertinent tack—forbidding price discrimination to different customers of the same commodity if it lessened competition or created a monopoly. And, as if inspired by the new legal tool, antitrust activity resumed vigorously after that.

But even amendments badly needed can be only weakly tacked on, hanging by a string. This proved to be the case with the earlier Clayton Act, which was found wanting in its approach to restrict stock purchases that would create "unreasonable" restraints of trade or monopolies. So, in 1950, the Celler-Kefauver Amendment to the Clayton Act was passed to curb a corporation's buying of stock in another company which would substantially lessen competition or tend to create a monopoly.

That amendment, fathered by an unlikely team of legislators from different ethnic and regional backgrounds, seemed to complete the statutory circle. The Celler-Kefauver Amendment, as in the case of the Sherman Act of six decades earlier, was passed on the crest of a big merger movement. It turned out to have sharper teeth than any of its predecessor statutes.

I have gone into some greater detail on the antitrust laws at this point because they and their interpretations by the courts and the federal agencies have painted a whole new backdrop for the takeover trend in the latter half of the 1960s and the early 1970s. The effect was, on one hand, to restrict large vertical mergers and, on the other hand, to spur surprisingly the incidence of horizontal and smaller-company mergers and acquisitions.

So far, then, we have two pile drivers—the big acquisitive instincts of desperately eager men even to this day and the accumulated restrictive statutes by government that have been injected in stages into the enterprise arena.

But that, I am compelled to tell you, is only the beginning. There are at least nine more.

Pile Driver #3—This one is so close to the pulsating heart of the country that it will be bound to keep business takeovers a part of the national business scene for many years. The shape and manner of mergers and acquisitions may change, and probably will, but the constant need to harness the country's great production ability is a stimulus that simply will not be denied.

Does the push for production to meet an ever-growing population, more disposable income, more sophisticated needs by the public inevitably have to mean more business consolidations? Yes.

It all began about the time of World War I, a war which

for the first time showed everyone the outlines of the great production capability that the United States had. Then scratch 10 or 12 years from the big depression onward. That brings you close to World War II, when the production monster really came out of hiding and the world reeled at its awesome dimensions.

Our hurried turn from wartime to civilian economy from 1945 through the 1960s, when the gross national product rose from $121 billion to $932 billion, was in its simplest terms an overt example of our great thrust to produce rapidly in a mass manner. And, since the business of the economy was to emphasize the most efficient form of growth, it became constantly necessary to seek out the new, large-scale systems. This meant that consolidations of manufacturing enterprises were vital in order to utilize men, machines and material so that the greatest suppliers could serve the greatest markets.

And, besides, the last big war taught us the value of the scientific-minded entrepreneur, whose success contributed to the victory. And then, in peacetime, the flexibility of his mind and his creative engineering brought us a flood of new technological breakthroughs—television, new methods of photography, the transistor and mini-electronics, compact autos, new food products, antibiotics and other new life-giving drugs, the laser, etc.

As the merger trend opted for ever greater production prowess, so it did for combinations of scientific men, combining the technological entrepreneur with others of his kind, men who had one foot jangling in the world of science and the other hopping on Wall Street.

Pile Driver #4—The other side of the previous pile driver, an immense consumer appetite for goods and services continued onward and upward virtually unabated for 25 years after the last big flareup ended. After the demand for the necessities and luxuries of peaceful existence was met, there was hardly breathing space before a whole new set of consumer-demand criteria appeared to descend upon the American market.

New products seemed to foster yet increased demand for other products and services. Television, stereo-sound reproduction, the transistor radio all created a need for more and more of the same, and with accessory products that were needed to help one savor even more the joys of the original product. Shortened work-weeks, more leisure time, more travel, more education contributed to an important increase in the desire for items and equipment with which to take advantage of these newly acquired benefits of contemporary society. And, as producers and retailers strove to meet the exploding demand on all sides, they saw the answer to their supply and distribution needs right at hand, in buying out competitors or like companies.

It didn't just stop at that, either. Primary-materials producers went into the fabricating or packaging field via acquisitions; fabricators retaliated by buying into the raw-materials field; manufacturers also became distributors and retailers; and retailers became manufacturers. The "vertical" merger, in which a supplier becomes either his own customer or is represented in various levels of the tiers of distribution, became an important element in the merger movement. In fact, it seemed for a while that there were as many of that type of consolidation as they were of the "horizontal" merger, in which similar companies are combined.

Pile Driver #5—One of the most important of all, the basic emotional and economic need of many company managements to convince themselves, their stockholders and their competitors that they can grow on a steadily ascending curve, even under another ownership. This seemed to be initially the case with the first-generation founders, who, after spurning numerous take-over offers, suddenly succumbed to one, as often as not regretting it to the end of their days. "Mergers are egotism uncoiled," sourly observes one company finder, after long experience.

But, if the father-founder failed to accept the blandishments of acquirers, not infrequently his son who succeeded to the business despite nepotism did accept and blithely exchanged his birthright for the equity of a blue- or gray-chip, listed stock. In fact, one of the principal traits of many of the second-generation ownership seems to be a great yearning to build up a company's image and fortunes not for personal or family glory but for the greater glory of selling out at a good price/earnings multiple.

Of course, a leading reason for selling a business is simply the realization by the founder and/or his son or sons that they have a limited capacity to thrive in a market that daily appears to be becoming more complex and competitive. Despite all their protestations to the contrary, bankers prefer to loan money either to larger companies or to those that have an undeniable potential for growth. It is no coincidence at all that some of the most active merger-makers are banks, yes, even that little one on your corner.

Pile Driver #6—A major and dynamic factor is the immense participation of investors in the securities markets both directly and through mutual funds.

Growth, it follows, is reflected in a broader circulation of a company's stocks, while earnings have a direct effect on the appreciation of stock values. So mergers and acquisitions inevitably raise stock prices, not always immediately, perhaps, but certainly eventually. What individual investor's pulse doesn't speed up when he learns that a company in which he owns stock is going to be involved either in a merger or an acquisition? If he could only know about it in advance, he could make a killing.

But the widespread activity of some 30 million investors in the stock market goes much deeper than merely that. If the tiny, private investor responds to a takeover development involving one of his stocks, the same is true on a much grander scale with the many institutions, mutual funds, banks and insurance companies which hold vast portfolios of stock.

Then it is no great revelation that the mutual-fund portfolio managers, as a prime example of the big institutional investors, are not only performance-oriented but must produce tremendous price appreciation in the contents of their portfolios. Hence, they will be very conscious of fast appreciation in earnings and in the price of the stock, particularly when these rises can be shortcut via a merger or acquisition.

Vast, almost cataclysmic swells and descents are created in the stock market when one of the big, big funds, insurance companies or other major institutions makes a major sale or purchase in its portfolios. It affects not only the price of that stock across the board but also on the stocks in that entire industry and even in the statistical showing of the entire market list.

Pile Diver #7—That brings us now to the catalysts or the entrepreneurs who dominate the merger scene like strutting colossi. Or, as Harold Harolds, my merger-specialist friend with the psychological bent, puts it, "The guy with the big guts, who has a tremendous selling ability and the instincts of a conqueror and an unlimited belief in his own capability. He walks into the middle of a fluxing situation and suddenly it is electrifying."

This type of guy starts with or creates a company that has public stock, enabling him to have a constant reading on the score, a window on the world at large for the results of his business. He has, of course, an automatic audience in the analysts for brokerages who are seeking an exciting story which they can convey to the fund managers.

The merger-maker recognizes first that he can show earnings and price appreciation more quickly by acquisition than by internal expansion. Too, he recognizes that many of the small companies that have developed in the post-World War II period are subject to a myriad of insoluble problems, such as limited growth capacity, inability of founders to cope with an increasingly difficult market, the country's tough inheritance-tax laws. So he pounces—on a frequently willing and pliable victim.

The upshot quite often has been the development of a conglomerate, the showcase of the merger revolution. What is the conglomerator or other busy merger-master really after besides the obvious ploy of acquiring assets and power? The answer:

Pile Driver #8—He is playing, in most cases the Earnings-Per-Share Game.

How's the game played? Simple. The merger-master of the conglomerator type knows that since he has a big window on Wall Street (those young, dewy-eyed, money-mad security analysts who are just panting to tell a hot story to the funds), he can best tell that story in terms of ever-increasing earnings per share. Not his method the gradual earnings-per-share rise through building from within—that's for the slow ones, whose blood is thin. His is the frontal thrust, the takeover of other companies whose earnings per share he could immediately add to his own, so that he is virtually an instant success, repeatedly.

Now, within that game is another game played by Wall Street.

As the conglomerator obtained a sort of arbitrage on price/earnings multiples by his frequent acquisitions—each time he bought a company he seemed to be offering a lower price/earnings multiple as a purchase price than his own stock was selling for—the Wall Streeters were interpreting that story to their big and little customers as a great American success saga in terms of tremendous growth in sales, earnings and especially earnings per share.

Their stories to all, and especially the big institutional buyers, were borne out in the technical language of Wall Street, a language with its own lexicon and, more important, with a respect which it did not deserve even among the initiated and the sophisticated. But, be that as it may, the result of the game and the game within the game was a meteoric rise in the stock prices of the conglomerates.

But that game suddenly changed. At the tail end of the 1960s, 1968 to be precise, Litton Industries, one of the brightest conglomerates, with the halo that only a scientific entrepreneurship provides, unexpectedly announced a decline in earnings after many months of gains. This was followed by similar negative reports from such conglomerates as Ling-Temco-Vought, Gulf and Western, "Automatic" Sprinkler, and others. Stock prices began to falter.

They began to falter even more when the Nixon administration almost from the outset of its tenure began heaving big legal shells at the conglomerates, using a combination of court rulings and agency interpretation of the antitrust statutes as their principal thrusts. Bigness, reciprocity, restraint of trade, monopoly, oligopoly, merger leading to more mergers, the risk of using debt equity to take over companies—all these charges were effectively used to curb the conglomerate tide.

And so the conglomerates cut back on their acquisition efforts, not only because of the Washington offensive but because Wall Street, once so hot on the conglomerate phenomenon, was going through the most agonizing reappraisal of all: Had it been taken in or had it just been plain foolish?

And for the conglomerates the big window on Wall Street was snapped shut, the earnings-per-share game postponed.

Pile Driver #9—Quite naturally the foregoing leads us into what happened when the traditional business community looked on with growing dismay as the conglomerators cut their swath. What happened? Plenty. The Establishment reacted slowly, but with stunning impact. It moved in a massive, successful effort, so paralyzing in connection with such attempts as that of twenty-nine-year-old Saul Steinberg, chairman of Leasco Data Processing Corporation, that the ridiculously youthful-looking Steinberg will not admit that the combined power of the Establishment is what caused him to withdraw from his plan to take control of the Chemical Bank and Trust Company, the country's sixth largest commercial bank. It was, instead, he flatly told this writer, the certain restrictive forces destined to come from the pending one-bank holding legislation.

Nor was the Establishment's great restraining effort any less effective when Loew's sought to take over Commercial Credit Corporation and was beaten to the lush spoils by Control Data Corporation or when Northwest Industries tried vainly to acquire control of Goodrich.

Everyone, or almost everyone most directly involved, denies that that is the case. But there are simply too many people who are willing to swear privately that they know that the Establishment ganged up to quell those acquisition efforts by the conglomerates or near-conglomerates. Some of these people, who admit that their lips must be sealed, are employed by the very Establishment itself.

Pile Driver #10—The human animal being what it is, the natural forces of human espionage, intrigue and skulduggery will continue to act as both a spur and a deterrent to takeovers. Two broad areas of undercover efforts must, however, be cited at this point and in the context of this particular framework. Clandestine moves are made, on one hand, by the protagonists themselves in mergers and acquisitions, while other secret, unethical and even immoral acts are performed by the people indirectly involved and even on the fringes of mergers.

Here's the difference, actually. The sale of one's business is very different from selling a piece of real estate. If, for example, you want to sell your house or a building you own, your chances of selling at a good price are enhanced if you pass the word around that it is for sale.

Not so when you want to sell your business. The last ones that a seller wants to know about that are his banker, his lawyer and his accountant, all of whom would prefer that he retain his company so that they will continue to have their perquisites. And he certainly doesn't want his employees to know in advance, because their work will be affected and they will look elsewhere for jobs. So he is reduced to quietude in his negotiations, to a sort of skulduggery, a sham that he is doing something other than he is, to lying and cajoling about things that he is ashamed of but feels himself compelled to foist on others.

That is, until he can come out in the open to his banker, his lawyer, his accountant, his employees and to his doctor and his dentist, who are always looking to him for either good stock tips or for the assurance that he is, afer all, a bulwark in the nation's economy.

But the others, the bankers, the lawyers and the accountants, not to mention the company finders who might bring a likely buyer or seller to a likely seller or buyer, or the company's executives, are engaged on their own level of skulduggery. These range widely from assurances that the seller should sell or that the buyer should buy based on their own personal motives, such as losing or gaining a lush new account, or earning a finder's or a consultant's fee, to selling some inside information by an executive either for an honorarium or a promise of a better job when the merger is consummated.

The instinct to do in a covert manner what is best for oneself is as great a personal and vital an instinct as exhaling and inhaling, or eating, drinking or reproducing, or seeking some measure of security in life. And as far as business takeovers are concerned, that instinct is a force to be reckoned with. Few mergers or acquisitions are ever completed, or for that matter killed, without it.

Pile Driver #11—An overreaction along adverse lines against mergers and acquisitions appears to mark current thinking, but, surprisingly, it may not at all be the deterrent you think it is. For one thing, there is always an overreaction against any national trend that produces unexpected developments, not merely reverses, such as conglomerates.

The same communications lag is evident in entertainment, politics, art, when mass forces fail to react quickly to what is apparently a new trend. A knowledge gap is created, an inefficiency in understanding why a major change took place in something that the public has accepted with much enthusiasm. This is in no way intended as a prediction that conglomerates will return to all their peripatetic ways, but only that the acquisition and merger trend will be with us for a long, long time, despite the generally adverse reaction which has been directed against them recently.

For another thing, mergers do not themselves have a meaning of their own. They are not self-sustaining but are sustained only by the forces that fuel them, some of which have been described here. The merger-acquisition technique is actually a tool of enterprise. It has, in fact, become perhaps the most dramatic expression of our free form of enterprise, although perhaps not the one of which we are most proud.

There are, of course, many people who believe that takeovers are the antithesis of free enterprise. They may be right, but they fail to realize that the acquisitive instinct in many people is a vital human trait that finds its expression in a hundred ways. In the case of a businessman, he will inevitably find his way to either buying or selling a business sometime in his career, or at least come close to being involved.

In the meantime, despite the government antitrust push, despite the disaffection in the financial community and the public's overreaction, the incidence of mergers goes on, if at a declined rate.

Want to try on a few figures for size? Here are the total number of American business mergers in specific years:

1920	—	206
1930	—	799
1940	—	140
1950	—	219
1960	—	844
1966	—	2,377

1967	— 2,975
1968	— 4,462
1969	— 6,132
1970 (est.)	— 5,200

Thus, the merger rate declined in 1970, bowing to the pressures of an economic turndown, the erratic stock market and tight money, after annual gains of 37, 50 and 25 percent in 1969, 1968 and 1967, respectively. But the number of consolidations in 1970 remained the second highest of any previous year.

5

Marriages, Corporate Style (A Breakable Code for Buyers and Sellers)

What, you never heard of the therblig? Shame, shame. And don't just plead your extreme youth, either, you fibber. Therblig was one of the minor phenomena of its day, that is, back in the mid-1930s through early World War II. It really stirred things up for a while. There were people in business who used to swear by it and even at it.

Therblig was named after its inventor. Spell it backwards and you have it, Gilbreth.

Now, you might just remember Frank B. Gilbreth the industrial engineer, sometimes referred to as the "father of scientific management," who also had a hobby of writing books about his rather populous family. One was called *Cheaper by the Dozen*, in which he related in quite hilarious terms the stresses and strains of raising 12 children. Clifton Webb did a fine job of portraying Gilbreth in the movie version.

The therblig, honest, was part of a word system that Gilbreth developed to make sense out of business management. The point

48

was that by developing nomenclature to identify every element of industrial activity you could solve all the problems of running a factory or a business. In particular, therblig represented a unit of production activity in Gilbreth's new lexicon. A time-and-motion engineer would use the word "therblig" when, for example, he wanted to express a unit of production effort, an element involving, say, reach, grasp or position on an assembly line or in a finishing plant or boiler room. The therblig concept, in other words, was intended as a real panacea. There was only one minor problem. It didn't quite work.

Yet the therblig was important in its time. It stirred the mental juices and probably generated some creative thinking that helped to produce today's more scientific management.

The point of all this is that the concept of mergers and acquisitions is as important in the business and financial world today as the therblig concept was in the industrial field some decades ago. But, like the therblig, the merger-acquisition factor has no self-generative, self-sustaining identity of its own. Instead, it reflects a basic set of forces that set it in motion and turn it into a handy vehicle for corporate growth. Putting it another way, takeover activity is simply the shortest distance between two points—where *you* are and where *you* want to go.

If in that statement I seem to stress the personal "you," it is quite intentional. If there is one conclusion to be drawn from an analysis of business mergers and acquisitions, it is that they are motivated by human egotism. Decisions to marry, corporate style, are no different from marriages between human beings. They are both a synergistic reaction to a surge of emotion by the principals.

Martin E. Kantor, executive vice-president of D. H. Blair & Co., one of the better-known investment bankers, likes to put it this way: "The most important decision in a merger is not intellectual. It is a gut reaction. In spite of PERT (Program Evaluation Review Technique), Critical Path, Budgetary Planning, Analysis in Depth, and all the other expensive techniques available to corporate management, the gut reaction of the decision-maker on each side is the only indispensable ingredient."

Mergers are like marriages because they are essentially deals between people, not between business entities, Kantor adds. "This is why the most successful merger companies are headed by a powerful merger-maker, who negotiates his own deals, moves fast, makes decisions."

The committee system is a deterrent to mergers, as it would be to marriages. How many babies would be born, Kantor wants to know, if girls submitted every proposal to a family committee?

Any argument?

But does all that mean gut or strong emotional reactions by chief executive officers are just as likely as not to develop into merger actions?

Back in 1963—and the principle has been enunciated even more recently by many executives who like to give the impression that they are more committed to the more difficult but perhaps more honorable role of building from within—the Financial Executives Research Foundation declared in a research study, "Mergers and Acquisitions: Planning and Action": "Merger or acquisition is only one route in a corporate diversification or growth program. Internal product, management or facility development is still the predominant course for corporate evolution."

That point might produce quite an argument among many businessmen today. In fact, only six years later, something odd had happened to the merger movement. It had become infested with a bold new organism—the conglomerate—and conglomerates in 1969–1970 were being investigated seemingly on all fronts. They were under attack or furious study by 11 federal agencies or congressional committees, the subject of at least three major lawsuits by the Justice Department and were viewed as the perpetrators in a war to reshape American industry.

What exactly are conglomerates? *Time* magazine called them "those multipurpose, multi-industry companies that specialize in hodge-podge acquisitions." *Samson Trends,* a publication of Samson Science Corporation, said that conglomerates were "either mini- or maxi-clusters of companies which, in turn are homogeneous, heterogeneous, or shrewdly ingenious."

John Childs, senior vice-president of Irving Trust Company in New York, called some conglomerators "manipulators who are playing the earnings-per-share game to affect price/earnings multiples and are using complex forms of securities, some with high-debt ratios, for that purpose."

It seems to me, though, that all mergers and acquisitions—conglomerate or otherwise—whether overtly a product fit or an attempt to attain additional market share by entering new areas of endeavor or intended to bring in the promising new management of an acquired company, are actually meant to enhance the earnings per share of the combination.

Yes, you might say, but the Method—just look at the conglomerate's method: Unlike the others which have additional motives, the conglomerate, you might well point out, is nothing but a blatant effort to add the earnings per share of other companies to its own by issuing a new stock or borrowing funds that will actually be repaid through the earnings of the acquired companies.

It seems to me that the conglomerate is a possible revival of the therblig theory, that it is a unit of effort, not of production, like the original, but, say, of corporate expansion. Wild? Maybe. But indulge me, be big about it, for the moment.

I can then evolve something of my own nomenclature for the protagonists on the merger stage, as well as for the production vehicle itself, the corporation. I am therefore taking a leaf from Gilbreth's own word system, freely but very freely translated into the present-day merger syndrome.

You have been pretty well brought to the altar or are seriously thinking of it. If you aren't a businessman, put yourself in the place of one. You are either young-old, somewhere between thirty and sixty, fatigued or just ready for some security or new excitement in your life, because you have achieved your goal but want some equity that the government can't take away from you in the form of stiff inheritance taxes, or you want to move on to some expanded horizons with a big public company or actually to cash in and move on to a new field. To your friends, you have ceased being a wonder boy and to your wife or girl friend, that deep passion in her eye has been replaced by what?—a disconcerting look of appraisal?

So my word in the new nomenclature for you at this stage is

"mull-on." This simply describes your current status—you are thinking it all over, you are ready, ready for something, you know not what, but you surely wish you knew.

You now decide definitely to sell or not to sell. That is an action in and of itself, whether you accede to a takeover or sell your business to a competitor or to employees, or decide to do nothing, which is a decision, too. In other words, you get off your mental fanny and you act! The word for that is "mego" (you and your ego, naturally).

But you (or you transformed into a businessman) decide to sell, and your reasons are perfectly obvious since we have already been through them several times. Since you have decided to sell, you naturally make it worthwhile. The code name for that is, of course, "selbig."

Now that you have sold, what are you? That may be the most important question of all, because there is an inevitable trauma that hits every seller of a business which he created or inherited and sweated over and nursed and loved-hated. Did you sell it all for a mess of Chinese paper, stiff spaghetti, or pottery, or what? Since you naturally want mostly stock, or all stock, so that you don't get clobbered by the IRS with its tax rules on mergers, you watch what happens to the "paper" for which you have traded all you have worked for. The real problem here is that you won't be able to tell for some years, even while you are earning your contingency—the remainder of your purchase price that is contingent on the earnings of your company in its acquired state. Three to five years, even longer, are needed before you can tell what your "paper" really has done. Let's call this stage "papermach."

And with all those stages completed except perhaps that final one of patiently awaiting the results of what you have done, you are conscious of an important flux of emotions. This denotes a change in your motivations—a complex shift from original entrepreneurship to a custodial status while you "enjoy" your monetary gains and seek to find deep within yourself some new direction for any lingering entrepreneurial drive. The word here, forgive me, is "afterglo."

Now let's shift to the buyer. Being one, he has already made his

decision. He really has no problem at this point. That, you can be certain, will come later. Now he is all-man, all-lover, all-triumphant. I suggest we codify him at this moment in time as "stud."

Having bought, he or you now seeks to examine at close range what it is that has been bought. It looks good, definitely worth the price—the physical assets are there, the accounts receivable, the forward bookings, etc. But perhaps you find some doubts about, say, the people (do they really resent you? will they stay on? are they willing to bend? these questions keep popping in and out of your head) or perhaps doubts about some of the machinery occur to you. "Doesn't some of the equipment seem to be a few years older than what the competitors have?" you nervously ask a colleague. "I wonder if they weren't more interested in depreciation and its effect on the balance sheet so that they could sell at a good multiple than in keeping pace?" you say out loud. Pace! That word epitomizes your doubts. Were they really behind the pack? The question screams right out at you. So the word for you at this stage is "gnaw."

But let's not be downright negative about it. Really. If it's true that one out of every three mergers or acquisitions is doomed to failure, as the Irving Trust Company claims ("The Corporate Marriage. 1 out of 3 ends up on the rocks. . . . When we play cupid for you, the odds are better that you'll enjoy the benefits of your merger happily ever after"), then it is likewise true that two out of every three are successful.

You attempt in every possible way to integrate properly the new acquisition into your own company. You don't miss a trick—orientations and studies at every level, deeply honest discussions on planning and budgeting. You change the corporate table of organizations to admit the principals of the acquired firm into your top hierarchy. The whole point is that you and they engage in a program of enlightened mutual entrepreneurship. I think we can now get away with "yeateam."

Now for the long pull. This is the tough part. It should take from one to five years, but I'll settle for three, in which to find out who has been smarter, who has put over the better deal. Or, put in a more wholesome way, it will take about that long to determine if the merger was truly synergistic—the sum of the two companies being more advantageous to each than if they hadn't combined. The main criterion, of course, will be profits, but there should be others. Did the acquired management contribute to making the merger successful and also to provide some additional contribution toward meeting the challenges and problems of the total company? Did the acquisition enable the corporation to expand its market share or to exploit its bridgehead in a new field? Did the new addition yield technical, sales or marketing skills to help the overall company? The right word for the long pull is "growpe"—a combination, you see, of course, of "grow" and "hope."

So far our therblig-type nomenclature for mergers and acquisitions includes nine words identifying various points of activity in the evaluation of the corporate marriage. Since these relate exclusively to the buyer and seller, there really ought to be some consideration given, too, to the shareholders and the public. In fact, in some ways these ought to be paramount considerations because what business accomplishes should accrue to the benefit of its shareholders and thus to the public, that is, if business is ever to achieve and sustain your confidence and mine.

Now, I know, as you do, what J. P. Morgan said, but I like to think that business has changed in more recent decades from the attitude of the "public be damned." On that point, let's go back to John Childs, the senior vice-president of Irving Trust Company in charge of mergers and acquisitions, who submitted to the following:

Q. Mr. Childs, broadly speaking, what are the social responsibilities of business involved in mergers?

A. It is the same as the purpose of our free-enterprise system—to transfer dollars into production and to raise our standard of living.

Q. Are mergers having that effect?

A. Some mergers are and some aren't. To explain that, let's analyze the different types of merger-makers: (1) the manipulators, who play an earnings-per-share game in which they manipulate earnings for the sole purpose of affecting price/earnings ratios; (2) the doers, who bring other companies into their own to produce added goods and services; (3) the scared ones, who, because they are being threatened by takeovers, are grabbing at others out of fear; and (4) the sheep, who are involving themselves in takeovers just to be in the swim—it's the thing to do.

Now perhaps you are beginning to see what I mean. Some companies involved in acquisitions are a combination of these types, but I like only the doers. Of course, I wouldn't say that, if I were president of a company threatened by acquisition, I would not try to beat the acquiring company to the punch.

But, in the long run, we have to think of what mergers and acquisitions will do for society. My conviction is that you don't create wealth by manipulating stocks.

Q. Do you mean "wealth" as money or—?

A. No, I mean wealth must be figured in terms of goods and services. That should be the goal of free enterprise, of which corporate consolidations are only one growth technique.

Q. Well, then, what's wrong with building up a price/earnings ratio through mergers?

A. Many managements don't understand that gearing up the price/earnings ratio of their stocks too high is like stealing from their own treasury. The shareholder gets only a temporary satisfaction and a fast comedown. To do this, management may form complicated types of capital structures which will ultimately mean losses to shareholders.

Q. I sort of gather that you consider playing the earnings-per-share game an escape from responsibility?

A. It certainly is. Many managements don't realize that increasing the earnings per share on an arbitrary basis is proof of a poor or false management decision. The professional life of a company president is about nine or ten years, and if he is inclined toward the earnings-per-share game, he can do horrible things in that period.

Q. So the responsibility of merger-makers to shareholders and to society is actually to provide a higher standard of living by raising productivity?

A. Management has to concentrate on the job of management. The real producers in this country, GE, Ford and GM, don't play the earnings game. They improve themselves in order to improve our way of life. That should be the goal in mergers, too, and it is being attained in mergers that are constructively aimed at this goal. In others, it is not.

So much for our interview with the intrepid Mr. Childs, who is considered an authority in the field of corporate mergers and financing. Using the points he cites, we can assign to the matter of what mergers should do for society the code "goserve."

Now that we have come this far, what do we have? Here's the lexicon or code words for the pre- and post-merger stages:

The seller:	*The buyer:*	*The company:*
mull-on	stud	goserve
mego	gnaw	
selbig	yeateam	
papermach	growpe	
afterglo		

How do you use it? In case you want to describe your particular mood or someone else's at a particular stage of a merger in which you or he are involved, you don't have to be wordy or spend a lot of time explaining it all. Just use the code.

I offer it all freely in the interests of better communications. Therblig, anyone?

6

Egomania, Money Mania, Merger Mania—How They Work

Let's face it squarely, without a quiver. Greed, avarice, chicanery, cravenness and conflict of interest lay curled at the throbbing heart of the merger movement in America, circa 1960–1970. Scarcely any element of the financial-business-government complex escaped without a blemish, but some emerged with more blemishes than others.

Although many of their principals like to brag about what they do to meet the pressing need for social improvements, the Wall Street community, the banking fraternity and some of the merger-makers do not exactly come off in the business history of that decade with any auspicious gallantry. At the core of their activities in the merger field is egomania, money mania and merger mania.

Strong words? No—realistic words. It is difficult to conclude otherwise from an even casual study of the decade's merger activities. Early in 1969 the head of a giant company being threatened with a tender offer which would lead to eventual control by a somewhat smaller concern called on the senior partner of one of Wall Street's most prestigious investment-banking firms. "Get this guy off our backs," the businessman told the banker, with whom he had done much business before, "or we'll all suffer."

Within 48 hours the investment banker called a meeting of two other partners of his company and the heads of another investment-banking house. They agreed to a policy of not submitting any block bids for the shares of the acquisition-minded company. Block bids represent buy orders for substantial blocks of shares, an important element in making the particular stock vital and appreciating. Naturally, withholding block bids then would have the opposite effect on the company's shares, and this is precisely what happened. And so the decline in its shares, along with other restrictive measures taken, helped greatly to cause the company to drop its intent to make a tender offer.

Some months earlier a conglomerate chief eager to add a large company to his offered to pay an "honorarium" to analysts of two mutual funds. All they would have to do was to show their confidence in his company's shares by recommending that they be purchased or by subtly supporting his bid in their advisories to superiors and clients. The offers were accepted. The takeover effort was successful.

Sometimes the greed and cravenness are generated at a more specific level, say during a person-to-person confrontation. A business broker who had been responsible for bringing a new subsidiary with sales of well over $100 million to a conglomerate was wondering weeks after the purchase had been successfully concluded when he would be getting his $500,000 "finder's fee."

He tried vainly to get through to the conglomerate's financial vice-president. Finally one day he waited down the hall until he saw the man come out of the elevator and enter his office. Then he himself strode in past a startled secretary and confronted the financial man. "Where's my check?" he demanded.

The vice-president glanced up with irritation from his papers. "Oh, it's you," he said. "What figure did we agree on?"

"Five hundred thousand. Don't you remember?"

"How could I? We never signed a paper. We'll give you a check for $100,000. You don't like it? So sue us."

The broker took it, of course. Foolishly he had thought that he could rely on a gentleman's arrangement, since he knew the people well. "With all my years of experience in the merger game," he sadly told this writer, "I should have had my head examined for trusting anybody."

The naïveté and the shrewdness implicit in that instance pale compared to those of other merger deals of recent vintage. Consider the five-and-a-half-week saga of events and the behavior of the antagonists and particularly the behind-the-scenes shenanigans that involved a proposed tender offer by Electronic Data Systems Corporation and Collins Radio Company.

This battle between two Dallas companies started on March 24, 1969, with an announcement by H. Ross Perot, founder of the $8-million-a-year Electronic Data Systems, that he would make a tender offer to exchange his stock for that of Collins Radio, a troubled giant with sales of $440 million. It ended May 3, 1969 with a glum announcement by Perot, a friend of John Mitchell, the United States Attorney General, and of President Nixon, that he was withdrawing the tender offer.

Five individuals and companies commanded the stage in that abortive attempt by a small although dramatically successful company to take over an ailing, venerable giant. Each acted on the basis of personal profit motives, rather than on considerations of shareholders or what would benefit the public or the national economy.

These were:

H. Ross Perot, thirty-eight, a former computer salesman who started his own company only five years after joining IBM. He sold Electronic Data's shares to the public only six months before zeroing in on Collins Radio but was delighted to see the public snap up 650,000 shares of his stock at $16.50 each. The investors then bid up that stock to something like 300 times the Perot company's earnings.

Obviously Perot's plan to take over Collins was based on the stock market's confidence in his own company and his belief in his own indomitability didn't flag almost until the battle was indeed lost. His first move was to approach Collins with a merger proposal. Collins' common stock was trading at less than 12 times 1968 earnings, Perot blithely noted, while his own had a market value of almost $500 million, compared to the Collins' market value of only $150 million. The relative multiples of stock for earnings were based largely on investor reaction to the two companies' earnings—dramatic in the case of Electronic Data and erratic in the case of Collins.

When Collins' management failed to accept the merger proposal, Perot then announced a tender offer. He would exchange his company's common stock with a market value of $65 for each share of Collins' common stock to a maximum of 82 percent of the larger company's outstanding shares. The exchange ratio would be 1.5 shares for each Collins' share, a seemingly generous offer.

From that point on, Perot assumed he was in, despite rumors that Collins would try to find bigger and better merger partners and that some of the large, institutional investors, such as banks and mutual funds, were not certain to be in his corner. This proved to be his downfall in the battle.

Arthur A. Collins, sixty, whose scientific skill and zeal had built his company up from its start 45 years earlier in the basement of his parents' home in Cedar Rapids, Iowa, to its position as a major electronics producer and government contractor.

Collins proved to be instinctively drawn to his laboratory, even during the height of the takeover battle. He had been personally responsible for developing many of the company's patents. His interest in concentrating more on the scientific than on the administrative phases of the business resulted in his being criticized for the concern's up and down earnings performance. Delayed government contracts and Collins' inability to tell an effective story of his company to investors were also what gave him a lackluster image and attracted the company raider.

The scientist was at first drawn to Perot at a meeting in January. Perot seemed to have the qualities that Collins lacked, and they might make a good team, after all. But scientist or not,

Collins' ego was bruised when he discovered that Perot meant to be the top man, even though his company was by far the smaller one.

Collins felt that he could rise above it all, pointing out that "we've ridden out a lot of rough storms in the last 35 years," but his lawyers convinced him that the threat was real. He prevailed on a longtime friend, A. H. Gordon, chairman of Kidder, Peabody and Company, investment bankers, to seek a tie-up with other potential merger partners. These included Harris-Intertype Corporation, Control Data Corporation, Burroughs Corporation, McDonnell Douglas Corporation, and University Computing Company.

An amicable reaction by Collins' management to the Perot tender would, of course, have rendered the offer successful, but Arthur Collins declined to meet Perot again once the tender had been proposed to the public. And Collins refused to be drawn into the various blandishments that Perot offered to him so that an amicable environment could be created for the offer.

Such Perot sweeteners included the possibility that Arthur Collins would not have to tender his own shares, so that he would not have to enter into the same taxable transaction as the other shareholders. Instead, Perot suggested, Electronic Data would, after the tender offer was completed, enter into a merger with Collins so that Arthur Collins could then exchange his shares. Another offer was that Collins would remain an autonomous subsidiary under Electronic Data and Arthur Collins could remain its president, and perhaps even be president of the combined company—under Perot, of course, as chairman.

Collins' reply was to end its silence by taking a large advertisement in *The Wall Street Journal* to list eight reasons why neither the company's management nor its directors would accept the tender offer and why they thought it was "hostile" to the company's interests. The major points were that Electronic Data's stock was high-priced *vis à vis* its earnings; that it was 91 percent owned by officers and directors; that it didn't pay dividends and had stated that it didn't plan to have any cash payout in the near future; and that its stock had only been publicly traded for six months.

In this way the battle neared a climax.

The other potential merger partners. What would they do? Perot had predicted that tight money would cut out any who might need to borrow money in order to make the merger and that conglomerates would be eliminated because of the big Justice Department push underway against them. The stock-market decline, too, he figured, would adversely affect price/earnings multiples so that Collins would not be able to get an interesting offer.

Control Data learned that the Justice Department did indeed have strong reservations on a merger with Collins Radio. The report that Perot knew about the Justice Department's position on Control Data, a big conglomerate, before Collins himself knew of it intrigued more than a few people. Did Perot have a pipeline into Justice? He denied that he had ever spoken to the department about Control Data. But he was known to be a friend of Attorney General Mitchell, had helped in the Nixon campaign, working with Mitchell, and had even employed Mitchell's law firm.

Another potential merger partner for Collins, University Computing Company, had good intentions. It would purchase about 300,000 shares of Collins on the open market as a gesture of support. But Samuel Wyly, president of University Computing, demurred when that company's own shares reacted in a decline to an announcement of lower earnings. About three weeks before it all ended, Collins Radio began merger talks with Honeywell, Inc. But that, too, came to nothing over fears of government opposition.

The institutional investors, including the Chase Manhattan Bank and Morgan Guaranty Trust Company. Within a few days after the tender offer was made, about 272,000 shares of Collins' stock were traded. Apparently institutional investors were buying big blocks of it in the belief that Electronic Data's bid would be successful. And, according to Perot, two weeks after the tender offer announcement, ten big institutional investors owned more than one million shares of Collins stock. This represented one-third of Collins' shares and would spell the difference between triumph and loss.

The largest institutional holder of Collins' stock, the Chase Manhattan Bank, held about 450,000 shares and had decided to oppose Perot's offer about a month after he had made it. Chase Manhattan and another bank, the Morgan Guaranty Trust, reportedly had been rather concerned about Perot's high-flying stock. But, according to well-tuned Wall Street reports, they had waited out those weeks in the hope that Electronic Data might ante up its offer from $65 to perhaps $90 or $100 a share. That might then have had the effect of raising Collins' stock from the pre-tender offer price of $50 to as much as $85 on the open market—an increase fat enough to enable the banks to sell their own holdings of Collins Radio at a good profit.

But this aggrandizing plan didn't work. Perot just wouldn't play. It took only a few days before Chase Manhattan, Morgan Guaranty and the other large institutional holders stiffened their opposition to Perot, especially when they saw that he meant not to raise his offer. In addition, Chase Manhattan began looking around for another firm which could merge with Collins, presumably, according to informed sources, a company in which Chase had substantial holdings.

Perot, of course, was finished. Electronic Data explained publicly that it was withdrawing its tender offer, not because of the opposition it had generated, but because a new $75-million revolving bank agreement with eight banks contained a clause providing that any change in Collins' management would bring a default on the loan. Perot and his staff didn't even bother to check out with the banks involved as to whether the clause would be invoked if the tender offer were successful. And so ended Perot's dream of creating a massive new rival to IBM by combining his company's computer know-how with Collins' wide electronics-communications experience.

Of course, no one is quite asking business to be noble—but the behavior of virtually all the participants of the Perot-Collins set-to was hardly such that it will draw much new respect for any of them. Personal interest, egotism, lack of creative imagination and unhesitating use of influence stamp the episode as one of the baser ones in the recent trend of mergers.

As far as mergers are concerned, it seems, the rights of the management are used with more high-handedness than at virtually any other point in the entire range of management's functions.

"This crazy merger business is one that I have lived in for 20 years," says Howard Suslak, president of MacDonald and Company, one of the country's leading corporate-development advisory concerns.

> You find out that when men say no, they mean yes. And when they say yes, they really mean no. And when they say maybe, they definitely mean yes. It took me those 20 years to unscramble this mad cipher. Mergers bring out different qualities in men, especially their greed, avarice, frustration and hangups. Very rarely have mergers brought out qualities of altruism, heroism, charity and love.

What processes of entrepreneurial dynamism, mental exercise and visceral turmoil compel a company head to become a raider or otherwise to seek to acquire another company?

Here is a composite profile of many company principals who become locked into such a quest as drawn by a varied group of sources, including bankers, merger specialists, psychiatrists and other observers of the merger scene:

> The majority of the chief officers of American companies are for the most part frightened, insecure men—frightened by their own sense of insecurity, frightened about their own and their corporation's futures, particularly when they have to steer their corporate ships into an uncertain economy. They are probably most frightened about the gap between what they like to think they have accomplished and the reality of what they have accomplished.
>
> Are they really successes? If so, why the continuing barrage of criticism from certain quarters and the consequent pangs of self-doubt?
>
> The majority of them doubt their own ability to keep pace with the standards that they have set for themselves and which they are now locked into. In an earlier year, when the complexities were not so great, the standards were attainable. Now, it is another matter.
>
> Because of their past success and the pressures of lenders, the big and the little investors and the knife that the press always holds at the ready, the chief executive officers find that they really have undertaken the task of achieving gains in each quarter and even month by month, allowing them no room to consolidate their position or to try to cope with the downturns in the economy.
>
> It is surely a rat race, they conclude, in which it is probably impossible to come up a winner. In fact, it invites certain disaster. The only

question is what shape the disaster will take—will it be a decline in the quarter's earnings, a lower price/earnings ratio in the stock, disenchantment by the board of directors, or a raid by another company?

In the midst of his hectic duties, the executive wonders whether the board of directors will look for a younger replacement at less money. There are, he knows full well, plenty of young tigers waiting in the wings, certain that they can do a better job than the "chief," who was effective in a simpler time but obviously can't cope today.

What happened to his "dream within a dream"—of retiring in a record year and in a blaze of glory? And with it all, he is paying a price, because for everything one does, he has to pay a price. His price is the growing decline of his family's homogeneity, because he has been working so hard and his time and attention allotted to them have dwindled.

At fifty-five, he finds his wife has withdrawn or he himself feels distant toward her, his children have removed themselves to another level of consciousness or they have become "oddoes." If his family life remains intact despite the problems of his business life, he is lucky. He may even have become so accustomed to a lack of real communication within his own home that it ceases to be a problem and simply becomes another layer in a life that has increasingly become centered around what already appears to be a fruitless attempt to realize that "dream within a dream."

Assuming that he has not fallen into a trough from which there can only be one exit—removal from his post—he then begins to think of ways in which he can yet achieve that dream and even exceed it. Some will turn to revving up the company's internal growth, even beyond its intrinsic capacity to increase its normal rate.

But a growing number of company chiefs then become very much attuned to making an acquisition or a merger, usually in that order, since the former is less hazardous than the latter. He lets the word out and in due time he becomes involved in the merger and acquisition game. Suddenly he seems to be a new man. A heretofore unknown fountain of drive, imagination and even youth springs up in him. A hard, opportunistic smile breaks out on his face.

But others find themselves the subject of a raid by others who see a golden opportunity to capture the spoils of a once-good company that is floundering under a disheartened chief. Sometimes, though, the raid is aimed at a successful company for reasons that might involve what is considered the right timing and the right market.

As he sees that he and his company are under siege, the chief gradually snaps out of his trauma and tries to take action. But at least half of the time it is just too late. The uneven battle leaves the company head wondering what he can possibly do to defend himself and

HOW CHIEF EXECUTIVES
TURN INTO BUSINESS PIRATES

Brain Drain

Am I really a success?

Maybe I'm a victim of
making my own standards
too high?

Should I take the
offense or the defense
in a raid?

Why not make a bid for
another company to
show performance?

Why not indeed? Times
have changed—
"acquire is the
name of the game."

Maybe I ought to play
the game?

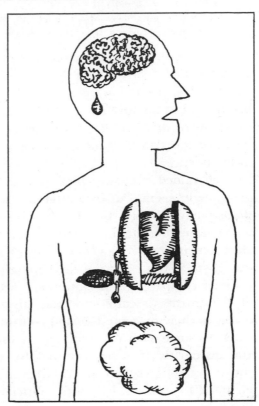

Heart Squeeze

They never leave me alone
long enough to consolidate.

Will I be replaced by a
younger model?

Wonder when I can spend some time
with my family? It's been so long.

Don't they know the whole
country is in rough shape?

If I could only look like a
hero again—a merger maybe?

That would make them look
twice at me, like they used to.

Stomach Gas

Do I always have to show gains?
Always? Always.

Are they planning to put me out
to pasture?

I'd sure love to retire in a
blaze of glory!

Do I have the stomach to be a
raider?

Maybe not—but there's no
other way.

often he will seek to find another merger-oriented company with which to make a marriage and thwart the raider. Such a desperate move works sometimes, but usually it doesn't.

The beleaguered company chief is then left to face the invaders alone, staring bleakly into an uncertain future.

The company raid is often a battle in which a man's greatest qualities and worst faults assert themselves. The quality of courage deepens and we are shown an aspect of a man shaking his fist against an advancing horde. Unfortunately there are more examples of dirty tactics, cravenness, unethical and even illegal behavior revealed than there are instances of courage and shining independence.

Some raided-company chiefs will fight back gallantly, rightly or wrongly seeing an evil attempt in the tender offer or the shares being secretly bought in brokers' names. It might even be an attempt to undermine the company by selling off its assets after securing control and then causing severe unemployment and loss of stock value for the shareholders.

Other company heads, however, react with horror not because of the threat to employees and investors but because of the threat to their own prestige and continued control over the company. In some such cases the tactics used show tremendous fear and insecurity. It is not unusual for such a company head to run to his congressman in Washington or to the Justice Department, or to seek out his local politician to engage their help in the fight.

In Ohio a stop-the-raid law was enacted against out-of-state corporations in 1969. When a out-of-state corporation acquires ten percent or more of an Ohio company's stock, the law compels the buying company to announce its real intentions and to submit the matter to the Ohio Corporations Department. A one-year notice of its intentions must in effect be posted by the out-of-state firm before it can take action to carry out that intention.

The statute effectively rules out takeovers of Ohio companies by firms or individuals outside the state. Delays, administrative procedures which are implicit in the law would certainly kill any such action. Are shareholders in an Ohio company consulted on their reaction to any purchase offer? How can they when a state agency and some Ohio legislators will .decide things for them?

Will every state have such laws in time, as raided companies or those which fear raids put the squeeze on legislators? Eventually such a state law's constitutionality will be tested, and there is at least an even chance that the statutes will have to be wiped off the books. In the meantime, however, laws of that type help to perpetuate management status quo, which may or may not be a good thing, depending upon the management.

Many chief executive officers even in these latter days of public ownership take an arbitrary and proprietary attitude toward their roles instead of considering themselves to be trustees for the shareholders. It is exceedingly difficult for a lone investor or even a group to hold out against a management proposal. Mustering the votes against it is the challenge, and the difficulties, both financial and administrative, have prevented 99 percent of such intentions from succeeding. The plain, unvarnished fact is that still too many company heads regard their co-shareholders as only people to whom they write letters or talk to or talk down to at annual and special meetings.

Does the term "raid" have a negative sense? Of course. But in today's swinging business environment, not everyone feels that way. A raid tends to generate new life in a sluggish company. It certainly makes it more aware of changing business currents. But quite often an all-out defense against a raid is aimed at maintaining mediocrity, incompetence and the status quo, that is, if management can get away with it.

"Stockholders ought to be in a position to throw out the management of a company," Martin Stone, president of Monogram Industries, Inc., of Los Angeles, told *The Los Angeles Times.* "Some companies are private fiefdoms, with managements perpetuating themselves. Stockholders' one protection from shoddy management is the raider," Stone said.

Strong words, but the fear usually expressed by a raided company is that the raid will all turn out to be just a parasitic exercise. Since there are companies that stage raids and do not have the ability to sustain the debt securities that they used to make the deal, the raid sometimes justifiably raises the specter that the pirate will use the assets of the victimized company as the spoils to pay off his debts. This has certainly happened. But the fear and the threat have been used with telling effect to generate support from lenders and shareholders alike against the interloper.

A recent ploy by established companies anxious to protect themselves from the raiders is to try to forestall them by effecting voting-rule changes. It works in this manner: Raiders often will buy five, ten or 15 percent of the stock of a company they like on the open market, submit a tender offer to the company's shareholders in order to obtain more stock at a premium over market price and then formally propose a merger to the management. But a voting-rule change to increase the percentage of shareholder votes needed to effect a merger can throw an effective curve at the raider. And it can even block his feint and blunt his real swing.

In 1969 the New York Stock Exchange expressed some concern that this type of maneuver by raid-conscious companies might prove discriminatory against large stockholders, who don't necessarily have raids in mind. This admonition failed, however, to prevent an increasing number of companies from asking for and obtaining shareholder approval for such changes in their charters.

We have been concentrating on corporate manias—ego, money and mergers—or the quaint ways in which company chiefs frequently behave on behalf of what they consider to be their management obligations.

Now let's move on to a more intimate, maybe even seamier side, the hidden level of personal behavior in the playing of that popular corporate pastime, "Merge, Acquire, or Tender Be the Raid."

7

Seven Categories of Shenanigans

He had been an accountant for a long time and had a good, solid professional reputation. Yet his attitude that morning toward the company finder who had come in with a letter of authorization from a buyer was more than faintly skeptical. It was, in fact, Machiavellian in the sense that he listened archly and reacted coldly. Checking to see that the door was tightly closed, he carefully explained his position.

"All right, my friend. So you've got a letter from a company interested in buying my client's firm. You want my help and you offer to give me a piece of the finder's fee. Great. But why should I risk losing a client who's been paying me over $25,000 a year for the past six years? You're not guaranteeing that your buyer will retain me. Of course not, how could you? So I'm going to fight this acquisition every way I know how. And if you should quote me, I'll deny I ever met you."

In another instance an attorney who had seen better years was nonetheless superb in finding every possible objection during the preliminary discussions. He saw little in the offers that his client couldn't obtain if he remained independent.

"My client, with whom I have been associated for over a quarter century, is a sensitive and proud man," he said. "Perhaps it is outside my professional purview, but I think I am safe in saying that he would not thrive in the environment that would be created if he sold his company."

As he finished, he was gratified to see his client's warm, grateful gaze at him. It was almost cowlike in its purity. That afternoon the lawyer's phone rang. It was one of the top executives of the company that was interested in buying his client's concern. It was an unequivocal offer, made without hesitation or shame. It was a simple commitment to hire the legal firm in which the lawyer was a partner for a minimum of five years after the merger was completed. The fee would be 50 percent greater than the law firm was getting now for its services to the company involved.

"Why didn't you say so in the first place?" demanded the lawyer. "That puts a different light on the matter. You see, it's not a question of selfishness at all. It's a matter of being able to help our client. Anyone that sensitive and proud needs our type of legal service and now we would be in a better position to nurse him through the adjustment period and afterwards."

The associate acquisition director of a large company had to make his pitch or keep it forever festering in his bosom.

"I shouldn't give you this information," he told the representative of another acquisition-hungry company, "but I will—providing you cut me in on a finder's fee. Agreed? All right, then, here's a list of recent deals presented to our company but which were rejected by our directors. Attached to it are financial analyses of each and other background information."

As he handed over the papers, the acquisition expert told himself that there was no conflict of interest involved. But, of course, he knew that there was. He was taking personal advantage of information, records and analytical work done by others which remained the property of his company.

How often do these things happen? Are they the rule rather than the exception? Statistically the incidence is small, so that they are the exception rather than the rule. But they *do* happen. They happen more often than is ever reported or disclosed. And they often violate the ethics of the professions in which their practitioners are engaged, and sometimes they violate the laws, too.

Such shenanigans are rarely disclosed, because both parties, the perpetrators and those who allow them to be perpetrated, keep them confidential, since it is in their best interests to do so. They come to light only occasionally under the harsh spotlight of official investigations, particularly those in Washington, or when there is litigation. All right, you might say. That's bad, that's unfortunate, it's just not to be condoned. But isn't it possible that this sort of thing is just the typical errata or "unethica" that occurs on the fringes of all business? That, wherever you have people reacting under the pressure or lash of stress, you will find a few violating the moral code and occasionally the law?

Perhaps, but let's examine the seven categories of shenanigans that seem persistently to crop up during, before or after merger-acquisition negotiations.

How do your hackles react to these:

1. *The desire for personal gain by executives of a company that may be sold develops into a conflict of interest.*

Shiny plums are held out by the buying company—juicy contracts, lucrative retirement plans, fat-cat job-security benefits—to insure a continuity of management. Many an otherwise decent and honest executive has stepped over the line in trying to decide what are reasonable salary and employment benefits and what are excessive inducements.

2. *Shareholders get secondary consideration. Management gives its own interests priority.*

This is, of course, related to the previous type of ethical lapse and was also mentioned in an earlier chapter. But it is such an important consideration in a merger—and so often results in selfishness and aggrandizement—that it deserves a category of its own. Stockholders are often as much to blame as the management because they sit by silently when it happens, especially when the business trend is good and they see some degree of appreciation in their stock because of the consolidation. But what about the future? Why are stockholders generally so lackadaisical, anyway?

3. *Theft of trade secrets, manipulations, embezzlement and even sabotage emerge like a foul wind from insecurity and unfulfilled expectations in mergers and acquisitions.*

Disloyalty, disenchantment, frustration and resentment over the new management's policies will prod some executives to seek new pastures. But others hang on, feathering their own nests, using their jobs as a base to make additional income and not stopping at unethical and even illegal acts. Many a court case has been based on such alleged activities.

4. *Takeovers with deferred payment, or contingency, arrangements, to the seller sometimes lead to ethical problems.*

In such cases the ultimate payout to the seller is based on his company's future earnings performance. Sometimes, the pressure to enhance earnings causes acquired executives to load up capital expenditures to produce short-term results at the expense of long-term needs.

But the buying company's executives can be and are just as tricky. They can saddle the new subsidiary or division with big overhead charges, management fees and other financial burdens in order to cut back earnings. These maneuvers can be like a double-edged sword cutting two ways. Who wins?

5. *"Looking for a raider on the Q.T." has become a devious game played by such a varied coterie as unhappy shareholders, ambitious company executives, greedy company finders and financial people with thyroid problems.*

The common denominators that spur such individual efforts are clearly unhappiness, overzealousness, selfishness and avarice, either singly or in combination. There is always the hope that the company under a different ownership, preferably one that recognizes and rewards the intelligence and information that are imparted by the person or persons who signaled the raiders, will produce a bright new environment for it. But all too often such intrigues fail to produce the desired results.

Aren't raids sometimes dictated by good reasons? Of course.

But perhaps the morality of it depends upon the motives and actions of those involved. Just what are they after?

6. *The role of stockbrokers and officers of large financial institutions can be an overaggressive one, disrupting a company from its chosen course and inviting acquisition-minded suitors.*

Here's how this kind of game works: Partners or their underlings in a stockbrokerage discover an undervalued stock which looks as if it could fly and tout it to mutual funds or other financial institutions. Then they visit the management of the company with the sleeper stock and suggest ways in which the concern could capitalize on its potential.

If the management is stubborn and insists that the course of operations it has chosen is best, the touters might then go to a company known to be on the acquisition route and suggest the reluctant company as a likely takeover pigeon.

The practice isn't illegal—yet—but it raises a number of disquieting questions about the role of Wall Street companies and financial institutions. The matter of short-term speculative trading by institutions has been decried by Ralph Saul, president of the American Stock Exchange. And the subject has been under study by a group under the aegis of the Securities and Exchange Commission.

7. *Finally, the winner's and loser's complex that underlies every merger or acquisition is probably the most overriding reason for personal misbehavior in company takeovers.*

Who wins in the merger game and who loses? On the surface, everyone in the field will insist that good intentions and honest dealings are the rule. It is impossible, they tell you, to pinpoint the winners or the losers at the outset of each deal because of the imponderables and the unknowables. These include the future turns of the company's image and fortunes, the efficiency of the company's management and the degree or the lack of duplication of manpower, physical and other assets between the owning company and its new subsidiary.

But privately you get a very different story, as you often do.

The hidden problems such as private debt or superannuated inventory or covered-up or inflated expenses of the seller and the true intent of the buyer and whether he will use the assets of the purchased company for the general benefit or for some ulterior motive—these are what determine more often than not who the winner and the loser will be and how forthrightly or deviously the individuals will behave. Be sure of one thing. In every merger there is one winner and one loser. Don't let anyone convince you otherwise.

Well, that's it for the different categories of shenanigans. Did your gorge rise? Control yourself. There's more to come, because now we'll elaborate, with true incidents and the right kind of background music—soft, enticing, mind-soothing—but including some harsh counterpoint.

Conflict of interest and the forgotten shareholder. "A lot of the self-protection moves are made among the top brass of selling companies," says a leading management consultant. "The president of one company I know began to feather his nest so well as the negotiations to sell his company progressed that it became obvious to his directors that that was his main consideration. They fired him and then proceeded with the sale."

A court battle developed in 1968 over the Crane Company's effort to acquire the Westinghouse Air Brake Company. The takeover move by Crane's chairman, Thomas Mellon Evans, a skilled and scarred acquisition man, proved to be abortive. But A. King McCord, chairman of Westinghouse Air Brake, charged that Evans had extended to him an "unethical inducement" to throw his support behind the merger offer.

"I would receive an option to purchase Crane stock and benefits after retirement, possibly by a consulting arrangement," was how McCord told his shareholders that he had been tempted by Evans.

During the trial McCord said that the stock options offered might in a decade have been worth $200,000 to $300,000 to him. "I was shocked," he said. "I told him [Mr. Evans] that it was entirely improper and that I do not wish to discuss this any more."

In rebuttal Evans jested: "I guess the offer wasn't inappropriate enough."

Sometimes the dangling is done by the head of the selling company and accepted by the buyer.

The president of a medium-sized electronics company owned little stock in his firm. But when a big producer started making wooing sounds, the electronics chief suggested that he might be interested if a new and better job could be set up for him in the merged company. When, shortly afterward, he was offered a group vice-president's spot in the merger, he announced his support of the consolidation.

The stock option and the inflating of the table of organization to provide cushy jobs are attractive inducements. But sometimes it becomes a matter of sheer survival for top officers in a selling company to ensure that their heads will not be chopped in a merger. The point of this, simply, is that the top men may be compelled to bargain for themselves in a merger since if they don't, their own future can be quite uncertain.

To underscore this type of uncertainty, in one case an Eastern banking group not only supplied the needed funds for a science-oriented firm to continue in business but also took over its management. And then, within a short time, the bankers summarily canned the three scientists who had founded the company.

Where is the fine line to be drawn?

Ling-Temco-Vought and Teledyne, conglomerates both, have a policy that no personal arrangements can be made with executives of a prospective acquisitionee until the deal is consummated. L-T-V believes that it would appear to outsiders that the acquired management is being bribed if personal deals are made before merger terms are settled. However, it's not quite that simple or cut-and-dried. L-T-V knows how vital it is to retain management of an acquired company and so makes a sort of exception to its policy. Thus, while it insists that no personal deals can be made until the merger papers are signed, it does provide for continuity of management agreements to be negotiated at the outset of the acquisition talks.

When, for example, L-T-V first contacted the Jones and Laughlin Steel Corporation with its intent to make a tender offer for the stock of the big steel producer, it also offered to give the Jones and Laughlin management team a majority voice in a trust that would vote L-T-V's stock in the steel company until February 1, 1971. The executives liked the unusual arrangement because it gave them a management continuity, and so they threw their support behind the tender offer.

Teledyne stresses shareholder protection in its policy that no personal arrangements can be made with the acquired company's management until the total deal is mapped out. But Teledyne's management, too, was sold on the need to retain acquired management. G. A. Roberts, who became president of Teledyne, owned very little stock of Vasco Metal Corporation when he was its president prior to its acquisition by Teledyne. But the buying company gave him a 10,000-share option at the then current Teledyne market price. And Teledyne's management considered the act ethical as long as the option was in line with company policy on executive options and the stock was optioned at the market value.

The answer to where the fine line is to be drawn must be that there can be no conflict of interest when acquired management receives salary, option benefits and jobs and when it is patently in the interests of shareholders to have those executives remain after the takeover.

Theft, embezzlement, trade secrets, etc. The company man who used to wear his loyalty on his sleeve before the merger sometimes finds himself bitter, unfulfilled and disgusted afterwards. Insecurity and frustration seem to dog his days under the new management. And if he is discouraged and unstable enough to resort to fraud, he can inflict plenty of damage on the newly combined company.

A longtime number-two man, who had once been promised a share in the business, was dismayed when the owner of a company became ill and then sold out to a larger concern. The vice-president—let's call him Bill—lost his title, his office and his secretary, in that order, when the new broom swept through. Bill had a year to ruminate on his personal disaster, as he did what he was told and, from his own standpoint, made it pay off. But about when the year was up, the new management began to find some severe inventory gaps as they sought to reevaluate the company's assets.

First auditors and then detectives were called in. An investigation of several hundred employees narrowed down to about two dozen executives. Once he was confronted, Bill admitted every-

thing. He had stolen $100,000 worth of merchandise since the merger took effect. "Why not?" he asked. "Wasn't the money coming to me? I was supposed to get a piece of the action."

Another such case involved not just one man but several, all in the same mixed-up state of depression and desire for revenge against the new management. For two years after it was acquired, a company kept losing money, more each year, and it was blamed on new computers that had been put in just before the acquisition. After a team of investigators was hired, the search pinpointed the ,company controller. With the help of other executives and department heads, he had falsified certain computer records, he admitted, and the group had embezzled something like $2 million in those years. All the people who participated had come from the old company and felt no loyalty to the new one. They resented the new regime, because they were convinced that they had no future in the changed setup. So they decided to build a new future by stealing. They found it, too, in jail.

The tricks of deferred-payment deals. Use of these contingency-payment arrangements has increased greatly in the merger field, mainly because many of them are tax-free when they involve deferred exchanges of stock.

But they are important to the seller because they insure that the acquired management will stay around long enough to cash in on the purchase. "Hanging around long enough so I can collect my marbles and scoot," a typical attitude of certain entrepreneurs who sell their businesses, just doesn't work under this kind of arrangement, since they must work to collect all their marbles.

This type of payout arrangement is most applicable to those acquisitions of closely held concerns in which the executives are also the big shareholders. The gimmick in the plan is the fact that those with the greatest stake in the acquired company's future are tied to continuing to show good performance under the new management.

Naturally, the matter of just what constitutes legitimate expenses and net profits can become sticky—and it often does. For example, a large West Coast manufacturer found that an acquired company insisted that its profits in a contingency arrangement included the money obtained from the sale of a factory. The result was that the buyer was compelled to pay an additional block of stock with a value in six figures. The reason: the contract didn't spell out how "special items" were to be treated. The additional stock was given to the acquired management so that no resentment would be allowed to mar the relationship.

As I. John Billera, president of U. S. Industries, the biggest corporate acquirer of any American company in 1968 and 1969, put it: "The seller knows what he is selling. We as the buyers can't always know what we are buying. But the contingency arrangement makes sure that the buyer isn't going to exaggerate his earnings, because the executives are going to have to live up to them and exceed them. That's great protection all around."

Yet it happens both ways. The seller sometimes inflates his earnings by such things as "special items" or "nonrecurring items" while the buyer tries to saddle the acquired management with prorata expenses.

Occasionally, or perhaps more often, it all comes out early in the acquisition talks. A successful smaller company was in the process of being sold by its middle-aged founder. Everything was progressing nicely until he reached into his pocket and handed a neatly written list to his counterpart in the buying company.

The buyer's face turned pink, red, then slightly purple, in that order, as he read it. "What the hell are these?" he demanded.

"Oh, those are just a few fringe benefits that I want to retain when you take title," said the seller.

The other man read out loud: " 'Keep up my major charities. Retain the accountant for at least five years. Continue to take my wife on all trips.' Does this mean that we are supposed to pay for all these, too?"

The seller nodded. "Of course. Why not?"

The buyer leaned close, pointing to the final item on the list. "What's this? 'Keep Mrs. M. on the payroll at $12,500 a year.' Who's Mrs. M.—what does she do?"

"Mrs. M.? Oh, she doesn't do anything. She's my mother-in-law."

Question: Do you think that deal ever went through?

Raiders, the role of stockbrokers and financial institutions. I suspect that my photograph won't be pinned up along Wall Street for grouping all three of those in the same catchline. But it is hardly a secret anymore that tender offers or other types of "raids" have been engendered on more than a few occasions by Wall Street houses, banks, mutual funds and even insurance companies. The effort is an exercise in ego satisfaction, a thrust against things as they are and in favor of what they might be, when it involves disenchanted stockholders or frustrated company executives or hungry business brokers eyeing the finder's fee, or a distressed former partner, or you name whom.

What about the stockbroker or officer of an institution who sees finding the right acquirer for a sleeping or plodding company as synergism in its purest state? Especially when his own firm has taken a strong position in that company's stock and then indulges in a hot merchandising campaign to sell those shares?

Witness what emerged from separate hearings in 1969 of the subcommittee on antitrust and monopoly of the Senate Judiciary Committee, headed by Senator Hart, Democrat of Michigan, and the subcommittee on antitrust of the House Judiciary Committee, headed by Representative Celler of New York.

Both committees were looking into the 1968 acquisition of the Reliance Insurance Company of Philadelphia, a $330-million giant, by a then pygmy, Leasco Data Processing and Equipment Corporation, which had revenues of only $14.4 million. Also being questioned were officers of a New York Stock Exchange firm, Carter, Berlind and Weill, later known as Cogan, Berlind and Levitt.

Both sets of congressional probers found nothing in the way of wrongdoing on the part of Leasco or the stockbrokerage. But the hearings established for certain the curiously efficient and double-barreled role that a stockbrokerage's officers can play in a merger.

In mid-1967 an exciting document circulated among managers of financial institutions and executives of conglomerates. It was "conceptual" in nature, thus challenging to the entrepreneurial instinct, and valuable, because it unearthed real treasure. Edward Netter, a partner in Carter, Berlind and Weill and an expert on the insurance industry, had written a study revealing that numerous insurance companies were not cash poor and were not dull prospects because they held large deposits of "surplus surplus," or "redundant capital." And insurance stocks did not reflect these treasures which, in one case, that of the Insurance Company of North America, was estimated at $510 million. Reliance Insurance, in 1966, had $80 million worth.

Insurance-company managements, like the public, seemed oblivious to these hidden assets. Most of their capital was invested in stable common stocks and preferred stocks which yielded a small return. So where did the hidden money wells gurgle? As investments accumulate, the redundant capital grows. Insurance companies are required by state law to set aside a portion of their portfolios as surplus as a hedge against new insurance policies. But the surplus over that portion of their investment growth could and did jump far beyond what was expected. However, strict regulations existed in the states on how to invest the "surplus surplus."

There was a good way of getting around this and Netter pointed it out. Some companies had set up holding companies, in which the insurance concern was a wholly owned subsidiary. Enough capital could be retained by the insurance company to satisfy state rules, but the redundant capital could then be declared a dividend and paid out to the holding company.

It intrigued many people on the study's mailing list. Leasco, for one, was interested. In the meantime, Carter, Berlind and Weill was busily merchandising the study to hold talks with possible large purchasers of insurance-company shares.

Now, let's try a chronological list of developments as revealed in the Celler subcommittee records and in its hearings:

January 11, 1968. A Leasco memo with that date recommended acquisition of a certain insurance company. In testimony, Saul Steinberg, Leasco's president, identified the company as Reliance. The memo's author was Michael Gibbs, a Leasco vice-president, who had frequently consulted with Netter, Steinberg said. The memo contained language that was very similar to Netter's report. The memo also had a page listing "outstanding stock" and "ownership," citing 600,000 shares with the note, "Institutions holding the stock that CBW [Carter, Berlind and Weill] can approach." In questioning by Representative Celler as to why the brokerage's clients were listed according to their Reliance stock ownership, Netter denied that it was for the purpose of acquiring the shares for Leasco.

Said Mr. Netter: "I think a representation to a company such as this might be an investment-banking judgment that at a certain price, at a certain value, institutional holders might be induced to sell their holdings. I don't think an investment banker can ever say they control "X" number of shares which they can produce at this, that or the other."

"Early in 1968." Steinberg testified that during that time Berlind representatives urged Leasco to make a tender offer for Reliance. But Leasco held off, uncertain as to its move.

March 13 to April 2. Leasco during those weeks bought 132,600 shares of Reliance.

April 16, 1968. This was the date of a letter written by Arthur Carter, then president of the securities firm, to Steinberg, spelling out the terms of a finder's fee contingent on the acquisition of 51 percent of the Reliance stock. CBW would be designated the tender agent or co-tender agent for any offer made to Reliance's shareholders. The brokerage quite obviously was seeking to increase its income from finder's fees.

In the fiscal year ended June 30, 1967, it had no such income. Two years later, or for the year ended June 30, 1969, merger fees totaled $2.5 million, out of total income of $13.2 million.

June 11, 1968. A "heated discussion" was held at the Harmonie Club in Manhattan between officials of CBW and Leasco, following frequent earlier meetings.

Leasco ultimately paid for the Reliance shares about $70 a share, in convertible preferred and warrants, down from the earlier suggested $120 and then $85 a share. Leasco, which Steinberg said had been "shocked" by the price it was asked to pay, was told that CBW's customers had paid up to $58 a share for Reliance stock.

During these negotiations CBW also was recommending to its customers that they buy Reliance stock, the testimony showed. In a major sale, the brokerage's retail and institutional clients bought 404,500 shares of Reliance at $50 a share in a single trade on May

16, executed by CBW on the floor of the American Stock Exchange.

June 22, 1968. Leasco announced its tender offer for Reliance stock, after weeks of rumors. Reliance's stock had climbed from $30 at the year's beginning to more than $59 by June 22. Trading in the stock had averaged 78,200 shares a month in 1967; 180,500 in March 1968; 240,000 in April and 1,631,300 in May.

Arthur Levitt, Jr., who became president of CBW when Arthur Carter left to start his own firm, told the Hart committee that the brokerage had recommended for some time prior to the Leasco acquisition of Reliance that its clients buy stock in fire and casualty insurance companies. "These companies represented substantial investment opportunities," Levitt said.

He added, "We looked upon these companies and looked upon this industry as an area that could very well benefit from a merger and we made such recommendations to our clients, both individual and institutional, but we did not make reference to a specific takeover that we had contemplated when we took an interest in the situation."

But during the Celler subcommittee hearings, Kenneth R. Harkins, chief counsel for the House antitrust subcommittee, questioned both Levitt and Netter with this result:

HARKINS: "Mr. Netter, during the period January 11 through June 11, 1968, you and other representatives of Carter Berlind and Weill encouraged your clients to purchase Reliance Insurance Company stock. Is that true?"

NETTER: "Yes."

HARKINS: "And is it not a fact that Carter Berlind was encouraging its clients to purchase shares in Reliance at the same time that Carter Berlind was attempting to negotiate an agreement with Leasco where Carter Berlind would be tender agent for Reliance stock?"

NETTER: "No, that is not true."

LEVITT: "Yes, it is true."

HARKINS: "It must be."

And so it goes.

Trying to Live as One

"Few of our 700 people or even our 22 executives were aware of the merger, but the word began to leak out toward the end of the six months of negotiations. Then when it was suddenly announced, we were all a little stunned. What would happen to us? What would happen to our quiet, little company—it had been like a family affair for so many years," she said.

The woman, a Miss Rankin, had been with the company for about a dozen years and doubled as personnel director and administrative assistant to the president. She had never married but supported an invalid father and had put a younger brother through medical school. An intense perfectionist, she put so many zestful hours in at her work that another executive with an acid tongue said, "Rankin has an orgasm with the company every day."

Now, describing her experience and those of others in the firm since it had been acquired by a $1-billion conglomerate six months before, she was unemotional and analytical.

When the announcement was made, my attitude and that of almost all the other executives was that we were just going in the direction of the future. The real big company was the only one that was equipped to handle all the problems in business. Our company had gone public a few years ago but it was clear that it was floundering. One year we had a four-percent net after taxes and the next year 1.5 percent. As the heads of a public company, Howie and Carl devoted their time to outside activities and neglected their own business. Carl, who is the president, was annoyed that he had to spend so much time talking to Wall Street analysts and I think he's very happy that he doesn't have to do it anymore.

A few days after the merger was announced, there was a great rush for raises among the executives. They felt that if they were earning more money, they would look better and more desirable to the new owners. But the boss handled them well. He said that he wouldn't give any raises out of panic.

But the hoped-for advancement and higher salaries didn't develop. Most of the executives lost their fear even if they didn't find themselves better off personally than they had been before. Miss Rankin found that the new owners had personnel policies like the government's—ratings and job standards and twice-a-year salary reviews. The maximum, however, was a seven-percent increase a year, compared with the acquired company's former 15 percent.

The treasurer and controller, who had been a company employee for only three years, said:

They require a tremendous volume of reports from us and send us a lot of reports, too. In fact, they deluge us with mail of all kinds, a great deal of which doesn't apply. They seem to have a fetish about communications. I guess that's because conglomerates are supposed to have bad communications with their divisions. But, in trying to avoid this, they're overcompensating.

They compel us to submit a monthly operating statement including a detailed balance sheet and a summary profit and loss statement. This is due two days after the close of every month and it's hard, damned hard to get all the figures in time.

Two days after that, they want a "wholesale" operating report—it's a much more detailed profit and loss statement, showing inventory value changes and an analysis of selling expenses. They use a crazy form that we have to convert ours to, creating a meaningless report and it makes me go out of my skull.

The treasurer also mentioned several "curious" things. The conglomerate didn't seem to get excited if "we had a big month." Instead, the new management works up a master report projecting sales, expenses and net income, based on the acquired company's own submitted report. "They get excited when the two mesh or come within ten percent of planned sales and five percent of net income. In other words, they make such a big deal about coming in on target that if you exceed it greatly, this doesn't make them as happy."

Another thing he found was that "we don't pay our own bills anymore, except really small ones." All the others are submitted to a computer in their headquarters which does the disbursing. "But it doesn't work smoothly—there are too many errors—and we have to ask for adjustments and corrections," he said, with some satisfaction.

And the system of having "Papa pay all the bills" has another strange effect. "They don't seem to watch or care about your expenses even though they are concerned about keeping to planned budgets and sales. It tends to make our people fail to watch their expenses as closely as before."

Carl Baker, the head of the company that sold to the conglomerate after 25 years of operation, had changed since I saw him some months before the acquisition. A tall, angular man who normally walked and talked quickly, he now didn't talk quickly, but he walked even faster. We strode around his plant, not saying much to each other, while he gestured about to show some of the major changes, such as new equipment, on-line installations for quality control and inspection, and so on, all done since the acquisition.

In his office he closed the door and said, "It's been an interesting experience these past six months. I'm really not free to talk to the press according to the policies of the company's public-relations department. But I've known you for some time and you know that you can't use my name or identify the company. I guess I can talk."

He relaxed and I thought his face would come apart. His features fell into composed lines and curves and he sighed and said:

An interesting experience. You know, when we announced the deal, there was a feeling in some quarters that I, my brother, Howie, and my father had sold out. People felt that we had betrayed them, because they had bought our stock when we went public and now we were selling the company. . . .

Of course, there was another embarrassing angle to it. The papers made a thing about the fact that we got $20 million for the company. That's a lot of dough, no matter how you slice it, but for weeks afterward I used to walk into the restaurant without trying to meet anyone's eye. I guess I was ashamed that we sold out for so much. . . .

I guess I really knew that the company wasn't ours anymore when a guy with a homburg and a briefcase walked in here a week after the papers were signed and started looking around and talking to everyone without first coming to me. I found out later that he was their group vice-president, in charge of companies like ours. A real tough cooky with ice cubes in his veins.

They're bottom-line guys, all the way. Nothing else counts although they make a big pretense out of caring about other things. I mean like personnel relations, they're very conscious of it, and deluge us with pamphlets and bulletins. They want us to start a house organ and keep telling us about their grievance procedures for employees. . . .

They're not at all what you'd expect a conglomerate to be. They're organized, full of procedures and reports for everything, and they control everything out. They don't know our type of business, but they're learning it fast. They don't exactly keep after you on everything—but you know they're watching closely from up in that great, big glass building of theirs. . . .

I guess so far they like what we've done. But I hope we can continue to do it.

Somewhere between 30 percent and 40 percent of all mergers and acquisitions fail to come up to expectations, says a consensus of merger experts.

The exact figure may be moot in the view of strong merger advocates, but few will deny that a large percentage of consolidations do not produce the degree of synergism or full variety of benefits portrayed in the smoke-filled rooms where mergers are put together.

Mergers' main criterion is earnings, particularly earnings per share, followed by return on invested capital. But there are others, including the resulting change in stock values, market share of the acquired company, employment, executive and rank-and-file salaries, production, product or service innovation and so on.

What inevitably happens in a good many cases is that changes are gradually foisted on the acquired company, often profound, philosophical and even psychological changes. The result is that in many cases, even when evidence is at hand that the acquisition has not worked out well, logical arguments are advanced to prove that you are simply comparing apples with oranges.

"What fascinates me about this business is that the average person measures a company's growth by its earnings per share and the acquisition leaders know it and cater to it," observes Louis Perlmutter, vice-president of Octagon Industries, Inc., a New York corporate-development consultant.

"So the acquirers cut expenses, salaries, costs, and even change the operations so that it earns more money—or gives the appearance of earning more money. But what the acquirer has done is to create the appearance of growth—an apparent growth—and he can then move on to his next acquisition," Perlmutter adds.

But within the first weeks or months the acquirer usually plays his hand. It isn't always the sudden appearance of a "a real tough cooky with a homburg and a briefcase" that shows that hand. It may be a series of directives, a wholesale tour by a team from the acquiring company, or a written or telephoned reaction to monthly reports from the subsidiary. And it may even be absolute, stony silence—for a while.

In any case, the attitude of executives who become part of larger companies by acquisition has two stages.

The first is a hypoed stimulation, a strong sense of hope, combined with a degree of uncertainty and concern. The hope is that new funds will be plowed back into the acquired company for expansion, for more research and development, for entry into new markets. And that the new owners might have wider horizons, more knowledge and sophistication than the old ones so that the marriage might turn out to open a new window on the world. In the process, naturally, the executives hope they will find new vistas for themselves as well as more money, better stock options and a better deal in general.

The second stage—we might call it the "prenatal blues"—comes somewhere between six and nine months after the merger or acquisition, and it might even come later than that. By then the attitude of most executives has experienced a reversal in its ratio of stimulation and concern. Now it is mostly concern, a growing sense of some impending, adverse changes of a personal nature, combined with some remaining degree of stimulation.

This drastic adjustment in emotions isn't necessarily the result of negative moves made by the new management. It may come from that, of course, or from restrictive policies laid down by the control-minded new bosses. But usually it arises from the lack of movement on a personal level by the acquired executives or from a lack of hoped-for events, such as the tipping of the money cornucopia in the direction of the acquired company, or the lack of any big, new direction by the acquirers.

The first year is, in many cases, actually too soon to "prove out" what effects the merger-acquisition will have on the shook-up, acquired executives. It is a time when they find that they must mostly set their own directions on how to behave and how to work, how to adjust to the new overtones that pervade the place, in the absence of any clear new orders from the acquiring management.

So much remains unresolved, it seems to everyone. The expectant hush that filled the offices has long since disappeared and been replaced by a general disillusionment. "Where is all that highly vaunted dynamism and drive of that gang?" might describe a typical reaction. Then, "Don't they care now that they got us?"

And then it comes! It comes in the form of announcements, directives, unexpected newspaper articles, visits to your office from engineers or management consultants or headquarters specialists, abruptly called meetings with your boss in which he solemnly reports a consolidation with or a closing of a plant or two or three, an introduction to a new president or a request to come up to headquarters and meet the guy who henceforth will set all the policy decisions and even sign the expense chits for your department.

Ernest Henderson, 3rd, the son of the late chairman of the Sheraton Corporation of America, was out less than a year after the big hotel chain was acquired by the International Telephone and Telegraph Corporation. Henderson is now devoting himself to setting up and running a string of convalescent care centers.

J. Edgar Bennett suddenly surprised his closest friends. Four months after the Lorillard Corporation, the 210-year-old tobacco company, was bought by Loew's Theatres, Inc., Bennett announced his resignation as Lorillard's president and left for a vacation of several weeks with his family in the lush sun of St. Croix in the Virgin Islands. His parting words before flying to the Caribbean: "I am resigning because of a conflict of management philosophy."

Few mergers of recent years have had so devastating an effect on their principals or, for that matter, on their stockholders and creditors as the 1967 merger between the Pennsylvania Railroad and the New York Central Railroad into the Penn Central Company.

After two years of political wars between the former managements of both lines in the new company, climaxed by a $100-million loss in the first quarter of 1970 in its railroad operations, the board ousted Stuart T. Saunders, the former president of the Pennsylvania, who had taken the chief spot in the combined company. The former head of the New York Central, Alfred J. Perlman, who had become the number-two man in the combination, had been shoved out by Saunders earlier.

Obviously, for a business behemoth like Penn Central with assets worth $7 billion to be unable to pay its employees and short-term bank debts in mid-1970 indicated clearly that the management of the merged company had been not only faulty but mismatched. The concern's transportation subsidiary obtained approval to reorganize under the Federal Bankruptcy Act, but by then the damage to people and shareholders had been done.

Other railroad combinations also appeared headed for similar reorganizations because of profitless and poorly managed assets. Daniel Willard, it seemed decades later, had been right when he devised what came to be known as "Willard's Law" on why railroads have been among the slowest to join in the merger trend. In the 1930s Willard, the former president of the Baltimore and Ohio, declared that "the reason that there haven't been any railroad mergers is that no railroad president has wanted to merge himself out of a job."

People are jarred, uprooted, handled cavalierly and selfishly, but sometimes jostled into better careers both within the new, enlarged company and outside it because of the consolidation.

Louis Epstein, the former president of the Colonial Corporation of America, an apparel complex acquired three years ago by the Kayser-Roth Corporation, found the new situation not to his liking, moved out and became president of Meller, Inc., a New York Stock Exchange firm. And according to his own light, he is "doing better than ever."

But Louis Putze found a better slot for himself opening up each time his company was acquired. Putze, the former president of Controls Company of America, moved up with each of two successive acquisitions of that company, first by the General Precision Equipment Company and then by the Singer Company. Putze became deputy group vice-president of Singer, in which he was instrumental in the administration of several different divisions (actually full-fledged companies) with estimated annual sales of $600 million compared with running a $60-million concern such as Controls Company.

Yet the effect of takeovers encompasses not only people but a company's fortunes, sometimes creating a harsh upheaval of people and the local economy.

"Your job and mine will continue as in the past," announced W. Cordes Snyder, president of Blaw-Knox Company, a Pittsburgh producer of heavy equipment, over a company public-address system shortly after the word was issued that Blaw-Knox was being acquired by White Consolidated Industries, Inc., of Cleveland. But within a year those became empty words, even for Snyder himself.

The concern's headquarters staff of 230 people was cut to 40. Thirty of the 65 supervisors resigned, were fired or retired. About 30 were transferred to other White offices. Snyder himself resigned within a year. His vice-presidents began straying away within months. And the eight operating divisions were shifted around the country. A no-man's-land was created of stringent economy cuts and directives sent to managers to move out by discharge or transfer large numbers of employees.

That wasn't all.

Actually Blaw-Know's management had welcomed White Consolidated's purchase offer. The Pittsburgh company had had more than its share of knocks, with business problems that had made the company a target for bargain-hungry acquisitors who always scour the marketplace looking for buys. So when White appeared on the scene, promising to keep Blaw-Knox as an autonomous division and to put money and talent into it, it seemed that a bright cloud had suddenly appeared. But within a year or more Blaw-Knox's problems multiplied and its fortunes declined even further. White's heavy-handed manner and the marketplace's concern about what was happening at Blaw-Knox severely cut new orders for steel and aluminum mill equipment from about $55 million in 1967 to a total of about $4 million in the first six months of 1969.

Occasionally the new broom sweeps just a mite too clean.

In one acquisition, the president of the acquired company felt that the pressures were such that, at his age of sixty-four, he might as well retire. But within months after he did, the company's sales plummeted. No one seemed to understand why, including the new owners, until it developed that the answer lay in the fact that the midnight poker games had ended.

What did that have to do with it? Simply that during the poker games in which a number of top management people had participated, the president, a former company sales manager, had regularly passed on advice and tidbits and tips to his sales vice-president. Those informal but valuable training sessions had abruptly ended with the president's retirement.

The brunt of mergers and acquisitions will sometimes appear to affect a city in a particularly damaging way. In Pittsburgh, for example, nine of 23 major corporate headquarters have disappeared in recent years because of the takeover of local companies. One reason is that, in industrial cities such as Pittsburgh, many old-established, traditional companies find it hard going to demonstrate any dynamic thrust toward new market shares and then fall prey to outside acquisitors.

The old-line concerns have plenty to offer to takeover experts, including high book value, low price/earnings ratios, so-so stock prices, low-debt ratios and cash. In Pittsburgh the takeover binge has resulted in the setting up of a program to preclude this type of underutilization of company resources by businessmen so that their city wouldn't shine as a beacon to acquisitive companies.

What's particularly rough about a company headquarters leaving a city?

Lots: Since the acquiring company customarily enforces changes in which lawyers, accountants, bankers and service companies should be employed by its newly acquired subsidiary, the loss can have a severe impact on local companies that serviced the vanished headquarters. The upshot of this can be startlingly traumatic to a service concern and even lead it to make acquisitions of its own.

This was the case with the Herblick and Held Printing Company, a Pittsburgh firm which had lost contracts to print financial reports for a number of departed Pittsburgh corporations. To soften the blow and give it a new hedge in another market, the Pittsburgh printer itself acquired a Cleveland printing company.

It was also the case with another service company, this one a Midwest industrial caterer. It, too, suffered the loss of business relationships with several local concerns after they were acquired by outside companies, which then made their own service arrangements. The local factory caterer thought it over—and then allowed itself to be acquired by a diversified, institutional feeding giant.

The rampant merger rate may also be seriously affecting employment, if a recent Wisconsin state study is any barometer. Governor Warren P. Knowles asked the Graduate School of Business of the University of Wisconsin to undertake the study because of the growing rate at which Wisconsin companies were being sold to out-of-state concerns. The study found that in 55 percent of the acquired companies there had been a slowdown in employment growth, or in new jobs, since they were merged into other companies from 1960 to 1968. Professor Jon G. Udell, director of research of the graduate school, who had conducted the survey, recognized that some employees were transferred out of state because of the mergers. But he said that the figure tended to undermine the theory that a merger would accelerate the growth of the acquired firms because of greater resources.

The average annual rate of employment growth of Wisconsin companies acquired by out-of-state concerns declined by 1.8 percent, as compared with an average annual increase of 11.6 percent for the same companies in the immediate years before the mergers took place.

In sifting the findings, Professor Udell came up with the fact that payrolls also had declined after mergers.

Despite inflation, during 1960 to 1968, in 53 percent of the acquired companies the annual payroll had slowed down or not grown after the merger as quickly as it had before. The average payroll for companies acquired by out-of-state conglomerates expanded at the rate of 15.6 percent before the merger but only by 2.1 percent after the merger.

Assuming, then, that takeovers uproot people, affect payrolls and alter the local economic picture, are they worth it all from the standpoint of purely financial performance? In other words, do they improve the profitability of acquired companies? In many cases they do, but results of this kind are withheld by most acquisition-minded firms. Few are eager to reveal the earnings of subsidiaries. They will be compelled to, however, as a result of new congressional actions which call for a breakdown of financial performance of company divisions.

In many cases, as has already been mentioned, earnings are hiked literally by surgery on people, costs and assets. For example, under the hard hand of International Telephone and Telegraph, the Sheraton Corporation of America dropped 20 marginal or unprofitable companies, reorganized its operations and showed improved earnings. One further move obviously dictated by ITT's management was the replacement of Sheraton's president by a member of ITT's management staff.

Within four years after the Bonney Forge Company became a division of Gulf and Western in 1965, its sales and earnings had doubled, partly through making more acquisitions and partly through internal expansion. In this case the president, William Jackson, was retained to run the company as a division.

With post-merger profit performance as an exception, probably the most important question on takeovers is whether the acquired firm will retain its autonomy or will not and invite a creeping form of monotony to settle in for its employees, particularly its executives. The question is an important one, because a preference for independence remains a highly prized reason for the reluctance to sell their businesses by company owners and executives.

Forty-six of 90 companies surveyed by the National Industrial Conference Board in 1969 said they planned to maintain their independent status. Thirty-five ruled out acquisitions of any kind. The others said that they would consider only acquisitions that wouldn't hinder their freedom. As one man put it. "Independence itself is a reason for wanting to remain independent."

Although most acquiring companies maintain a general hands-off policy in the early months, as they become more and more involved with the acquired company the matter of autonomy—which is both much promised and much expected—tends to disappear. Some acquired companies have come to the bitter realization that autonomy is something they must fight constantly for. Others have given up the fight because they have learned that ownership is tantamount to involvement. Give one up and you can forget the other. That principle, hard as it is to swallow for numerous company executives who have signed their names to a purchase contract, is an essential in the merger game.

Sometimes it is possible for a bought company to retain its autonomy by making sure that it, and not the new parent, has the technical or nitty-gritty knowledge of the business. But this, too, is often a losing battle. Perhaps, it seems, the only way to keep the new owners out of the business is for the acquired company to continue to meet its stated plans and, even more important, to continue to make money—more and more of it all the time.

Yet this, too, is no assurance that the new bosses will sit by placidly and not flex their muscles. A good example is what happened when Rollins, Inc., a diversified service company, acquired the Orkin Exterminating Company in 1964. Orkin, a family-owned business, was racking up good profits servicing some one million termite-sensitive customers. But Rollins' executives were appalled at the new division's archaic practices. Service all those customers without a computer? Handle contract renewals only at the beginning of the termite congestion period and then sit out the rest of the year? These questions stirred Rollins' management to try to shift renewals around so that new business could be written during the termite season and renewals could be made during the off-season.

A Rollins' executive said, "We stopped having the termites run the business. Now we run the termite business."

But it would hardly be fair or accurate to say that all the acquiring companies or the conglomerates exert a tight control over their acquisitions so that autonomy withers. That is the case in many instances, but a good number of companies have found that granting autonomy to well-managed divisions makes sense, keeps headquarters costs down and creates incentive.

Consolidated Foods, which by government order in 1965 was compelled to divest itself of 100 supermarkets and 26 drugstores with combined sales of $200 million a year plus, has gone deeply into such nonfood acquisitions as the Electrolux Corporation and other consumer goods companies. Today, according to its management, it is an "autonoplex"—a complex of "autonomous businesses and we much prefer this to being called a conglomerate."

Conglomerates generally are inclined to grant greater autonomy to their divisions than are the acquisition-minded companies that keep to a narrower product or service spectrum.

But the very freedom that the highly diversified company grants has also resulted in bringing down on its head fading profits and even losses, with consequent rumblings from Wall Street and investors. The reason, of course, was the plain fact that the parent company granted too much autonomy and exerted insufficient controls.

The alternative is more control and less autonomy—and it is quickly put into effect once the adverse results provides a stimulus for it.

What ratio ownership and involvement? Will it lead to autonomy or monotony? The line between them is a fine, fine one, but who ever said that business, especially the American mode of business, which has to perceptibly grow every year without fail, is for the simple and the placid?

In any event, the business marriage has been consummated, time passes—and now the real punishment begins.

The People Crunch:
The Grating,
Not the Grateful, Life

The life of the individual in the world of mergers is tough,
constantly grating and ever uncertain. The push is on performance,
but performance criteria are what the boss makes them and he
makes them often. So you never really know whether you are in
or out. Getting through each day is an accomplishment of its own.
Consequently you are smart to enjoy each minor triumph, each
moment of satisfaction, while it lasts.

Am I being unreasonable, negative, sensational, specious,
narrow, unconstructive? Try these:

Gene Brewer, a fifty-five-year-old genial but naïvely idealistic
man, had been with U. S. Plywood Company for 32 years and
president for four years. Yet in 1969, after he resigned in a policy
battle with Karl R. Bendetson, the tough, introverted chief
executive of Champion Papers, Inc., which merged with U.S.
Plywood in 1967, the new switchboard operator in the office of
the $1-billion company could hardly recall Brewer's name.

"How do you spell that, please?" she asked. When she heard

that he had been president, she exclaimed, "Oh, yes! I think someone pointed him out in the halls once."

When American Motors Corporation sold its Kelvinator division in July 1968 to White Consolidated Industries, fewer than 200 of the 600 employees at Kelvinator's Detroit plant were retained by the new management. Most of the rest were either transferred or retired, but about 100 were let go.

A good example was Matthew P. Biedron, fifty-one, who held a $20,000-a-year job after 34 years in the refrigerator division. One day he got the news and his plans to retire and to send his sons to college simply disappeared. For weeks he walked around in a state of shock. He lost 15 pounds. His main problem, aside from his age, was that he didn't know how to go about looking for a job. But he learned. He eventually found one which paid a slightly higher salary.

The ones at the top rung find it the most slippery right after a merger is completed. Norton Simon, Inc., named in honor of the conglomerate builder who could easily have vetoed the name if he had been so inclined, was established in the three-way merger in 1968 of Hunt Foods, McCall Corporation and Canada Dry Company. Three months later James Fixx resigned as editor of the lagging *McCall's* magazine. The month after, Henry Bowes left as president of McCall Corporation. And then, in August 1969, William McKenna resigned as chairman and chief executive of Hunt Foods.

It's not just the top ones who quickly find themselves on the griddle. Frequently it's their entire headquarters group, too. It happened within 60 days to the Norge division's top team and staff when the Borg-Warner Corporation sold the division to the Fedders Corporation in mid-1968 for $45 million. Fifteen top Norge executives were discharged and about 55 of Norge headquarters staff of 250 were laid off.

The word quickly filtered back to Borg-Warner, where the news of what had happened to former colleagues brought shock and dismay. Borg's top man contacted the new owners of Norge and expressed his unhappiness. Fedders replied simply that it would try to find other jobs for those who had been taken off the rolls.

Those are just a handful of examples. We'll have more. Meanwhile . . .

The boss of a $2-billion conglomerate (thinking out loud recently):

> It shocks me and delights me when I think that we now employ almost 100,000 people, directly or indirectly. I sometimes wonder what they all do. Maybe I ought to pinch myself when I think of the size of this empire that we built—all since 1950. But 100,000 lives! What a responsibility. Sometimes I feel like I'm personally carrying all of them on my back. Then I get hot. How many of them are actually earning their pay—or just thumbing a ride?

A secretary in middle management of the same company (talking to some friends):

> I tried hard to like my job here. When they bought out the company I worked for and transferred us to the city, I thought it might be nice to have a change of scenery after six years. But the novelty wore off and the long commuting is annoying. I really don't like my job here, anyway, and I'm looking around. They're so chintzy and at the same time they have so much red tape. In our old company, when we wanted some supplies, we just went out to the supply room and brought it back. Here we put in a requisition and then wait four weeks. But what I dislike most is the bigness of this company and the fact that you don't feel part of anything. I feel I'm just a number in a computer in the accounting department. I know that a lot of people feel the same way I do. What's the point of working in a big, shiny building if you don't feel you belong?

Sometimes an employee doesn't even last out the first week of a merger. People at the top and in the middle seemingly are in a more precarious position than those at the rank-and-file level.

What can anyone do besides sweat and wonder? Adapt, if possible, until the message comes clear. That may take many months.

Fred Detweiler didn't want to go through that routine. He told James J. Ling, the conglomerator who had just acquired Temco Aircraft Corporation, that he could see no sense in Ling's offer to merge with Chance Vought Corporation. But, although Detweiler had done a pretty good job as president of Chance Vought, Ling insisted that the company could be better managed. He successfully engineered the merger and Detweiler moved out.

That was in 1961. Detweiler could have remained, because he received the standard offer to stay on, but he left three months before the merger took effect. He just didn't like the steamroller tactics that were standard Ling practice. So he also sold his stock and looked for another job.

The story should have ended happily for the then fifty-one-year-old Detweiler, but it didn't. It took him some time to line up another job and, in the process, he had some disturbing times. He wound up in a totally different world. At fifty-seven, he became director of administration at Austin College, in Sherman, Texas, earning about one-sixth of what he used to as head man at Chance Vought. But he found that, despite the severe change in income, he could get a lot of satisfaction in his new life.

Others stuck it out but eventually found the erosion in their roles and the decline of their egos impossible to accept. This is the sort of thing that happened to Stanley F. Kaisel, who sold his company, Microwave Electronics, to Teledyne Corporation in 1965. It was one of the first Teledyne acquisitions before Teledyne was to become a conglomerate of over 100 small electronics, metals and oceanography companies.

The first year was easy for the forty-seven-year-old Kaisel. With his own company having sales of under $5 million and accounting for one-tenth of Teledyne's total sales at the time, Kaisel had virtually complete autonomy and reported directly to Teledyne's chairman of the board.

In those days Teledyne, as did most of the conglomerates in their early years, provided a loose, airy environment for its acquisitions. Performance goals were left up to the subsidiaries. Corporate management behaved as though it had planted a lot of different seeds and stood by with a smiling interest to see what would sprout. Why set up standards of return capital invested when each acquired company was blossoming in its own way, was in a different stage of development and needed only an enlightened parental hand?

But things changed—how they changed.

As Teledyne expanded, it set up group management, with one man responsible for supervising a number of acquired companies. Their method of management varied depending upon the executive's own experience and philosophy. Kaisel got a tough man over him, one who did everything according to the book.

Kaisel then experienced a series of shocks. The corporate financial people started breathing down his neck and kept it up relentlessly. Then Teledyne purchased a building for $2 million which Microwave had leased and charged it to that subsidiary's capital account. This made Kaisel's performance look bad in terms of a lowered return on Teledyne's investment in Microwave and also crimped his executives' incentive bonuses, which were tied to the return on capital.

Worst of all, as Teledyne became a giant, Microwave's ten-percent contribution to sales dwindled to one percent. Kaisel and his company simply lost position in the total complex. His personal incentive also underwent a decline, since having become only a minor factor in Teledyne's performance, he could hardly do anything that would favorably affect Teledyne's stock. He quit after three and a half years to become a consultant.

A parting shot, with some very evident truth in it, was delivered in May 1969 by John C. Lobb, former president of Crucible Steel Corporation, when he resigned as executive vice-president of Colt Industries, which had acquired Crucible the year before.

"When duplications are eliminated, the company that does the buying usually decides that its own guys are better than the fellows in the acquired company—whether they really are or not," Lobb said.

Naturally the ability to survive in a corporation, especially a large one with a big yen for swallowing up others, depends to a great extent on one's nature. Some people can absorb the bad and the good and live more or less happily with it. Others can't and won't.

Robert Krausz was one who could and then couldn't. But, to be accurate about it, there was a five-year spell between the could and the couldn't.

A California entrepreneur, Krausz sold his company, Rantec Corporation, to Emerson Electric Company, of St. Louis, but began to find that living within the big electronics complex could present some problems. He reported first directly to Emerson's president and then to a subordinate. He didn't like it, but he didn't mind it very much as long as he could have some good degree of autonomy in operating Rantec.

This, however, became elusive. Although Emerson was hundreds of miles away from Rantec's offices, this remoteness became a complicated matter when it involved lots of red tape, needed approvals and constant communication. Then, too, Krausz learned that some of Emerson's financial and other controls didn't jibe with Rantec's situation in its own locality. There was more, too. The Rantec executive group found itself chaffing under the irritation of high personal incentive and loosely related company dicta. Stock options had been more lucrative before the merger and the stock showed a bigger rise in those days.

But, as in the case of Stanley Kaisel, his Microwave Electronics and Teledyne, Krausz's role and Rantec's sales assumed lesser importance as Emerson grew, so that the corporate office did not always feel impelled to respond quickly to Krausz's calls and queries. He quit, probably with a deep sigh, after five years with Emerson.

The ego factor, which, almost without exception, is the most compulsive force that makes a businessman sell his company, also has a backlash effect. It is at the heart of the entrepreneurial instinct, an instinct that hardly dies when the entrepreneur's business is bought. Instead, it undergoes a protracted period of frustration. In many such cases the ego pangs are so severe that the only release can come from the man's breaking out of his organization trap. Not a few self-made men are simply impossible as organization men.

The regimen of submitting monthly, quarterly, semiannual and annual plans and budgets and then being called to account if there is much of a deviation from them represents a straitjacket that is unbearable. But that is not nearly so onerous to them as the need to get permission to undertake things that they could before the merger with the snap of the fingers or by quickly convening the board and informing it what was being done. Life in the post-merger state for such people becomes a chamber of horrors, each one bigger than the other.

If that's the case, why do such men get involved in mergers in the first place?

Does having the inflated ego preclude having a strong sense of pragmatism or even common sense? Sometimes, it does, but lately stringent changes in the stock market and money markets have compelled entrepreneurs who would like to go public to venture into mergers instead.

"Ego makes many a small entrepreneur go into a merger, and many a merger or acquisition is triggered by the man's need to brag about the fact that he has become a rich man," observes Robert J. Burg, a New York financial and merger consultant. He says:

> If he is the sole owner of the company, he wants $1 million. If there are two, they want $2 million. If three, they want $3 million. Or the multiples thereof, if a larger company is involved. They all want to be millionaires and they want the publicity, too, so that everyone knows about it.
>
> Up till then, most of their assets have been tied up in physical assets and suddenly, through the sale of their company, these become liquid, personal assets. They have arrived.

Or they think they have. More than a few find that even when they can be entrepreneurial in operating their companies as part of a larger one, their style is being crimped. The freedom is gone and there is insufficient flexibility in their new setup to keep them flying to the extent they have been used to. They are, in two words, caged birds.

Some entrepreneurs go through this routine more than once. Morris R. Jepson sold two companies he founded to High Voltage Corporation and to Armour and Company, and resigned from each. "Our commitment," he told *Fortune* magazine, "is not to a company but to technology. And my key people come right along with me, from company to company."

Others go into a merger, find it an unhappy situation, and then go out and buy their own company. Hilliard J. Coan, whose family founded the Hill Supermarkets on Long Island, agreed to a merger with E. J. Korvette, Inc., the dynamic discount-store chain, and then became chairman of the board and one of the largest shareholders in the combined company. But in less than two years he was out after an unsuccessful struggle for power with Eugene Ferkauf, Korvette's founder and then executive committee chairman and largest shareholder of the combined company. Coan then put some of the millions he obtained from that merger into buying control of First National Supermarkets, a Boston-based chain.

And sometimes the entrepreneur has to get out because the company that bought his should never have done so. It was a mistake, a real, 100-percent fiasco for the seller, because it made the deal hurriedly and without adequate investigation.

Says Irving Yahr, a 40-year veteran of putting together small and medium-sized companies in New York's frenetic garment center,

> If an owner has made some bad mistakes, doing a merger or acquisition is the only way he can get rid of it. He hooks on to something else. If he goes on by himself, operating his company and making more mistakes, it will only wipe him out. So it is a game between buyer and seller. And it is easy to get cheated—more often the buyer than the seller.
>
> But the seller who gets rid of a weak company to a buyer who is sometimes simple enough to think he is getting a wonderful deal every time, is sooner or later on the spot. And then he's got to go.

As pointed out in the preceding chapter, the rank-and-file workers are affected by company consolidations particularly when plants are moved, closed or combined. But the more frequent adverse effect is on the executive, who is suddenly uprooted from what seemed to be a secure slot by a new team of either young-Turk executives from the other company or by group-staff men who couldn't care less about him or might not include him in their big plans for the "new company." Or might relegate him to a minor role.

Middle-management executives get it in the neck sometimes because they represent a needless duplication of executive function in the acquiring company. If such people have been living high, the dislocation represents a severe handicap to maintaining a family and leads to financial problems and an extended tour of job seeking.

And while he probably will not suffer the same trials of financial hardships, the top management man whose resignation or discharge has been smoothed by the granting of pension, stock option or other form of severance benefit probably has an even greater loss to pride and standing than the junior executive.

Rejection is a bitter pill for anyone. But for those whose credo has always been status, climbing the professional, social and economic scales, and frequently and fearfully not looking back to see how far they could fall, that fall is often a devastating experience.

Reported *The Wall Street Journal* in May 1969, in discussing the people swath cut by White Consolidated Industries when it took over the Blaw-Knox Company:

> Then there's the "wounded list." In the months immediately following the takeover, one executive developed a bleeding ulcer, another suffered a heart attack and a third had a stroke. A fourth executive experienced backaches, insomnia and a sharp rise in blood pressure because of tensions surrounding the change of ownership, his physician says. His health didn't improve until he resigned.

The plain fact is that entirely too many companies make acquisitions without taking into account the human factors. As a result, their corrective measures are very often cruel, wasteful and even foolish. Let me cite a few instances of human sacrifices that I personally know of that followed quickly, in some cases almost immediately, after the signing of purchase papers.

A broadcasting company bought a publishing company in a multimillion-dollar deal. Within a few months the new owners assigned an advertising executive to supervise both the administration and the revenue-getting phases of the publishing subsidiary. One morning he looked over the most recent results and made a simple pronouncement: "Let's try a new team and see where that takes us."

The publisher and the editor in chief were removed, the former resigning and the latter accepting a lower job because he was locked into a pension program. Between them, the pair had 45 years of service. But it didn't matter, in terms of either company investment or the individuals' commitment. And incidentally, installing a new team didn't "take" the new owners anywhere much. When last checked, they were considering putting in yet another new team.

An entrepreneur with millions and a professional chief executive with little money but lots of experience decided in the late 1960s to start their own business. The millionaire put up the money and the manager put the company together. After two years the business was practically on a paying basis, but the entrepreneur decided to merge it into a larger, more diversified company. The professional manager balked. He was convinced that they needed only another year to make it big and that it was unnecessary to sell out to obtain additional financing. But the entrepreneur, who had had his greatest days of glory when he had built a big company from the first one he had founded, had never lost his yen for the big time. He insisted that they make the move. The manager decided he would bow out. "I just don't like the people," he explained.

The boss lost his control. Launching into a 15-minute diatribe, he tore into the manager and described every weakness and fault he had observed in him from the moment they had met. "You ungrateful bastard! I offer you a big piece of the action! I give you a job! I practically take you in off the street! And what do I get from you?" The manager offered to stay on six or eight months to allow the merger to take place. But he was ordered to vacate as soon as possible and then all his options and benefits were withdrawn.

An example of multiple human sacrifice occurred when a conglomerate-type company that should have known better bought for more than $10 million a family business that wasn't going anywhere. Four members of the family were ousted in less than a year, as well as six middle-management executives, in a clean sweep that came because a discovery of inventory errors proved to be the topper after a series of other disappointments to the buyer.

Personally I knew it was coming.

How come? I was sitting in the office of the president of the company several months after it was acquired, chatting with him, when I happened to look up at a shadow at the doorway. It was that man with the bowler hat and a briefcase, the one that my friend, Carl Baker, had mentioned to me as the harbinger of his own troubles. Probably he was just a facsimile or a symbol of my thought association with what Carl had mentioned to me months earlier. Then the gaze of the guy in the bowler swept arrogantly across the face of the man I was interviewing and moved on to take in everything else.

The company president and I shuddered in unison.

It didn't happen for months after that, but when it did, it affected at least ten lives. But it gave a young salesman, who never expected it, a chance to become the company's president.

And, oddly enough or not, he's doing well.

But there's one saving factor. There is such a heavy demand for qualified executives today that men displaced because of company takeovers often find jobs as good as, and better than, those they vacated.

Except if they are beginning to get up in years. Those who have worked long for one company or are in their late forties or fifties hold a lower priority on reemployment. If they do get jobs, it is tough to match the previous income. Or even to regain the same level on the executive ladder. Why should a company invest in a man of that age when, in theory, at least, his remaining working years can only be half those of a younger man, plus the fact, never really forgotten in the super-realistic world of American business, that he is a retread?

So the sacrificial lamb in company takeovers is the more mature executive, who most often never quite recovers from the shove that he gets. He goes from one job possibility to another, filling out résumés, having "great" interviews and receiving many a promise. Only these never, or rarely, materialize.

As a result, the older displaced executive settles for something less than he wants and is entitled to. He compromises because he must. One such man, who at fifty was suddenly out of a job after working for one company for 26 years, found that as a longtime company department head he could only obtain a job as a substitute schoolteacher for three or four days a week. That gave him some income—plus unemployment compensation.

Another man, a former department-store president, was fifty-

five when he started pounding the sidewalks, going from one executive recruiter to another. He finally wound up as a minor
executive in a research agency. His salary was a fraction of what
it had been, but he was one of the more fortunate ones. He had
saved his money while making it.

The unemployment period can stretch into months and months.
A man who had risen to a vice-presidential post, then had been
reduced to a plant managership and then had been released
found that at the relatively young age of fifty-two no one whom
he had contacted in eight months would have him. A victim of
duplication on the new organizational chart, he could hardly
interest anyone if he applied for a vice-president's post. As a
foreman candidate, he was unlikely because he had been too high
up on the ladder and was asked, "Probably you won't stay, will
you?" And, getting desperate, when he applied for a $12,500-a-
year job, or half of what he had earned, the questioning look in
the interviewer's eye spoke more eloquently than the unasked
question: "What are you, down and out?"

Loss of income, displacement and idleness—these face many
older men caught in the trap of mergers. But not to sound too
idealistic, the human waste in contemporary American business
is atrocious.

Sooner or later a movement must be touched off by industry to
handle the displaced executive in a positive, constructive way.
It is already being carried on by individual executive-placement
firms, some of whom are being given assignments by businesses
attempting to assist their ex-employees. But it seems like only a
trickle of help when a flood is needed.

Now that I have apparently lambasted business mergers for
their adverse effect on people, I would like to balance the scales
a bit.

Businessmen are obviously becoming conscious of the quite
horrible "people crunch" that mergers have and some are taking
steps of a remedial or preventive nature. There is a trend among
the most actively acquisitive companies to recognize that there
are human hardships involved in business takeovers. A good
portion of them have a plan to soften the pain of moving em-

ployees to new cities. Honeywell, Inc., for example, tried to facilitate the burdens of relocating employees because of mergers. When 150 of its own employees had to move from Fort Washington, Pennsylvania, to Framingham, Massachusetts, the employees were flown before the move to Framingham for orientation tours that included meetings with community and school officials. Those who had trouble disposing of their homes in Fort Washington found the company willing to buy them. Honeywell also helped to arrange loans for the purchase of new homes, paid moving expenses and boosted salaries to make up for the difference in the cost of living. And the employment list at Framingham rose sharply as a result.

Not too long ago there seemed to be a brash lack of concern by companies attempting takeovers with the reaction of their intended acquisitions to their plans. But that, too, is changing, not necessarily because the merger advocates have gotten religion but because of the hard scrutiny of the government and the hypersensitivity of the stock market. Dogged pursuance of a takeover in the face of a fight requires the proper environment.

But there is little doubt that recent disappointments in acquisitions have also compelled acquiring companies to take a greater interest in the management quotient of takeover candidates. Every so often a small company will be acquired simply so that its chief executive or other top man might be brought into a bigger corporate fold. But, conversely, many a mistake has been made through bad appraisal or the lack of proper appraisal of people in an acquired company.

In as many cases as not, an honest attempt is made by a corporate management to use constructively the executives snared into the net that acquired the company. But few firms are as yet sufficiently sophisticated or willing to do this or have the knowledge, patience and determination that it needs. Yet if a prediction in this connection can be made, it is that the role of the staff personnel man and the management recruiter is due to grow in the years ahead, as mergers continue to increase and the needs for manpower grow more stringent.

The people situation in mergers and acquisitions is a fluxing one, with some rising hopes that improved handling of the human equation may yet alleviate the "people crunch."

In the meantime, however, until such an apparent millennium may arrive, why not consider:

A "Handy" List to Avoid a Career Disaster in Takeovers

John L. Handy, founder of Handy Associates, Inc., an executive-personnel management consultant, is a wily expert in the field of executive search and development, particularly in relation to mergers. "To avert a rude awakening when his company is acquired by another company," he told me, "a farsighted executive should examine his own situation from all angles. Here is a checklist of 11 questions he should ask himself in such circumstances."

1. Did the new owner buy your company for management talent, including yours?
2. Was your company acquired for nonmanagement reasons, such as financial advantages, manufacturing facilities, or a distribution setup of which you are a part?
3. Are you the key executive in a profit center of vital interest to the new management?
4. Are you flexible enough to (a) report to a new group of executives? (b) function in a new organizational structure, that is, a decentralized one? (c) do things "their" way?
5. Are your executive skills transferable within the new structure?
6. Is your salary too high in relation to the compensation scale of the purchasing company?
7. Is your salary relatively high in the market for your job outside the company?
8. Is your function duplicated within the parent company?
9. Were you known to be opposed to the merger?
10. Are you in a staff position?
11. Are you a "self-made" man with long tenure?

"If your answer is 'yes' to the first five questions and 'no' to the remaining six," says Handy, "you are in a strong position in the corporate merger. However, if your answers are off on even three or four points," he adds, "you had better begin to look around for other, if not greener, pastures."

10

The Paper Wonderland

4:15 P.M.

They tumbled into the conglomerate's office, not drunk with whiskey but with the exciting possibilities, yelling numbers at each other like football signals, laughing at the bargaining and cursing each other for the obvious cheating that each offer and counteroffer took, behaving raucously and childishly, as if they were playing stickball 30 years earlier on a narrow ghetto street.

"One hundred thousand shares of treasury common, you son of a bitch," Eric Wunder said, "you should only croak instead of enjoying it!"

"It doesn't even excite me," said Al Stanton, with an exaggerated grin.

"You are bluffing," Wunder said, his blood visibly rising in his neck. "I happen to know on good authority that cash money is something that you just don't have."

"I got plenty—" Stanton retorted, but he was spared from saying what he had plenty of. He had spotted the men's room just off the elevator in the elegant, mahogany-paneled offices and made for it. His stomach was heaving, as it had often lately, but now it was worse. He and Wunder had had a tempestuous lunch and had decided to pursue it in Wunder's office.

Ten minutes later, when tall, gaunt Stanton emerged, he found Wunder's cameolike young secretary waiting just outside the men's room. "He is waiting for you in the boardroom, please," she said, with a smile straight from a Gainsborough.

In his weakened abdominal condition, Stanton was taken aback by the girl's fresh, almost immaculate beauty. How could she avoid Wunder's crocodile bite? How could she even stand him? He followed her into a handsome boardroom, in which about a dozen men of various ages were engaged in a pantomime—no, a flawlessly smooth montage of unfolding and spreading out folders, unzipping heavy briefcases, comparing one law treatise with another, unraveling profit and loss statements. One man posted charts on an easel. Another prepared a movie screen. As he gaped in the doorway, Stanton was bumped gently on the backside. A bulky attendant with a work uniform bearing the conglomerate's initials wheeled in a sleek, boxlike device. A deskside computer?

"Come on, come on, don't stand there like a shmuck!" shouted Wunder at Stanton. "We got no time to waste, Al."

Wunder sat at the center of the shining oval table, staring impatiently around at this staff. Suddenly he snapped his fingers at 45, 90 and 135 degrees, so that they all caught the brisk sound and its breeze. Everyone collapsed into chairs simultaneously, staring alertly at their records and back at Wunder, ready for the go.

Stanton sat in the one open seat, directly opposite the conglomerator, realizing that all these people had been summoned and the preparations made in something like the ten minutes while he had been indisposed. It bespoke tremendous discipline and an awesomely smooth meshing of a corporate machine.

"What range of multiples do we use on crappy outfits like Al's here?" asked Wunder, jabbing a finger at a dour young man at the end of the table.

"Eight to twelve."

"Wait a minute, Eric—" Stanton began.

Wunder waved him aside with a big grin. "Kidding," he said. "You see that I haven't been kidding, though, about the multiple—"

"You're basing it on our last quarter, we had some non-recurring expenses—"

"All right. George, what's the mature date on those debentures we got left over from the Peruvian Shipping deal?"

George, who sat across from the dour young man, responded instantly without looking it up. "This April 30—"

"Okay, Al. Maybe that's it—we can give you a better deal with debentures that could give you maybe a 13 times multiple if you don't mind waiting three years to convert them to common—"

Al Stanton leaned across the table, his stomach turning. He *just* must be getting an ulcer, even though his doctor had thought not on two separate checks. "Look, Eric, I don't want to sell my business after 20 years for a bunch of paper that I got to wait three years to know if they're any good."

"What do you mean, 'any good'!" Wunder yelled. "All our paper is good, even if we just paper the walls with it. That's what you think about it, anyway, don't you? Dammit, you know what we built here in less than ten years? One of *Fortune's* top 20 industrials, by God, that's what we built here."

"Look, I don't mean to say that your paper is no good. It's just that I know we can do some great things together, but I can't give up the rights to my company unless I know what I'm getting."

"All right, all right. One hundred and twenty-five thousand shares of treasury and forget the warrants."

"No," Al Stanton said instinctively.

"Then it's 130,000!"

"You can't do it, Mr. Wunder," spoke up a stolid man with gray hair as he pointed a finger at a brochure in front of him. "That would leave us only—"

"All right, we'll buy a block on the open market and put it in the pot with the 100,000 treasury—"

Al found himself shaking his head even before Wunder had

finished. What was wrong? Suddenly the conglomerator's secretary was in front of him, again startling him with the exquisiteness of her face and figure. He caught Wunder's gaze on him as he shifted his expression from surprise to idle curiosity.

"Mr. Stanton," the girl said. "Mr. Ahl is outside asking for you."

"Who's Ahl?" asked Wunder. "Your number-two man. Sure, send him in, Miss Mayo, but just tell him to keep his trap shut, Al. He's just a spectator, not a participant."

"Mr. Wunder, the group is also here from Ardsley," the girl said quickly.

"Oh, yeah, send them in. But tell them, too, to sit down along the wall and just listen. Tell them if they want to get into the negotiations, they got to raise their hands like in school and be recognized."

Within three minutes the boardroom had filled with the arrival of about ten more men, including Bill Ahl, who was Stanton's executive vice-president, Henry Applegate, Stanton's lawyer, and a team of executives from the trucking division of Wunder's conglomerate. Stanton knew a few of them, being in the same field, and nodded politely, although his stomach was not quiescent and his head pounded. He knew that they had been summoned by Wunder, so that they could guide him, if necessary, in his negotiations with someone of their own industry.

A look of hope appeared on Stanton's face as he prepared to listen to his lawyer, Applegate, take on Wunder. But, of course, it was just the other way around.

"Listen to me, Mr. Lawyer, we want Al's fleet and warehouse system because that's all we need to make our carrier system a coast-to-coast operation. Now, we're willing to extend ourselves and our holdings to get it. Now, we're even willing to overlook your company's lousy earnings last quarter and—"

Applegate, a Wall Street attorney who had always impressed Stanton with his stern ethical code, removed his jacket, something that his client had never seen him do before as he leaned toward Wunder and responded to various suggestions of terms.

Stanton gazed curiously around to see where Bill Ahl was

and found him sitting directly behind him and against the wall. Ahl smiled encouragingly, but Stanton could tell that Ahl didn't mean it. Bill had been against his making a deal with Wunder from the outset. They could expand by themselves, buy the equipment they needed, without anyone else.

Wunder was now on a new tack: "There's nothing says we can't make it a package—cash, stock, warrants, and even debentures—"

Applegate shook a lean, correct head. "That's too complex a deal for us, Mr. Wunder. We need a simple exchange of stock for assets, with a multiple that is based on our average earnings for the past eight fiscal quarters."

Wunder rose angrily, a small, dapper man with spite on his spit as he cried out, "You goddam lousy lawyers! Now I see why Al wasn't listening to anything I been saying. Eight quarters! You—"

"Eric, Applegate's been my attorney for years and naturally I discussed it all with him before," Stanton said.

"This goddam lawyer is gonna screw up this whole deal. How can he give you a minimum figure when he hasn't even been in on our talk till now? Al, all of you, listen to me—"

All eyes were fixed on him as he stood at center table and pleaded for understanding of what he was trying to accomplish. He was building economic security for thousands of people, not just for today but for tomorrow and tomorrow's tomorrow. He was charting new directions for the American free-enterprise system, something that Europe hadn't known, so that it had had many dark years. It was a famous speech, having been made before two congressional committees, half a dozen security-analysts' groups, a number of private meetings on Wall Street. Perspiration dripped off Wunder's face as he spoke with a ringing sincerity. He paused for effect, but instead the door suddenly opened again and Miss Mayo, his secretary, stood there. Wunder demanded, harshly, "Yeah, what is it?"

The girl was undaunted and admirable to Stanton as she said, "It's Senator Manson. He's in your office and says he just must see you."

Wunder looked around with, yes, wonder, stunned by the

interruption. Manson, everyone knew, was the assistant chairman of a Senate committee. Would Wunder interrupt his downhill drive to hammer out a deal with Stanton in order to see a powerful member of a Senate committee? The suspense in the room was palpable, not a sound was heard except everyone's breathing in short gasps, as the perspiring conglomerate chief turned back to the girl and said:

"Miss Mayo, tell the Senator I said, 'Fuck you, Senator. Call me for an appointment like everybody else does!' Now, repeat to me, Miss Mayo, word for word just what you're going to tell him, Miss Mayo."

The cameolike, fragile and intensely beautiful Miss Mayo did. It was very impressive.

5:45 P.M.

Bill Ahl couldn't believe it. On his right there was an earnest young man who kept himself nervously busy with a slide rule, alternately stuffing it into his pocket and then whipping it out every time Wunder mentioned a new figure. Then he would lean over to a colleague sitting at the oval table and whisper a few words. On Ahl's left was a squat, pug-nosed man in a pin-stripe suit who studied some sort of a technical manual as though it held all the secrets being sought by everyone in the room. As the conversation shifted among Wunder, Applegate and Stanton, this man would find the right place in his book, point a finger or make a "6" out of the first three fingers of his left hand and hold it aloft to the team at the table.

"We figure that over 30 percent of your rolling equipment is practically past the depreciation time," Wunder said.

"The actual figure is less than half that," Applegate said.

"What the hell," said Stanton, showing new energy, "even at 30 percent that would mean that we have twice the proportion of new equipment that your own division has."

"Hah!" shouted Wunder. "There's life in the corpse yet. You had me worried for a while."

"If you thought I was a corpse, we wouldn't be here right now," Stanton said.

And so it went, seemingly getting nowhere. Every few minutes Wunder, after snapping questions at his growing team or consulting with one member, would make another offer. Gradually his patience appeared to be getting thinner.

This became apparent as he began to make his offers more and more without seeking the help of his own people. Finally, at about 7:00 P.M., he rose again and stretched and yawned.

"All right, you lousy bastard," he said to Al Stanton, "name your own figure. Whatever it is, you can have it."

Al shrugged. Applegate looked aghast. And a number of Wunder's own people stared at him in amazement.

"What the hell's the difference?" said Wunder, staring right back at his own legionnaires. "It's all paper, anyway, ain't it? We can print as much as we want in any color, any size, any design we want, can't we?"

He reached over at the briefcase of a colleague and withdraw a fistful of stock certificates. He fanned them out in his hands, a dozen of varying colors and designs. Suddenly he threw them up in the air and they cascaded over the table and faces of the men sitting around it.

"What the hell—it's only paper until we do the job and make the money that means the paper stands for something, right?" demanded Wunder.

Bill Ahl could tell from Stanton's taut position in his chair that he was outraged. He felt his own heart pounding. It seemed to him more than ever that Al must realize the type of man with whom he was considering an affiliation. How long did it take to see it? Bill himself had had no illusions from the moment the possibility of a takeover of Stanton's business began less than a week before.

A "friendly" banker had thought that they ought to meet. Bill Ahl wondered how friendly the banker could be if he had come up with the idea of putting together businesses founded by a shrewd man like Eric Wunder, who had built a $1-billion conglomerate in less than a decade, and Al Stanton, who had parlayed one truck into a fleet and then into a transportation concept.

Stanton, a complex man with a deep streak of inferiority that existed alongside a similar stratum of egotism, was intrigued with Wunder's acerbic enthusiasm. The little European looked at life in America like an old, wise child in a nursery but behaved in its marketplace like a tyrant. He had a brusque, Continental charm which helped him, when he elected to use it, but he really didn't need it. He was one of those post-World War II immigrants who saw opportunities in the United States through fresh, acquisitive eyes, and bit them off with crocodile jaws.

He immediately appealed to Stanton's desire to see his company become a giant by wedding it to his own trucking division. As he had inched toward bigness and tasted affluence, Stanton had been tortured by the fear that he already had more success than he deserved. He was afflicted, too, or thought he was afflicted, by a wife who had started as his switchboard operator and who daily convinced him that he should be happy with what he had and should not lose his health in a fruitless attempt to overreach himself.

When, in a burst of frankness after they had soon realized that they had more than just a lot to talk about, Stanton had casually mentioned that "even my wife thinks I've gone as far as I have any right to," Wunder's eyes had shown a streak of insight. "Yeah, old boy, I know just what you mean," he had said.

All this had been related by Stanton to Bill Ahl, the only other person in the world to whom he had confided all of it, and a chill had run through the engineer: "Al, I didn't know you were so anxious to double the size of our fleet and to become a coast-to-coast carrier," Bill had said.

"Sure, I would. Why stand still at 38—when the whole world is ahead of us?"

"But you don't need that guy to do what you want," Bill had said. "With the company's record and your reputation, you could get the financing you need and all the charters you need."

Al's gaze had turned vague at that point and Bill Ahl saw it all then. It was a matter of chemistry, that all-important prerequisite to a merger between men and companies, and he had walked away with a premonition of defeat.

"I'm listening for your figure," said Eric Wunder. "What's the matter. Now that I'm leaving it strictly up to you to hold a gun to my head, you're losing your guts?"

"Now you're being the shmuck," Al said, with a pained smile. "I don't have any idea what amount of paper we should get. I'll leave that up to Applegate. He knows a lot better than I do."

Applegate stared thoughtfully at the two of them. His satisfaction, a weird expression of glee on a thin, lined face tortured by self-repression, was very evident. "Yes, yes, I think we can work something out now," the attorney said.

8:20 P.M.

But even that took a lot longer than anyone thought.

The figure that the lawyer proposed was actually only one element, a minor one once it was established. There was the matter of contingency, part of the payment predicated on future earnings, the matter of continuance of key executives other than Al Stanton, and a hundred other details. Even Wunder's eyes began to bulge and he got cross, impatient, and nasty. When Bill Ahl spoke up once to protest one contention by Wunder's team, the conglomerate chief turned to Al Stanton and asked:

"Any reason why this guy can't go? Do we need him?"

"We need him, all right. He stays—absolutely," Al said grimly. "As a matter of fact, if he goes, I go, too."

Wunder shrugged, as if it were all too much.

He sat quietly now, a Napoleon empty inside after the victory because it had spent him. After a few minutes, he jumped up and went around to Al and said, "Come on, let's go have dinner." Then he turned viciously on the others in the hot, smoky room and said, "The rest of you guys stay here until you hammer out all the details. Don't move an inch. Don't even go to the bathroom. Order in your dinner and drinks. Al here and I will be back by midnight, by which time I want to know for sure that his crappy little company is part of Wunder Corporation. All that should be left for the two of us to do is to write in our names."

He then buzzed for Miss Mayo. She came in, as fresh and as startling to Stanton as she had been hours before.

Wunder stood then with one hand on Al's shoulder and one on his secretary's. With a smile that was impossible to fathom, he said to Stanton, "One thing more, you shmuck. Just to show you how I feel about you, to get you over your hangup with your wife and to seal our deal, I'm throwing in Miss Mayo, too."

And that, according to Bill Ahl, my informant who spelled it all out for me and who understandably has left the company since all this happened, is about how that merger took place.

11

From Howard Hughes to Dr. Hammer: The Top 25 Merger-Masters

Howard Hughes, the billionaire recluse, and Kirk Kerkorian, the Fresno farmer's son who turned into a big-league corporate manipulator, compete in the hot sun of Las Vegas to become the biggest commercial host of that glittering oasis. In separate deals they also match strides to try to swallow major Western airlines.

Saul P. Steinberg, stopped cold in his desire to obtain control of the Chemical Bank of New York before he could even offer a formal bid, jumps the Atlantic to spend $60 million to buy Pergamon Press, Ltd. His plan to take over the leading London publisher of books, technical journals and encyclopedias, sets off the bloodiest takeover battle in British corporate history. It leads to suits, countersuits, executive ousters and a crisis in a staid civil body, the London Panel on Take-Overs and Mergers. Forty thousand feet over the Mississippi, Meshulam Riklis leans back in Olympian solitude in his private, twin-jet Sabreliner and smilingly contemplates new ways of exchanging "Russian Rubles" (his own term) for companies to add to his $2-billion complex. And in an East Side Manhattan duplex Charles G. Bluhdorn grimly watches "rushes" of new movies of his unprofitable Paramount Pictures subsidiary in a $316,756 projection room.

But all of these are minor in scope and pale in mood to the aspect of Dallas financial wizard James J. Ling early in 1970 as he contemplates a $289-million paper loss of his company's acquisition of Jones and Laughlin Steel Corporation. This was after Ling-Temco-Vought had spent $425 million to buy a 63 percent interest in the nation's sixth largest steel company.

Neither Ling nor L-T-V, however, had counted on (1) a decline in Jones and Laughlin earnings so steep that it failed to provide dividends to shareholders in three of five fiscal quarters, (2) two strikes that pared the steel company's profits, (3) a severe drop in Jones and Laughlin's stock values, and (4) being slapped with the biggest antitrust suit by the Justice Department in a decade. The Texan, on whom fortune had seemed to smile at every move, was now bitter and uneasy. What had happened to that fabled Texan luck?

These, in some more recent situations, are a few of the men at the top of the contemporary merger movement in America. About 25 men rock that merger activity.

They do it individually, peripatetically, leaving surprise and dismay in their wake. Their economic and human power is tremendous, extending far beyond the limits of their already large companies. Collectively they have changed the course of American business, jarring it by sheer force of energy, creativity, impatience, crust and bravado out of its rut of recent decades, and have made diversity of product and service a new, viable means of growth. Centralized control, which was beginning to bear a stigma in the late 1960s, because the economy was slowing down, suddenly gained new attention as a result of their freer, more enlightened management, although it was not always a more efficient one.

They let fresh air into dusty executive chambers and boardrooms, jolted the Establishment, titillated if not satisfied millions of investors and exposed and skewered the mystique of proprietary ownership's rights.

They also fell flat on their faces, not once but often. Their noses got caught in the doors thrown shut in their faces, their knuckles got skinned and bloodied from the books being slammed down on them and their treasuries and reputations were dented by the fines and legal suits when they tried to push around the laws of the land.

They are an odd but hardy lot. Each is a rugged individualist who likes his own ideas best, with a life-style, however, that varies greatly from the next one's except in its ostentatiousness. They love to show how well they have arrived, from Ling's $2-million Dallas showplace to Riklis' $400,000 New York town house to Kerkorian's private, walnut-paneled DC-9, his 10,000-square-foot ranch house that cost $500,000 and his 147-foot-oceangoing yacht and to Cortes W. Randell's world's fastest ocean racer.

They range in age from thirty (Steinberg) to seventy-two (Dr. Armand Hammer) and run a wide spectrum in ethnic and national origins from white Anglo-Saxon Protestant to American Jewish or Catholic, Armenian, Palestinian and Austrian.

How did they get there in the first place? How do they operate? What makes them tick? Will they last?

Above all, perhaps, what do the careers and behaviors of some of the most important merger-masters prove in terms of contemporary American entrepreneurism? Are we fated to see spectacles of continuing self-aggrandizement of financial manipulators or are we hopefully in for an era of new-breed business management that will help to solve some of our most lingering economic and social ills?

Let's train a spotlight on about a dozen of those in the $1-billion club and see what it shows.

Texan Charles B. Thornton put together one of the most unusual companies in American corporate history and one of the fastest-growing on record. As chairman of Litton Industries, he is a management specialist who functions in a technological environment. It was just the combination that he wanted. In 1953 he and two other ex-Hughes Aircraft executives dropped in on

Lehman Brothers, the investment bankers, to borrow $1.5 million to buy Litton, a tiny producer of microwave tubes.

They presented a radical idea. A lot of scientists were floating around in business. Many had an entrepreneurial flair but were locked into situations that didn't allow them to satisfy their personal and professional drives. Now, if a diversified company could be set up around them, permitting them to carry on research toward practical ends and giving them incentive through participation in profits, there was a chance that an exciting and profitable enterprise could be developed.

Lehman bought the idea and Thornton and his colleagues bought the San Carlos, California, company. Its founder, Dr. Charles Litton, agreed to sell on the condition that he receive the purchase price, $1 million, all in cash. Had he waited and taken stock instead, he could eventually have realized $85 million within 15 years for his little company.

Within the next four years Thornton and Roy Ash, who became Litton's president, acquired ten companies in the electronics field. In the meantime, they made use of the Litton laboratories to test new ideas in radar, computers and inertial guidance. But Thornton, who became enamored with the new technologies, kept buying companies in the fields of business machines, medical electronics, oceanography and shipbuilding. The common denominator was technology and the common incentive for both those acquired and the Litton executives was entrepreneurism through stock options, capital gains and income based on performance.

Had anyone ever really thought that scientists were just wild-eyed theorists, living in a world of their own? Not this bunch. The combination resulted in a tremendous company which, after only 15 years, reached total corporate sales of just about $2 billion. The idea of buying technology companies and technological talent had paid off. By 1969 Litton had 120,000 employees, including 12,000 scientists and technicians, working in 227 plants in 14 countries, making some 10,000 different products. Earnings had remained high—that is, until 1968.

That year Litton, which had become known as a model conglomerate, reported its first quarterly earnings decline and its stock dropped precipitously. Suddenly, in the eyes of Wall Street and many thousands of investors, not only Litton, the prestige one, but all conglomerates were through. And then, as if to confirm it, the conglomerates all started reporting either lower earnings or declines. Time and nature had caught up with most of them, in a perhaps inevitable happening as it would with any business segment, and cleaning house and consolidating their position became the logical moves. The entire field's stock, too, dropped to two-year lows, in a sensitive response by investors to the situation.

But Thornton wasn't much dismayed. To him Litton wasn't a fast-buck outfit, its pillars were sunk deep into long-range potentials and he remained confident of a big earnings rise in the 1970s. He certainly wasn't dismayed about the conglomerate way of life. In view of exploding technology and product obsolescence, he felt, the properly financed, well-managed and diverse company was the inevitable direction in which American business must go. Nor were conglomerates a threat to small companies, he remained convinced. Capably managed small companies should have no trouble thriving amid the growth of conglomerates. These or any other giants don't throttle the little outfit—only poorly managed small companies do.

An interesting thing about Litton is the fact that many of its executives have left to become company founders themselves, starting either limited technology companies or conglomerates. So many departed that they began calling themselves "Lidos," for Litton Industries Dropouts.

Thornton's attitude was expressed by a regretful shrug. Litton's simply attracted management recruiters who sought executives for those companies which were eager to grow as multinational companies. While many Litton men stayed in spite of more lucrative outside offers, more than 25 departed and became chief and top executives of other companies in related fields. It was a testimonial to Thornton and Ash, but it gave Litton a chance to bring up some ambitious young men.

Merger-makers can come in pairs, too. One of the top brother acts in American business consists of two of the most active acquisi-

tors on the country's business scene. In something like 20 years
Laurence A. Tisch and Robert Tisch, the two chiefs of Loew's
Theatres, Inc., have built a $1-billion complex of hotels, movie
theatres, real estate and tobacco products. Their biggest coup
was the November 1968 acquisition of Lorillard Corporation for
about three times the amount of Loew's 1968 sales—$450 million
of debentures and warrants.

That was a curious deal. Lorillard, bombarded by government
broadsides on the tobacco-cancer issue, decided that it would not
mind being absorbed by a smaller company if it permitted the
cigarette company to submerge its identity to the financial community. By doing so, admitted Manuel Yellen, Lorillard's chairman, "Our business would continue to grow."

The Tisches *almost* had another big one. Commercial Credit
Company's management was horrified when Larry Tisch informed it that he had been buying the company's shares on the
open market, already owned ten percent and now meant to take
over the company. Commercial Credit managed to attract Control Data as a preferred suitor and the Tisches pulled out after a
brief but spirited contest in tender offers. The brothers were
probably disappointed, but they walked away from the deal laughing. They netted a profit on the stock of $28.5 million.

The Tisches' parents had owned a summer camp and a family
clothing factory. In 1946 they sold these properties and, after
Larry discovered it in a classified ad, they bought the Laurel-in-
the-Pines Hotel in Lakewood, New Jersey. Two years later the
father and mother turned the hotel over to the boys, who had
just finished college. Soon, because of their efforts, the menu
was "beefed up," the entertainment was "jazzed up." The huge,
ramshackle Laurel began drawing a lot of customers who had
just been driving by or had been frequenting the burgeoning
nearby motels.

The boys did so well that they were shortly able to buy several
other small Jersey resort hotels. Then they caught the smell of
the sea breeze not far away at Atlantic City. Within four years
they had shown enough profit to take over two great Atlantic
City hotels (the Traymore and the Ambassador) that had seen
better days and then, using profits they made on those, to buy

the leases on two midtown Manhattan hotels (the McAlpin and the Belmont Plaza). Then in 1956, they built without the need to obtain any mortgage the $17-million Americana Hotel in Bal Harbour, Florida.

The Tisch boys showed unusual imagination, even for entrepreneurs. Between them, by 1969 they had amassed a personal fortune of more than $300 million by following two principles. One was to have a basic sensitivity to values. The other was to acquire undervalued properties and to give them new life. An instinct for hard work and a sense of giving their building construction a showmanlike look also helped.

They took the then unusual step of building a large ballroom at the Americana to attract the convention business, which would be more dependable than just hoping for the best during the tourist seasons. It proved to be just that.

After buying the Loew's theatre chain in 1959 from MGM, they launched an intensive campaign to make maximum use of the real estate. They leased out some sites by shutting down old theaters in the downtown district, opened new ones in the suburbs and even put two smaller theaters side by side on the same spot on which one big one had stood. The timing was right, because people starting going to the movies again.

In a little over two years seven hotels were either built or modernized, six in New York, including the Summit, the Americana, the Howard Johnson Motel, the City Squire Inn, the Midtown Motor Inn and the Regency Hotel. Occupancy in Loew's 17 hotels topped 80 percent or about 12 points above the industry average. The hotel end of the business, starting back with Laurel-in-the-Pines, became the country's third largest.

The brothers don't care much for the term "conglomerate," believing that they are merely businessmen, "in the old sense of the word," as Larry, the older by three years, puts it. They point out that their job is to take assets and earn a solid return. They buy companies not because they are glamorous but because of their potential. The brothers always take the maximum depreciation allowance, they say, so that earnings are never overstated.

Both take a close personal interest in the business, studying sales reports and cash receipts every morning. When they were involved in the building of six New York hotels, construction moved along according to plan, perhaps because Bob practically lived in the construction shacks, going from one rising tower to the other and checking progress on each level.

But they make mistakes too. For example, the blue and white Summit Hotel on Manhattan's Lexington Avenue was a takeoff on the Miami beachfront type of garishness. In the case of Lexington Avenue, the Summit proved to be too long a walk to the beach. Once the Tisches realized their error, they moved to tone down the Summit's look and then obtained an 80 percent occupancy.

Like the other conglomerates, Loew's was much loved until in 1969 its stock dropped 25 percent from its year's high of 61½. Some of this spilled over from the Justice Department's attack on Ling-Temco-Vought and ITT, but the Tisches decided to sit awhile until the antitrust furore subsided. In the meantime, the Loew's Asset Fund, whereby the brothers hope to "obtain a fund of $200 million other than from bank borrowings for a major acquisition," has steadily mounted in value.

Commenting on the furore that involved the takeover trend, Larry Tisch angrily told *The Wall Street Journal,* "If you stop takeovers, you'll see the decline of American business. Why perpetuate poor, inefficient management in industry after industry?"

The brothers get along well, at least in outward appearances. They socialize and play tennis together and profess much faith in one another. They were always friends, even back in their parents' summer camp as baggy-pantsed kids. That friendship has endured in a much bigger game.

Harold S. Geneen has been called both "the greatest corporation executive in America" and a "man-killer." He also put together some of the period's biggest mergers which became prime targets for antitrust enforcement.

The chairman-president of International Telephone and Telegraph Company is deceptively quiet and pleasant-looking, speaking rapidly in a soft but clear voice. His round face, too, has a seraphic look, even when he continues his executive meetings into the late night, breaking for dinner at midnight. But Geneen is the man who built the company from $700 million in 1959, when he left his post as executive vice-president of Raytheon Corporation to join ITT as president, to $5.5 billion by 1969, mostly by making big acquisitions. He demonstrated the additional and unprecedented feat of increasing net income every quarter for 42 consecutive quarters.

Geneen also, despite his benign appearance, loves to give his executives almost unattainable goals and then draws accomplishments out of them by beating boys into men. This harsh treatment has either driven executives out or made them grimly succeed at their tasks while retaining the scars of the rack. Sometimes it did both.

The big international electronics and telecommunications supplier was founded in 1920 by the Behn brothers, Sosthenes and Hernand. They developed it to world prominence, but a combination of rather unstable foreign holdings and unsuccessful ventures into domestic consumer goods obviously demanded a new hand at the throttle.

Prior to Geneen's coming to ITT, its efforts to build a domestic business had included such then famous subsidiaries as the Capehart-Farnsworth Corporation and the Coolerator Corporation. But Geneen did better. He got Sheraton Hotel, Avis Rent-A-Car and Levitt and Sons, the big builders. His aim was to build up domestic earnings to the point where they would at least equal those from the successful foreign ventures. And he chose the acquisition route to do it.

And how he chose that route. Few entrepreneurs in recent American economic history did it with such gusto. He bid $400 million for the American Broadcasting Company in 1965. Then, after the Federal Communications Commission approved the merger, the Justice Department appealed to the U.S. Court of Appeals to cancel it, but the court refused to act. Geneen withdrew in a dramatic New Year's Day statement in 1968, blasting the continuing delay and explaining that the proposal was no longer in the best interests of the shareholders.

(Litton Industries, incidentally, also had approached ABC, in December 1965, with a purchase offer of $80 a share, but Leonard

H. Goldenson, the generalissimo of ABC's diverse empire of television and radio stations and movie theaters, chose ITT's offer of $85.50. Geneen's decision two years later gave him a severe disappointment.)

But the money offered by Geneen for ABC was as nothing compared to the $1.5 billion in a proposed tender offer that he made in 1969 for the Hartford Fire Insurance Company. The Justice Department again attacked this plan and sought an injunction against it. A federal court refused the injunction, as well as one requested by Justice against ITT's 1969 merger with Grinnell, a large producer of fire-protection systems.

In March 1970 Geneen was eloquent in proselytizing for the Hartford deal, trotting out a few of his loyal executives of acquired companies and other friendly sources, such as banks, to testify on his behalf at a hearing before the Connecticut Insurance Commissioner. The issue was whether the tender offer was, in the commissioner's eyes, a valid economic one for the state's insurance industry.

Geneen, an old smoothie who bears his battle scars well and moves from battle to battle like a well-oiled tank, simply promised the moon. He assured the commissioner that Hartford Fire's employment would not be cut, that its headquarters would remain in Hartford, that he would not take any funds out of the concern, that he would not cut employees' pension and fringe benefits, that he would not interfere in management, that he would not reduce insurance levels in any lines for at least five years, that—

Even the commissioner admitted he was impressed and later approved the takeover.

But the litigation involving ITT's takeover of Hartford Fire and Grinnell will probably drag on for years.

Geneen's approach to the conglomerate philosophy or way of life is simple: "We think a philosophy of varied industries can lead to a more efficient corporate vehicle than the traditional pattern and one, moreover, that develops management capabilities and flexibilities that no one-industry approach can provide."

In ITT's case the credo seems to have worked. Net income rose from $32 million in 1960 to $180 million in 1968, dividends to shareholders from 50¢ to 85¢ and stock values on the low-high ratios from 16–24 to 44⅞–62½. And net sales had increased almost eightfold by 1969.

But Geneen, unlike Thornton, is a professional manager, not an entrepreneur. His marrow is more attuned to achieving management and corporate efficiency, even perfection, than it is toward making money that he can personally bank or salt away to lead the affluent life. As he told one of his close associates, "When you stop working for money, that's the real life." Perhaps he gives his executives superhuman tasks so that they can enjoy "the real life," the striving to make ITT the best-run corporation in America.

Despite all his setbacks, James J. Ling may well be the greatest player of the merger game. The former electrician from Dallas, who dropped out of school at fourteen and never learned anything about finance, eventually taught everyone something about finance. From a small electrical business he started in 1955, selling shares in his company at the Texas State Fair, he built a conglomerate supergiant, consisting of electronics, aircraft and airlines, sporting goods and meat-packing and steel manufacturing that catapulted his Ling-Temco-Vought, Inc., into one of the 25 largest concerns in America by 1968. Its $2.7-billion sales, its $36.3 million in net income and its employment of 114,600 persons—all in less than 15 years—was a fantastic feat of corporate expansion brought about by some of the fanciest financial "redeployment" seen anywhere. No company had grown so fast or so much in decades. And no company ran into such troubles during that time.

After a series of acquisitions through 1965, climaxed by the purchase of Okonite Company, a wire and cable producer, for about $30 million from the Kennicott Copper Corporation, Ling then moved into the really big time by acquiring Wilson and Company in 1967, and Braniff Airways and Jones and Laughlin Steel Company, both in 1968. In between, he had made an unsuccessful swipe at both Youngstown Sheet and Tube and Allis-Chalmers. Those post-1965 moves exploded L-T-V's position from 204th of the country's top 500 industrials to twenty-fifth and edged him into position to realize his ultimate goal of breaking into the top ten.

Until the roof fell in.

Jones and Laughlin's fortunes declined. Ling, it seemed, had poured many millions into the steel industry just as it was poised on the famine phase of its traditional feast-famine cycle. And then the Justice Department sought to void his ownership of Jones and Laughlin, since expanded from a 63-percent interest to 81 percent. Then his own company's earnings hit the skids, because of Jones and Laughlin's decline and those of other L-T-V entities. And Wall Street, as it often does, quickly showed its distaste for the entire proceedings. L-T-V's stock plummeted in January 1970 to 27½ compared with the 1969 high of 97¾ and the 1967 high of 169½.

Ling was understandably upset. It had all seemed like a great idea and a great chance to add to his and L-T-V's luster. As usual, Ling's moves had been stunning in their surprise. He was the "boy" corporate genius whose financial antennae were admired as the most sensitive among the conglomerators. Because he saw the steel industry in general and Jones and Laughlin in particular as offering tremendous potential as yet untapped and assets that could be "redeployed" to great benefit, he offered to buy the Jones and Laughlin shares at $30 apiece over the market price.

But he failed, and so did his advisors, to track the possibilities of steel stockpiling in May in anticipation of an August 1, 1968 steel strike. By the end of the year the industry's recent fat profits had been pared by the stoppage, but Jones and Laughlin's results were virtually disastrous.

What was worse, the government's zeal in carrying forth its antitrust enforcement under section 7 of the Clayton Act had an additional dimension. It was to be the first attempt to extend the statute to conglomerates. It was obvious that this was the opening shot in a campaign against conglomerates and so it was—four suits were later filed against others.

The application of the Clayton Act's section 7 to the Jones and Laughlin tender offer was patently inexact, but was nonetheless pressed by the Justice Department with much determination. The law outlawed mergers that might substantially lessen competition or tend to create a monopoly. This could hardly be the case between L-T-V and Jones and Laughlin, which had never competed, but the Justice Department contended that the merger would reduce "potential" competition, lead to opportunities for "reciprocity" (where joint ownership sells products and services to itself to the disadvantage of others) and create greater concentration of manufacturing.

The government brought the suit against L-T-V on April 14, 1969, asking for a court order to require the conglomerate to divest itself of all its interest in Jones and Laughlin. In January 1970 the concern, saddled with a slew of problems both external and internal, reported a 90-percent drop in operating profits and a loss of $8.3 million. On March 7 Justice announced that it had settled its antitrust suit against L-T-V on the basis that the conglomerate would sell either its interest in Jones and Laughlin or both Braniff Airways and the Okonite Company within three years.

That was not all, even though Attorney General John N. Mitchell hailed the settlement because it called for "the most substantial corporate divestiture of any antitrust decree in recent years." L-T-V also agreed not to make any further acquisitions of companies with $100 million in assets without government or court approval and not to permit Jones and Laughlin and its subsidiaries to engage in any reciprocal deals.

Jones and Laughlin's assets of $1.1 billion dwarfed those of Braniff's, about $371 million, and Okonite's, about $164 million. Ling decided to dispose of Braniff and Okonite. These were problem companies anyway, at least in more recent years and under Ling's ownership, and had contributed only small profits to the corporate coffers. Norton Simon, Inc., had expressed an interest in Braniff, as had other airlines, so that Ling was certain that he could realize between $140 million and $200 million for it. Okonite, too, he figured, might bring as much as $75 million.

The settlement, despite the fact that it put restrictions on the big conglomerate and removed two entities that might have provided more revenue in the future, lifted Ling's spirits. He was now admittedly back on the acquisition trail again. He noted, in a statement released when the settlement was announced, that "Ling-Temco is still permitted considerable latitude in terms of possible future opportunities where acquisitions are feasible and otherwise indicated for the company's diversified growth."

So he was limited as to what he could buy, fenced in by the $100-million restriction, but there were plenty of companies left around the country with assets under that figure. What was more, he had an excellent chance of realizing more than $275 million from the two-company divestiture, which would help to reduce a mountainous $750 million in L-T-V bank debt. And he could now involve himself and his team in the Jones and Laughlin operations to obtain a turn-around situation.

But what was apparently most intriguing now to the tall, handsome but moody Texan was the opportunity to renew his policy of financial "redeployment," which he described this way: "What we do is that we acquire companies and spin them off as one or more public companies, usually keeping the majority ownership, thus redeploying the assets to best advantage."

In this type of financial expansion Ling had become probably the country's most astute practitioner. For example, in 1965 the L-T-V Aerospace Company, an L-T-V division, earned under $5 million and had a $6-million book value. Thirty-five to 40 percent of its stock was sold to the public, providing a $30-million market value for the stock, but the parent company still retained 60 to 65 percent of the outstanding stock. Three years later the subsidiary, then a public company, had sales of more than $500 million, net income of about $15 million and contributed $25 million to the parent company's balance sheet. The move also provided new incentive for the aerospace company's management.

If Ling seemed to be bouncing back, events soon proved it not so. By early 1970, L-T-V's debt had shot up to $1.5 billion. This came after an announcement of a $38.3 million loss for the previous year. L-T-V then eliminated its dividend on the common stock. Now the pressure was on from lenders, directors and shareholders, and it found release in two board meetings in May and June at which Ling was first moved down a rung from chairman to president and then another rung, possibly to oblivion, to vice chairman. In the first action, Robert H. Stewart, a Dallas banker, was named nonsalaried chairman, and in the second, Paul Thayer, president of the L-T-V Aerospace, was named chairman, president and chief executive. Ling now appeared to be in limbo, severed from active participation in the company's operations. But for as many who believed that he was through, there were others certain that the conglomerator's career was just in a hiatus that could end at any time.

Despite all their modest starts, the conglomerators inevitably veer to bigger and bigger numbers. Numbers are in their blood and it all usually starts with zero and explodes from that. Hence the common expression, "They do it all by arithmetic," should not faze them, but it does, it does. The conglomerators are all sensitive—their constantly exposed flanks erupt in a rash that comes and goes depending on the breezes. Eventually they approach the astronomical in merger incidence, sales and accumulated debt. Geneen, since taking over at ITT, spearheaded the acquisition of 157 companies, 48 of them in 1969, with a round dozen pending as the year ended.

Not far behind in the numbers parade is another prototype conglomerator, Charles Bluhdorn, who put together Gulf and Western Industries, with 127 acquisitions between December 30, 1957 and January 1, 1969. But conglomerates largely make their acquisitions through long-term debt, so that the big number of acquisitions wasn't the only high figure that Bluhdorn and Gulf and Western amassed. Long-term debt mushroomed from $11.5 million in 1964 to $930 million in 1969.

This was to cover such takeovers as New Jersey Zinc Company, mining and chemicals, for which he got an $83-million loan from the Chase Manhattan Bank, or about three times Gulf and Western's net worth; E. W. Bliss, a large machinery manufacturer; Desilu Productions; Paramount Pictures; South Puerto Rico Sugar Company; and the Consolidated Cigar Company.

By 1969, after 11 years of operation, Bluhdorn had brought his conglomerate to sales of $1.5 billion but operating earnings had declined to $51 million from $67.7 million the year before. The high long-term debt didn't much faze the excitable, highly com-

petitive Bluhdorn. But what did get through to him in 1969 and 1970 were the government's push against conglomerates and the first decline in earnings in Gulf and Western's history. He reacted to the first by clamping down on the takeover throttle in both those years. His reaction to the second—a 37-percent earnings drop in the 1969 final fiscal quarter and 25 percent for the entire fiscal year—was to report in somber tones that it stemmed from profit erosion in the manufacturing, metals and chemicals, leisure-time and consumer-products divisions.

Paramount Pictures was his most controversial acquisition, because its own fortunes had swung to extremes for years and also because Bludhorn was scarcely considered knowledgeable in the ways of Hollywood. Paramount reported a $22-million reduction in pretax income in 1969. But Bluhdorn pointed out that this was deliberate. Paramount had the highest box-office revenues in 1969 in its 57-year history. However, Gulf and Western, anxious to "restructure and rejuvenate Paramount," had decided to defer temporarily leasing feature films to network TV and had instituted a new accounting system to achieve a more accurate matching of film costs to revenues and to make a more realistic appraisal of the concern's performance. This new accounting method was already being used by a majority of the other movie producers.

This sacrifice of income plus Bluhdorn's decision to relax in the face of the antitrust push compelled him to treat 1969 as a "major cleanup year." This represented a new maturity for him. Few at the year's beginning were willing to accept him in that role and it was easily understandable. Bluhdorn, let's be fair about it, was hard to take, all energy, brashness and voice. An Austrian who came to this country in 1942 at twelve, he went from one job to another, taking night courses, becoming a citizen and serving in the U. S. Air Force. He worked as an order clerk for a plate-glass distributor, then as a $60-a-week clerk in a one-room export-import house specializing in commodities. He learned a great deal in this last job, so that, when he was twenty-three, he invested $3,000 to open his own business, confident that he had finally found an avenue for his restless drive.

The international commodities market seemed to offer that

opportunity. Prices rose and fell frequently during the course of a day and a watchful opportunist could buy, sell and make a killing in hours. In a matter of months he was importing $1 million worth of coffee a day.

By thirty he had made his first million. By 1958, when he was thirty-two, he had sought and found a new vehicle into which he could channel his new kitty and which would be more stable than the chaotic commodities market. He began buying small auto-parts companies, figuring that their products would have dual end uses, in both the original and the replacement market. By 1966 he had welded a complex of 33 auto-parts warehouses and 150 auto-parts distributors. Within this fold he also added companies that made parts for jet engines and survival equipment for astronauts and he had also acquired New Jersey Zinc. Total package: $300 million in sales.

But Bluhdorn remained essentially European, emotional, gesticulating, given to exaggeration in talk and movement, equally enthusiastic in exhortation and in recrimination. *Life* magazine referred to him as the "Mad Austrian." Wall Streeters still looked askance at his constant practice of using securities to buy companies, frowning on the streams of "confetti" that emanated from Gulf and Western. But it was his acquisition of Paramount, which many analysts felt had a great potential which had not been tapped for years, that brought him both Wall Street and investor enthusiasm. Gulf and Western's stock on the day that the acquisition was announced hit the most-active list and a new all-time high.

Then, a year or so later, he caught the backlash of the growing disaffection with conglomerates, fed by Litton's unexpected decline in its quarterly earnings. But, by then, Bluhdorn had built a strong organization, saw his new 44-story glass tower that would house Gulf and Western's headquarters rise at Columbus Circle in New York City and knew to his satisfaction that he had indeed arrived.

In October 1970 I saw Bluhdorn in his glass tower and found him solemnly, if restlessly, bound to his retrenchment program. Maximizing the return on assets by sorting out what was good and what was bad in his $1.5-billion empire was his objective, he told me. Every division would have to stand on its own and those that didn't perform "will not be part of this company in the next four or five years." The long-term goal? Proof of the viability of the conglomerate concept through Gulf and Western's example.

Was he defensive about the kicks on conglomerates? That he was, especially since his own had done relatively well in 1970's first nine months by showing a slight gain in profits and sales. "There have been abuses among the conglomerates and some haven't performed as well as others," he said. "People tend to lump all together and judge the entire field on the basis of a few. We have made many acquisitions and not all of them were good. We have had to be doctors. But given time, we have brought improvement to every company that we have bought."

He was concentrating on expanding from the inside instead of from the outside, but in his office he was still as restless as ever. It was clear from his slouching, sitting, pacing and frequent requests from employees for this or that. Also clear was his pride in his new team and in the growth potential for his auto-parts system, his cigar company and his food complex.

He was particularly sensitive about his profit-expense problems with Paramount Pictures. "Today, it represents no more than 5% of our assets and we're no longer wedded to the Hollywood glorification of companies outbidding each other to spend the most money," he said. "I've got a president in Paramount now who not only watches nickels, he watches the pennies. Our whole global budget this year will be less than $25 million, or less than we used to spend for two pictures. 'Love Story,' the number one best-seller novel this year, due in the theaters at Christmas, cost only $2 million to produce. It will set an example for lean movie-making for the whole industry. And we paid only $50,000 for the movie rights for 'The Godfather,' which was also the number one best-selling novel, because we snapped it up early."

Gulf and Western now has neither the cash nor the stock to pay out for new acquisitions, so that even the most attractive corporate property probably wouldn't whet his appetite. He was just plain out of the acquisition business, he concluded. But that, observing his obvious restlessness and recalling that he had bought 80 companies in the last five years, was a bit too much. How, I wondered as I left, would he feel about acquisitions when he decided that his sorting-out stint was over?

Meshulam Riklis, like Bluhdorn, was born in another country but became an important member of the new breed, the conglomerator, who taught many native American businessmen a few tricks that they never would have believed. They scoffed while they learned. Riklis became as smooth a teacher as Ling or Bluhdorn.

A Palestinian, Riklis came to the United States in 1947, taught Hebrew at night while working during the day as a security analyst. He attracted interest from people with money who staked him to buy his first company. He bought another with the assets of the first, a third with the assets of the second, pursuing a program of the "effective use of noncash." Thus, by using securities of already acquired companies or employing their assets as collateral for loans, he operated in the same channels as both Ling and Bluhdorn. In the process Riklis built a hydra-headed business empire, with sales of about $2 billion, consisting of Rapid-American Corporation, McCrory Corporation and the Glen Alden Corporation. It included such well-known subsidiary companies as Schenley Industries, BVD Corporation, Best and Company, S. Klein Department Stores, Stanley Warner Theatres, International Latex Company, McCrory-McLellan-Green Stores, the Lerner Stores Corporation, Joseph H. Cohen and Sons, Otasco-Economy Auto Stores, Leeds Travelwear, and others.

In 1969 and 1970, besides a good, fast look at Armour and Company, by way of a possible takeover of General Host, which owned a big interest in Armour, Riklis decided to consolidate his position. It was, he told me, not so much a consolidation (which implies either a "necessary retrenchment" or a hold-off of activities for other reasons), but simply the most current phase in a long-range plan. That plan was to build three large entities, McCrory as a retailing conglomerate, Rapid-American as a holding company and Glen Alden as an acquisition vehicle. The three entities were now substantially shaped, but the current period was needed to refine them. Obviously, he stressed, Glen Alden would be the active acquisitor of the three.

Riklis mixed overly generous drinks as we ate lunch in his dining room, just off his office at 711 Fifth Avenue. In all the seven years that I had personally known him, he had never looked so sleek, so self-satisfied and so much at peace with himself and the world. He wore his hair and his sideburns long in the mode of the new breed. It seemed that for many months he was certain that his "house," often busy and even chaotic with new, pending or recently consummated acquisitions, had finally been put in order.

Not, he said, that he wasn't considering some new aspects of the "effective use of noncash," a policy that, he noted incidentally, had been almost preempted by some even more daring entrepreneurs. But those aspects would certainly involve subsidiary rather than outside concerns.

Had he changed his acquisition philosophy since he had put together his whole complex? He replied:

> No. The philosophy is based on what was true back in the beginning and is still today's economic need—the efficiency of big business, its ability to cover large markets, serve many people and to keep prices in line as much as possible. After World War I the country's economy had demanded that big business should become the style to fill the demands of the people, to provide better research and better products.
>
> But after World War II this went one big step further. The economy and the nature of business saw a big social change. Family and college ties were broken by the war and the displacement of people and even the second generation of management found that its ties were broken. What all that did was to open the door for the talented, ambitious individual to go out and do things and make a place for himself in business, in big business. The whole environment, in other words, opened a new outlet for the individual.

He was referring to himself, of course?
Of course.

> One thing Riklis never lacked [he said,] was self-confidence. I believed in my ability to plan and execute a program. When I sold Butler Brothers and had the money from it, our 1959 prospectus at Rapid-American said that we would take this money and build a retail complex and then the dollars we got in 1960 were used too. By 1961 we had the basic framework, McCrory, and just added to it so that today it is a big company. Of course, later we added the other big company, Glen Alden, but we are still pursuing the same plan. . . .

Despite all that has happened, including the government's tougher role on mergers, this form of business expansion will continue to be a major one. Certain things, of course, will be eliminated in the game. The minor-league players will not be able to take over big companies by issuing "Russian Rubles." Ninety percent of that is already stopped. And the practice of taking over companies against the will of management, by rape, will almost, but not completely, die out.

Government regulations on mergers are not regulations but a police job. The enforcement of the regulations is the result of complaints brought to the government, not the result of research. Bigness, monopoly? How can the government allow Atlantic and Richfield Oil to merge but not a few supermarkets in Ohio? But I am convinced that big mergers will continue, leading to big new complexes, because I think that government push will subside. The time for that is coming soon.

Others bestride the merger scene, too, with giant steps that may or may not leave an indelible footprint.

We met Saul Steinberg earlier, in other connections. Steinberg's case is one of those in which school studies, in this instance a class project of the IBM Corporation which he did while at the University of Pennsylvania's Wharton School of Finance, turned out to be the guiding factor in his professional life.

As a young man who wanted to become a millionaire before he reached thirty, he was much intrigued by his study of IBM. "The potential of data processing amazed me," he said when he became a success. "I had previously been interested in leasing. I thought, Put these two together and there is money to be made."

After college the chubby, effervescent young man worked for his father's rubber company in Brooklyn while simultaneously operating a chain of 46 leased subway newsstands. In 1961 he made the big move at age twenty-two—he obtained a long-term computer lease and used the contract to obtain a bank loan to pay for the computer and its servicing costs for five years. He also borrowed money from his father and started the Leasco Data Processing Equipment Corporation.

Its income in the first full year of operations was $45,000. By 1968, a year in which his company took over Reliance Insurance

Company, the net had risen to $27 million, with assets of $1 billion, which included, of course, Reliance.

As a company builder and takeover expert, he had done magnificently—that is, until his fruitless attempt to take over the Chemical Bank of New York. Everyone, it seemed, even business friends, closed ranks against him. But rebounding with great verve, he quickly made a successful feint at and then purchased control of Pergamon Press, a prize in London's publishing industry.

Seeing Steinberg in his own habitat, a thirty-fifth-floor office in the West Building, one of twin towers at 280 Park Avenue in New York, provides you with a quick insight into one of the more amazing things that are going on in American business today. Youth, youth. In that brilliantly modern, rococo and sumptuous office Steinberg sits flanked by his attorney and answers questions with an eager interest, his brown eyes shining. He seems very young, ridiculously young for thirty, more like a bright, well-fed president of a high-school student body or of the campus organization.

We spoke for about 90 minutes, mostly about the abortive Chemical Bank deal, but I am leaving his remarks for the chapter on those mergers which never were.

Another merger-master of first rank, standing high in the gallery of the $1-billion club, is Norton Simon, a dour Californian who doesn't talk much but up until his recent semi-retirement was the man behind the closed door of many a merger.

In 1931 the lean, craggy-faced Simon made his first move by buying a bankrupt orange-juice bottler in Fullerton, California, for $7,000. It was not the first time that an ambitious man picked up a bargain in a bankruptcy court and made something worthwhile of it. Simon did more than that. About 13 years later he had built up the bottling firm so that he was able to sell it to Hunt Foods for $3 million.

He developed a fine ear and eye for picking up limp companies and putting muscle into them. In his 30-year career of takeovers he strung together something like 30 companies, including Hunt

Foods, from which he went on to acquire McCall Corporation, the magazine and book publishers, Canada Dry Corporation and Knox Glass, the container firm. He seemed to have the magic touch on profits—every one of his acquisitions prospered under the spur of his clipped directions.

None of his executives could quite feel secure with him. He was known to be demanding, impatient and not easily swayed by excuses. Many major new executives were subjected to an intensive examination by a pyschologist. The technique here was simple. You were invited to chit-chat, to confide and even socialize during the interview. But when it was over, you learned to your dismay that you had implicated yourself by displaying weaknesses and faults. You had, in effect, impaled yourself on your own confidences.

Simon has had his failures. In 1967, after making a major investment in Wheeling Steel Company, he sold out at a loss of $654,000 in what was apparently a disappointing attempt to seek new opportunities in the steel industry. He did a little better when he obtained a 23-percent equity in Crucible Steel Company, where he took the seat of power. But his experience at Wheeling Steel, a losing company compared with Crucible's relatively steady earnings, caused Simon, who rarely talked to the press, to refer to the steel industry in stinging terms. As a small producer, he told *The New York Times*, it was difficult for Wheeling to compete "in the cartel-like atmosphere of the United States steel industry, particularly in the high-tonnage carbon-steel business."

Simon's acquisitiveness extends beyond business into the art world and he ranks close to the top of the world's buyers of fine art. In 1968 he stunned an audience at Parke-Bernet Galleries by breaking the price barrier for a Renoir painting by successfully offering—over the telephone—$1,555,000. But even that was no record for Simon. In 1965 he had shelled out $2,234,000 for Rembrandt's *Titus*.

Throughout his business and his art-collecting career Simon has shunned publicity, almost but not quite as much as Howard Hughes, because he obviously felt that personal publicity was meaningless. So it was difficult for both friends and critics to understand why in 1968, when his three big companies merged, the new corporate name turned out to be—Norton Simon, Inc.

The apparent rivalry that has sprung up between Howard Hughes and Kirk Kerkorian actually centers only around Las Vegas, where there is a direct confrontation between their biggest hostelries-casinos. There probably is nothing more than coincidence in the fact that Kerkorian has been following Hughes' footsteps in the movie industry (Hughes once owned RKO Pictures and Kirk now controls MGM) and in airlines (Hughes once controlled Trans World Airlines and Kirk now holds a big chunk of Western Airlines). That may still be enough to establish more than a coincidence, but Kerkorian disowns any real feeling of rivalry. Of Hughes he says, "He is a mountain, I'm a molehill." On another occasion he said, "I feel like a BB gun next to a shotgun."

Hughes, oddly enough, is widely known for the fact that he is not known well at all. Secretive, considered a sort of Texas mystic, Hughes made many millions from oilfields, tools, aircraft and movie-making. In 1968 he became involved in a $148.5-million tender offer for the American Broadcasting Company following similar interest shown by Harold Geneen and Norton Simon. He at one point apparently was so reluctant to appear in court that he was willing thereby to give up his control of Trans World Airlines.

Unpredictable and elusive, Hughes has a reported net worth of $1.5 billion against Kerkorian's $260 million. Even his advent into Las Vegas was done on the QT, but Hughes' grasp was hardly of a modest nature. He has an estimated $200-million investment in six hotels, an airport, a TV station, a 525-acre ranch and much open land. Hughes sold his 75-percent interest in TWA for $545.5 million in 1966, but retained his holdings in both Hughes Tool Company, one of the country's largest tool firms, and in Hughes Aircraft, a company owned by the Howard Hughes Medical Institute, which is one of the country's major foundations.

Flamboyant for all his publicity-shy nature, Hughes was once a test pilot for his own aircraft company, a producer of such movies as *Hell's Angels, Scarface* and *The Front Page*. He was also frequently seen in those days with Hollywood's leading actresses and elsewhere with prominent socialites.

Kerkorian is something else again. The American-born son of immigrant parents, he was as a boy outgoing, inclined to outdoor pursuits such as cars and sports, not good in school but good enough for auto-trade school, occasionally getting in trouble but helping to support the family even when he worked away from home. His father, an Armenian who came here from Turkey in 1905, made out well at first in Fresno and Los Angeles but lost all of it about the time Kirk began growing up.

At eighteen Kirk started tiny businesses of his own, a used-car lot in his own backyard, a car wash and so on. Then he turned into such a successful amateur boxer that he almost became a professional. He became interested in airplanes from a friend and got a job in which flying lessons were part of the salary. He obtained his commercial pilot's license in 1941 and served as a civilian and military flight instructor. At war's end he emerged with a kitty of $12,000, which he used as a base to buy surplus airplanes.

He combined this business with flying charter groups, made several killings on purchases of overage or damaged transports and started a small, nonscheduled airline of his own. This developed into Trans International Airlines, a fast-growing supplemental carrier, which went public in 1965 and personally brought Kerkorian $7 million in stock. The airline prospered and in 1968 Kerkorian sold it to Transamerica, Inc., the West Coast conglomerate, in a stock exchange of $148 million. Of that Kerkorian himself realized $104 million.

In late 1969, he acquired a controlling interest in Western Airlines, an interest worth $40 million. He liked the fact that Western Airlines had acquired some new routes from inland cities to Hawaii, a natural route for vacation-goers. He put out a tender offer, ran into some heavy flak from management, but wound up with more than 30 percent of the shares, enough for control.

He had come far for the Kirk Kerkorian who had been one of the bad boys of his neighborhood, reaching the age of sixteen before he was ready to enter eighth grade and being absent from school and getting into so many fights that he was sent briefly to a disciplinary school. Yet even in the early days he had the "trading instinct," perhaps a throwback to an Armenian forebear.

In early 1968, Kerkorian became engaged in a 60-day battle to take over Metro-Goldwyn-Mayer and in the building of the largest hotel and casino in Las Vegas, which would throw him into direct competition with Howard Hughes. MGM, once profitable and mighty, had recently come under the control of Edgar M. Bronfman, president of Joseph E. Seagram and Sons, after a pair of unsuccessful proxy fights by Philip J. Levin, a New Jersey real-estate tycoon. The Bronfman family then owned 16 percent of MGM, and Time, Inc., the publishing empire, had acquired five percent of the shares. Kerkorian became interested because he saw no reason why MGM couldn't be as profitable as, for example, United Artists.

He made a public tender offer in July 1968 for one million shares at $35 a share, which would have given him a 17-percent ownership, not enough to dislodge the combined forces of Bronfman-Time, Inc., but would have allowed him to put a big foot in the door. MGM rallied quickly. Its lawyers sought a restraining order on an apparent antitrust violation. Kerkorian, in order to finance his tender offer, had obtained a $30-million loan from Transamerica, which already owned United Artists.

Kerkorian, however, as an old boxer, had picked up a few new feints. He had quietly arranged for an additional loan of $32 million in Europe and then followed it up with another from similar sources for $30 million, thus removing the antitrust charge. The MGM lawyers, successful in the first round, lost the second and the bout. Kerkorian's offer was $7 a share above the market price for the stock, which had undergone a decline. He wound up with 32 percent of MGM's stock in less than two months after he had started his takeover effort.

As a fun-loving, luxury-loving rich man, Kerkorian had been fascinated by Las Vegas since he first visited the gambling center in 1945. In 1962 he bought a 70-acre vacant lot. Six years later, after collecting $2 million in rent from the hotel, Caesar's Palace, that had been built on it, he sold the land to the hotel operators for $5 million.

But he had bigger plans for the lush oasis. He started in 1967 to build the city's biggest hotel, The International, which would cost $54 million. The land alone cost him $5 million, located a half-mile from the Strip, and the experts laughed. It was too far from the action, it would never go they said. But Kerkorian pushed ahead and opened his 1,500-room hostelry in July 1969.

The gigantic, gaudy, triangular tower immediately began to draw well. When it opened within a day of Howard Hughes' new Landmark Hotel, the rivalry was set in motion. Kerkorian visited Hughes' opening. Coming out, he stared with evident satisfaction at the bulk of his 30-story edifice looming in the sky just a few blocks away. Las Vegas, it was clear, was certain not to be the same.

There are others in the $1-billion club of merger-makers. Textron, Inc., the granddaddy of all conglomerates, shot up to $1.5 billion in 1968 after sales of $382 million only a few years before. The conglomerate, a forty-two-year-old company, began its current course under entrepreneur Royal Little after World War II, when he linked a chain of tax shelters to phase the company out of its up-and-down textile business. In the mid-1950s, when some of Little's acquisitions turned out to be lemons, he engaged a banker, Rupert C. Thompson, to come in and devise a program of acquiring smaller companies. These were the small producers, with $40 million or so in assets, who dominated an industry and offered a good return on equity.

After this successful effort, George W. Miller, a top Textron executive, came in in 1968 as the new chief executive and devised a new plan that would make Textron swing the other way. He spearheaded a new offensive to take over larger companies, a new phase to push Textron to the size and market diversity that would make it a supergiant in the 1970s and 1980s. And one of the first moves was to take a good look at such firms as United Fruit Company, long sought after for its big cash reserve and no long-term debt, and its $400 million in assets. That failed to result in any deal.

There is, of course, U. S. Industries, the $1-billion conglomerate made up of 100 different companies, all acquired since 1965. I. John Billera, its chairman, has plans for quintupling the scope of the company by intriguing and retaining small entrepreneurs everywhere. This includes not only holding out financial incentives to them by contingency arrangements based on their continuing earnings performance, but also by having them vie for professional standing within USI's management corps. By this two-pronged effort Billera hopes to keep the millionaire entrepreneurs within the fold even after they have sold him their business. USI's acquisition and management approach might well be called "Getting Big by Thinking Small, or How to Keep 150 Millionaires Happily Slaving Away."

And there is the interesting situation of Dr. Armand Hammer, the physician who never practiced medicine after graduating from the College of Physicians and Surgeons but practiced high finance in the petroleum industry and turned it all into a great big gusher. Occidental Petroleum was almost an afterthought to Dr. Hammer, since it all came up during his retirement in California when a friend suggested some speculation in oil as a "fun" thing to do. So the doctor invested $60,000 in Occidental, a failing refiner.

In 1957 he came out of retirement to become its president. He brought in professional oil engineers, adding new markets, obtaining profitable oil concessions in the Mideast and drilling for oil rights in the heart of downtown Los Angeles. Within a decade the would-be retiree had raised Occidental's revenues from $1 million to more than $1 billion. And the Los Angeles project, with big oil pools supposedly gurgling under its busy streets, still looks like it might yet gush.

So much for most of the $1-billion club. What about some of the others, the lesser merger-masters who are well on the way toward joining the club?

They're a mixed lot, too, but they show promise of becoming

the odd-ball but smash successes of the front rank. For example, there's Eli Black, a former rabbi, whose family provided ten generations of scholars and rabbis. He developed the AMK Corporation, a conglomerate which shot over the $1-billion mark in just a few years. It knocked off the United Fruit Company and Morrell and Company, the big meat-packer, under the noses of bigger and more experienced acquisitors. Black's personal style is soft-spoken, meditative, scholarly.

And Richard C. Pistell, the former chairman of General Host Corporation, formerly the General Baking Company, who loves big-game hunting, tried unsuccessfully to bag a big trophy, Armour and Company, and blithely lost a big pile of dollars for his stockholders in doing so. Al Lapin, Jr., a New Yorker who moved to California, turned a small pancake and coffee shop into International Industries, a conglomerate of varied retailing franchises. J. B. Fuqua, a farm boy who became interested in radio because he didn't like farming, became a radio-station operator, then owner, then operator of a conglomerate of movie houses, TV stations, trucking and boating concerns.

And James E. Robison, chairman of Indian Head, Inc., operated in the image of his mentor, Royal Little, the creator of Textron. Robison's education by Little and his own skills showed in the development of a textiling, hosiery, glass-container and auto-parts conglomerate. Another Royal Little disciple, Jerome Ottmar, chief executive of Amtel, Inc., took over from Little's chairmanship to operate the successful conglomerate of automotive-textile-machinery products and of engineering, construction, novelties and forgings.

Eugene Klein, a used-car dealer, started it all with a $2,000 loan to build another conglomerate, National General Corporation, with diverse operations including movie houses and a company-owned popcorn factory. Nick Salgo, an investment banker, took Punta Alegre Sugar Company's confiscated sugar mills in Cuba, merged it in 1964 with Bangor and Aristook, a railroad holding company, and then made 20 acquisitions as head of the Bangor Punta conglomerate. Another $1-billion conglomerate-builder, Robert V. Hansberger, used 33 mergers to expand Boise

Cascade Corporation into a "congeneric" (the company doesn't like "conglomerate") diversiplex of leisure communities, conventional homes and factory-built homes.

Robert A. Levinson, chairman-founder of Duplan Corporation, a textile company that diversified widely by acquiring a dozen firms in four years, nudged the once ailing, old-line company into showing the biggest stock rise on the New York Stock Exchange in 1968. Cortes W. Randell, who founded National Student Marketing Company, the giant among youth consulting and supplying firms, also ran his stock up more than any other on the over-the-counter market in 1968, partly by making 30 acquisitions in a few years, but resigned early in 1970 because of "fatigue" and multiplying company problems.

Harry Figgie took "Automatic" Sprinkler to a high place on the list of conglomerates and then let his enthusiasm push him into excessive claims that failed to be realized on the balance sheet. Tinkham Veale, a horse fancier, maneuvered Alco Standard Corporation, of Valley Forge, Pennsylvania, in eight years from a $5-million chemical company to a $140.4-million technically oriented conglomerate. J. W. Van Gorkum, president of Trans Union Corporation, formerly Union Tank Car, tried conglomerating out of the tank-car leasing business by acquiring local credit bureaus, a land-development company and industrial fastener makers and found it all very much of a nonfluxing mixture.

And not to be forgotten, Martin S. Ackerman, the brash lawyer who developed Perfect Film and Chemical into the acquirer of Curtis Publishing Company, ran into a bunch of stiff upper lips in the publisher's Philadephia stronghold, killed *The Saturday Evening Post*, and then called it quits.

There they are, 15 out of many more, who have come up prominently on the second tier of merger-masters, with varying successes but lots of noise and bravado.

Now, having done that, let's go back and examine the species, particularly the top rung. Let's briefly review that main gallery.

12

"We Got Sucked in by Our Own Publicity"

"We—the Lings, Bluhdorns, Riklises, Thorntons—all got sucked in by our own publicity—and we fell flat on our behinds. We made some serious errors because of it and I don't think we have yet learned the real lesson. The only question is, How bad can our next mistakes be?"

This was one of the country's top conglomerators talking, spilling out some of his ire from his "gut," flagellating himself as well as the others on that top tier. He had made our talk contingent on a nondirect-quote basis, so that he could speak frankly without recrimination from the others or Wall Street or the watchful gang at SEC, Justice and FTC in Washington. But once he opened up, he responded with some enthusiasm and some apparent self-relief to the question: "Where, Mr. ——, do you think you and the rest of the conglomerates are headed?"

He kept alternating between "they" and "we," but—not that he really was trying to—he failed to differentiate totally between himself and the rest of them. He meant that he was really part of the group, maybe a little superior (hence the "they") but generally respectful of at least the four names he had already mentioned.

> The trouble is that they began to listen to their public relations, that the only direction was up, that you can go from one acquisition to another without stopping, not worrying about the equity that remains and letting the long-term debt pile up. You talk to a roomful of analysts and see their tongues hanging out, waiting for the big projection, and you give it to them. We are optimists by nature and if they invite us to "optimize," well, dammit, we "optimize."
>
> Then what happens to us? We pile up long-term debt, we overproject our earnings, we build up high hopes for our operating people and they let us down—and then it all shows up in the earnings. The analysts start puking all over the place, they catch hell from the institutions and suddenly the conglomerates are no good. "The Establishment is right," they say, "we're plunderers, we'll run the economy into the ground. The millions of tiny investors are getting screwed," etc., etc., etc.
>
> Then, of course, the government guys start nodding their heads, because here is evidence that they have been right all along. They really got no problem, those fellows. They just sit in their offices and figure out ways to kick us around. They aren't investors, bankers or operators of any kind. I'm not trying to knock them for the sake of knocking—but in some ways they're the least responsible of all.

Pausing for a moment and looking just a little sad, he continued:

> It's all our own fault. I don't say I suffer from gluttony, but we let our public-relations guys take over, or maybe we wanted them to. Personally I think that Jimmy Ling is the greatest of us all. He made the greatest use of everything he had and he built a company that will last a long, long time. But even he got sucked in by his own publicity, like the rest of us. What did he do? He wanted to buy Jones and Laughlin so he could get into the steel industry in a big way, even though he already had a lot of debt. So he goes out and borrows $500 million. In his circumstances it was the wrong thing to do. It was definitely a big mistake. No wonder he's got more headaches than anyone else.

I have reported these remarks in some detail because self-criticism and criticism by one of their peers would be about as accurate an appraisal of the conglomerators as they and we could get. I leave you to make the final judgment on that. In the next few pages, however, I will stay strictly to my own opinion, an opinion, I must add in all honesty, that is shaped not only by my own ideas but quite naturally by those of sources I respect.

First, let me indulge in a few points on the personal side of some of the principal members of the $1-billion club. Ling, Riklis, Steinberg, Bluhdorn, Kerkorian, Ackerman, Pistell and a few others have an incongruous note to them. Perhaps it is because they have not quite become accustomed to their success, the collar is a bit tight or a bit big, but they give the impression of having arrived a little disheveled and sweaty at their new house, all furnished, sumptuous and with not a loose bit of lint to mar its perfection.

Putting it another way, maybe the tremendous accomplishments of these men, the building of the giant corporate edifices, the linking of many firms that were in business before some of them were even born, the employment of many hundreds of thousands of people, and the faith rightly or wrongly which they engendered in people might be just too much for anyone to assume handily and gracefully.

When Steinberg sits in his lush office, curled up like a pudgy, indulgent schoolboy on a sofa and denies that he was stomped on by the Establishment, when Riklis has to keep reminding his audience over a word flub after 20-some years in this country, "I still can't handle this English, I wish you could understand Hebrew," when Ling straight-facedly insists to the administration what a reduction of merger needs is a special tax on mergers, when Bluhdorn insists that his only compulsion was that his parents were poor so that this developed his ambition and he snaps up 127 companies and doesn't like his press in the bargain, when Cortes W. Randell of National Student Marketing, he of the pure eye and the open-mouthed eagerness, estimates within the same five minutes that his sales for the same given fiscal year would be $140 million and then $200 million—well, it gives one some reason to stop and ponder.

At least, you might well say, they are acting like humans, not stuffed dummies. Fine. But the problem is that people in such high places fail to get the benefit of human kindness from others when they do falter, much as we might feel that they should. The bigger they are, the more brash and successful they are, the harder they fall and the more resounding the applause.

Perhaps that is part of what happened to the conglomerates and their principals. Just what did happen to them? Here's my version.

For years the established managements sat around on their "assets," refusing to bow to what might be called the "laws of nature and of gravity." Opportunities developed simply from the growth of the national economy, population and income, but many of the potentials generated were left to those who might dare and gamble. After World War II not a few of those who might have dared stepped into the vacuum. They defied the mystique that developed among the traditional professional managers that they were compelled to safeguard their assets even to the extent of ignoring sharesholders' needs and ignoring market opportunities. The entrenched managements, in other words, regarded their businesses with a sort of religious fervor rather than with economic objectivity.

The conglomerates got their breaks from two sources. One was the need by many small-, medium- and even large-sized entrepreneurs for a financial and management lifeline to grow. The other was the simple fact that there was a demand and a need for bigger companies to accommodate fast-growing markets.

This is not to say that there weren't many instances of takeovers of companies with unfriendly managements, a tough spot for anyone to be in on either side of the fence, or that some of the so-called market opportunities didn't develop as expected. But there was another favorable circumstance for the conglomerators in the fact that Wall Street, faced with an infusion of new, small investors and demands for performance, began to look with interest, admittedly much of it skeptical interest, at the new acquisitors. And the institutions with big portfolios, the so-called go-go funds, and all their analysts began to feel a vast new pressure for performance.

So the conglomerates began to grow, to acquire, to startle the Establishment, and Wall Street got rid of its skepticism and started to romanticize them. This lasted for several years, the institutions and bankers backing the conglomerates while at the same time agreeing with the Establishment about how unfortunate it was that the brash new gang had drifted into town.

Up to this point we have a law of nature asserting itself—where there is a natural need, there will be a natural supply to meet it.

After years of startling performance among the conglomerates, the excesses began to set in, roughly in 1968 and particularly in 1969. There was a flood of rhetoric from the conglomerates' chiefs, thick slices of verbal baloney, of excessive claims of growth, earnings, prospects, book values, net return on capital, etc.

The official results failed to confirm these brave projections and no one was more surprised than many Wall Streeters who should certainly have known better. Most shocked were the young analysts. They had fallen for the big guff, recommended the conglomerate stocks highly because the performance seemed to be there. The stocks began going down, down, down. And the go-go funds, in going after the bigger-fool market, found that they had run out of fools.

If the conglomerates came on strong and Wall Street could hardly hide its pleasure and all that was only the law of nature asserting itself, then the turn-about could only be considered the law of gravity taking over. That law, very freely translated, is that a successful company has to take in more than it pays out.

But the Establishment got the daylights scared out of it. It saw the graffiti on the subway wall. "Watch out—or the congloms will get you!" It seems certain that entrenched management, which, I guess, more accurately describes what is generally meant by the Establishment, will never quite relax again. It can hardly afford to.

There were three things that the traditional pros had found belonged to the conglomerate way of life. They didn't fully believe them, but they began to suspect that the conglomerates, the better-run ones, at any rate, could claim advantages over the Establishment like:

1. an earnings resiliency on the downside, particularly in relation to external forces out of control, like an economic downturn;

2. greater earnings appreciation on the upside, especially when all is well;

3. an ability to allocate and diffuse capital better for many divisions and subsidiaries.

But what could the conglomerates, in all good conscience, not claim? Few of their principals and executives will deny that they are less capable than the Establishment in:

1. keeping a control on the diverse nature of their business, particularly on expenses and on adhering to planned sales and earnings;

2. developing an *esprit de corps* so important in establishing joint objectives;

3. maintaining a good debt-to-equity ratio, so that credit lines remained intact and the ability to finance expansion is sustained.

Yes, I know there is some contradiction between the two lists, but don't blame me. I didn't make up either of them.

At any rate, let's examine the gap between the two lists and see what we can chew on. If the conglomerates have a better earnings resiliency and appreciation, how much of that capability will be lost because of poor controls? The answer must be "substantial," since controls harness the energies of the mechanism, without which you have a big energy dissipation and even immobility. Roughly speaking, it's like having a powerful car with a 350-HP motor but a faulty transmission. Conglomerates unfortunately, except for ITT as a notable example, and perhaps one or two others, have shown that they have not been able consistently and adequately to control their earnings ability.

For another point, admittedly the conglomerates provide the financial and professional backing for their component companies and this they do rather well. But small central staffs and a hot-eyed zeal to concentrate on the bottom line tend to discourage any solid company spirit that might easily be generated across the layers of line command. I personally know the heads of three conglomerates who are keenly aware of this, but assign it to a back-back burner on the stove. The matter of communications and exchange of mutual confidence is a major internal problem.

The third point, the matter of inability to maintain a proper debt-to-equity ratio, is something that has dogged the conglomerate breed for years. My friend, the candid conglomerator of a few pages back, referred to the headaches of Jim Ling. This debt accumulation in the face of profit erosion is one of Ling's major headaches and it will take more than a bottleful of aspirins to ease it. L-T-V, having accumulated a long-term debt of $750 million, was compelled in 1969 and 1970 to dispose of and juggle its subsidiaries in order to reduce onerous debt payments. It is hardly out of the woods yet.

You can look forward to more of this by the other big diversified companies, and it, too, is a major problem which must be solved by the companies that place the biggest stress on acquisitions.

The matter of fixed-interest stock doesn't appear on the two lists I gave you earlier, but perhaps it should, because it has been a prime issue in the drive against and disaffection for the conglomerates. The 1970 tax-reform act passed by Congress places roadblocks and higher costs before any company plans to make use of fixed-interest securities to buy the equity capital of other companies. Perhaps working to meet the pressure exerted by the Securities and Exchange Commission, which has threatened new accounting regulations for public companies, the accounting fraternity has drafted some new rules which would prevent a conglomerate from putting together or pooling into its own figures the profits and balance sheets of newly acquired firms.

The conglomerate community has reacted with horror to this plan. The beef is why in all fairness and justice should profits not be pooled and why should the big, successful companies with a good track record not be permitted to borrow the maximum of fixed-interest money that the banks and institutions can provide?

Answer the advocates of nonpooling: "Why should you have that privilege when stock dilution and funny money are what have come out of it all?"

Of course, as conglomerators themselves freely admit, some of the conglomerates have combined the two elements by arbitrarily and even artificially exploding their equity profits by tendering "confetti" for the equity of other companies. This has been one of the big complaints against the conglomerate way of life—that the "real value" of fixed-interest stock of debt securities used for acquisitions, and even of short-term debt committed for sake of takeovers, has not been established or recognized. In fact, just the reverse has happened—a decline in the values of such paper accepted both by the sellers and the investor at large.

At this stage of disaffection the investment-banking community, as shown by its attitude and behavior in half a dozen cases, will not go along with any conglomerate's move to merge with or acquire a company whose management is unwilling to merge or be acquired.

This became apparent starting in 1968, when Goldman Sachs and Company, one of the biggest of investment bankers, gave Northwest Industries its walking papers as a client because Northwest tried vainly to merge with B. F. Goodrich Company. Goodrich may have been the country's third largest tire producer, but it is a matter of record that Northwest, a new conglomerate consisting of a Midwest railroad and the former Philadelphia and Reading Corporation, another conglomerate, had recently paid Goldman Sachs larger fees. But let's face it bravely, Goodrich not only had been Goldman Sachs' client longer but represented the Establishment, which Wall Street bankers would rather follow than oppose.

There were other cases of conglomerates' seeking to take over or merge with companies whose managements were not happy about it, but the point was made indelibly clear: "Rock the boat at your own risk and don't expect us to help."

Perhaps needless to say, few of the big conglomerate chiefs intend from now on to do otherwise, at least in terms of pushing an unfriendly takeover. Actually they won't have to, because this would have been largely circumscribed by the government antitrust push. In addition, as in the case of L-T-V, the prohibition against its future acquisition of companies with assets of $100 million or more still leaves that conglomerate and others plenty of room to roam around in: most of the publicly and privately held companies in the country are under that level of assets.

Will the conglomerate survive? Of course, but some will change radically because of pressure to improve their structure and policies. Perhaps more important, the changes that they forced on other companies where established professional management had operated for years will create burrs to irritate under the establishment's hide for years to come.

As *The Economist*, the conservative London publication, put it,

> For a start, conglomerates have between them advanced substantially the theories and practices of running big business groups. A more dramatic change is the fear of God that the threat of an attack can put in a stuffy management like Goodrich; it would be sad if accountancy changes or antitrust law were to alter this. . . .
>
> Almost always, the target for acquisition is a modest, old-line company which could be put to better use. In this sense, the conglomerates have started a process which badly needs completing in an aging industrial country such as America.

Interesting what viewpoints an outsider can bring, isn't it?

One additional point remains to be made here. That is that the conglomerate chiefs have not only been their own greatest advocates but also their own biggest detractors. How do I mean? By asserting some of their more aggrandizing ways to such an extent that it hurt rather than helped their own performances. Sometimes they have even performed badly in a role which was tailor-made for them, with the claque just waiting. Only, at times, outside of the claque, there could be no applause. Only jeers and deserved ones.

I return now to my friend, the self-flagellating conglomerator, and to Jim Ling, who used to be the top conglomerate chief of them all.

> I said before that Ling is the greatest but not only because he was personally so good. That he is, but Texas took him to its heart. He was a local boy who was going to make it to the top and he did, except that he overreached himself. He didn't have to. Dallas and the whole state loved him—bought his shares that he peddled himself like they were hot cakes—and yelled their heads off every time he did anything. Why not? He was a great, young businessman who came up big on the national scene; he was not a sharpie, an Eastern sharpie at that, which Texans hate, especially those from New York.
>
> So the big-hat boys took to him like he was what they had been waiting for. They bought his stock, they gave him credit and they

bragged about him. Texas was building up its president, not Lyndon B. Johnson but James J. Ling.

He was Texas's Horatio Alger story in the flesh—and he probably deserves it. But he did one thing wrong. He made the big boo-boo. He got sucked in by his own publicity.

13

"—Psst, Have I Got a Company for You!"

In a large New Jersey hotel and inn, a merger "shopping center" was in full operation. Seventeen companies looking for mates separately courted 55 prospective business "brides" in 155 flirtations, each lasting two hours over a three-day stretch. The negotiations, the first conducted on such a wholesale basis, resulted in half a dozen deals and were held in such secrecy that none of the business "brides" was aware of the presence of the others. Like something out of Molière, the activities of the lovers were staggered so that each was deftly, even if only feet away, kept from the others. The company delegations were controlled by the organization's switchboard, which was separate from the hotel's own board, so that the timing of the meetings was precise and there were no accidental, embarrassing confrontations.

These days, in Miami, Palm Beach and points seaward, vacationing businessmen escape from the big cities to relax at the pool, bar, golf links or race track—or try to. Instead, many find themselves not only bragging outrageously about their business exploits to others like themselves but quite suddenly talking about buying or selling their companies to each other.

And sitting nearby at the pool or bar or puttering away at the golf course are alert eavesdroppers. These suave and not so suave men saunter over and easily join in, the lure of a possible finder's fee lighting up their faces as they drop seeds of suggestion into willing ears and happily pick up the pool, bar or locker tabs to please the penurious rich.

Don't look now, if you're having your coffee at Harvey's, Longchamps, or even at Horn and Hardart. Then, in a couple of minutes, glance over at the little guy with the wild look at the table next to you, stirring his coffee with one finger (he obviously forgot his spoon) and jabbing with his other finger back and forth between the financial section of *The New York Times* and *The Wall Street Journal*, comparing the reports. He probably has *Barron's*, too, sticking out of his back pocket. Wait. The manager just hurried by, his gaze naturally fixed on everything but the customers. He's got a small yellow sheet of Standard and Poor's peeking out his breast pocket. Wait, wait, now the busboy with the long sideburns. Under his arm as he juggles a heavy tray of dirty dishes there's something folded that says "Merrill Lynch . . ."

Are these just concerned investors? Maybe. But there's an even chance that they are professional or amateur merger matchmakers. Almost everyone nowadays, believe it or not, seems to be one or the other.

In fact, the corporate matchmaker activity in recent years has become a new American game, a sort of adult form of Monopoly, in which the winner takes home an armful of real, not play, money—providing he has signed the selling or buying company, usually the former, to an iron-clad contract assuring him his finder's fee.

This new American game, call it "Find Me a Company" or "Have I Got a Company for You!," is attracting more and more players all the time. It's a relatively easy way to make a dollar, most people think, but actually, once they really get involved, they find it takes a lot more work than they thought. It's not just a matter of research, but of getting the two companies together, not always an easy task, and sometimes of nursing the engagement along until the wedding banns are posted.

But it's an exciting business, because the rewards are great and much of it can be done by checking financial records that are readily available or by some phone calls and visits. Of course, the real pros organize it, research it and make a big, profitable, systematized business out of it. Nonetheless, there are literally thousands of professionals, amateurs or part-timers who are playing or are trying to play the company-finding game.

Here's one, for example:

M. M. Matson, a genial, burly former insurance salesman, spends only 100 days a year in New York to indulge a second career as a business broker or merger matchmaker. The rest of the time he enjoys a life of affluence and leisure in Palm Beach, where his $200,000 one-level Grecian-style home is one of the more lavish residential showplaces. The three months plus that he spends on merger-making nets him about $100,000 a year. He has had about a dozen deals in the last decade. These, combined with extensive stock and other interests, have in recent years given him a minimum annual income of $275,000.

Not long ago he stopped the frequent incoming calls on the telephone in his New York office to reminisce a bit, to chat and to prognosticate. Almost seventy, "wealthy but not rich," Matson declared, "I like to play golf. I've done well and I've even bought into three companies that I helped put on the merger road. I don't have the money disease, but mentally I'm just as great as anyone. The big boys don't faze me. I know them all and they know me. I can talk their language and that's how I can make deals for them all."

More merger deals are conceived and cemented in Palm Beach, Miami, Bal Harbour and Palm Springs than in New York, Chicago and Los Angeles. It's not hard to understand, the way Matson tells it. A good many of the big-city entrepreneurs go to the warm-weather resorts here or in the Caribbean or the Riviera to relax. The only problem with that is that most of them have never learned to relax away *from* their business so that they relax away *with* the business, so to speak, and soon find that they can't stop making deals, can't stop trying to put over something on the next guy, who is sitting there in the sun or the nightclub and trying to do likewise. So while their sons or sons-in-law are back in New York, Chicago or LA, slaving away trying to prove they, too, have what it takes, the old man is making the big deal on his vacation. He really doesn't know how to do anything else; the built-in generator just won't stop running.

Matson's claim to fame rests more on his insurance career, where he had cut a wide swath as one of the industry's best salesmen of his era. In 1958 he sold $100 million worth of insurance to companies and individuals, which placed him in the industry's top bracket for salesmen. He achieved such a reputation for getting around in the right circles that one day in the mid-1950s an executive for the Studebaker Corporation told him, "Matty, you've got the connections and you know how to make deals. We're in the acquisition business right now. See what you can work out for us—we'll pay you five-percent commission."

Matson did, eventually arranging ten deals, the first of which cost Studebaker $10 million and earned Matson $500,000. "So I decided to work with rich people on mergers," he said, "and it has done so well for me that I give it only one-quarter of my time."

After more than a decade at it, he is convinced that the merger trend will continue indefinitely, although those between big firms may be curtailed for a while. "Mergers," he said with the confident smile of one who has succeeded not once but twice in his lifetime, "will get bigger in the small field but smaller in the big field."

Most pros are, of course, full-timers but the matchmaking part of the merger game is a complex, bustling world of its own, made up of Wall Street, banks, financial institutions and literally thousands of company finders. These, who make only one or two deals a year, can be found in every major and minor city in the country, and in quite a few small towns, but there are some substantial companies in their ranks, too. Among them are MacDonald and Company and Octagon Industries, Inc., both of New York, and W. T. Grimm, Inc., of Chicago, which prefer to call themselves financial and corporate development specialists.

Wall Street houses and many commercial banks are also very

active in the field, compelling their executives to spend more of their time on making mergers than they have in the past. They have found that finder's fees, which scale down from five percent on smaller mergers and acquisitions to one percent on the big ones, are a lucrative form of additional revenue besides fees from underwriting and providing venture capital.

Some of the techniques used are subtle, nonpublicized and practiced with a sort of back-door method. Off-beat tactics are used by one of Wall Street's largest and busiest investment-banking houses to arrange for the acquisitions of a growing number of small companies, especially in the medium-sized and smaller cities. The details were related by one of this firm's corporate finance associates.

> I have had some unusual success by setting up a string of about a dozen contact men throughout the South, East and Midwest. I give each about 25 percent of my fee when we clinch a deal and it has been sufficient incentive to bring in a lot of acquisitions to our house.
>
> I find a guy in a community, say, the head of the school board or a city employee or a guy who sells municipal bonds, and I show him a list of local companies I'm interested in. I get the names from the Dun and Bradstreet middle-market and $1-million books—the ones that list companies that have assets of $1 million or so. The contact men are well respected and pillars of the community and they advise me on which businesses are the most likely to sell, what their inside story is, the family, the local feeling about them, and so on. If the prospect sounds good to me, my man makes the first contact. If the reaction is good, I let him carry it a step further and then I match up the company with another. Then I come into town and clinch the deal.
>
> These guys do pretty well with me. One is a lawyer in Indianapolis, who made more money from me than from his law practice. Another is a stockbroker in a medium-sized Pennsylvania city, a World War I hero. Another is a retired banker in Birmingham, Alabama. I try to keep a few of the respected, older guys on my string who have built up a lifetime of relationships and are sort of elder citizens who can come and go anywhere in the town. . . .
>
> The opportunities this way are unlimited for takeovers. There are thousands of businesses across the country—maybe thousands of them in Ohio and Pennsylvania alone—family-owned businesses that do between $1 million and $10 million a year. You would be just amazed at how many there are—Momma and Poppa businesses that got big— and who are wondering how they can get around the inheritance-tax

bite or if they can survive the second generation. They are just sitting there waiting for me and my contact men to come around.

This corporate finance executive, who lives and travels well, recently pulled into an Alabama city and found a message to call a long-distance operator in a smaller city in the state. He recognized the name of the caller, one of two brothers who had built a mini-conglomerate operating out of the small Southern city and apparently doing well enough to have installed (rather than rented) its own IBM 360 computer. When he called, one of the brothers, let's call him Wes, demanded, "You-all come down heah and help me, you heah?" and hung up.

When the Wall Street man arrived the next morning, he found Wes and his brother, call him John, yelling at each other across the computer room.

"What's wrong, Wes?" asked the financial man.

A towering fat man who had a penchant for local politics, Wes replied in a rage. "What's wrong? This goddam brother of mine screwed me up with all this heah computer crap"—wagging an angry finger at the equipment—"and ah won't win mah election!"

John, the calmer, older one, explained that they had apparently used the computer incorrectly or carelessly, so that their expected good earnings had instead turned into losses. The company had a number of important local stockholders who would be shocked to learn of the disappointing results. It could well mean that Wes would not be elected mayor in the forthcoming elections.

"Well," the corporate finance man related, "I knew just what to do under those circumstances. It was an emergency. I merged their unprofitable divisions upstream—and had them out of danger, including Wes' political ambitions, within 48 hours. And got a good fee for it, too."

Those who spend all or part of their waking time trying to figure out ways to shoot down the corporate sitting ducks are aided in this hunt by a massive annual volume published under the name of *Hudson's Corporate Mergers*. Each year this tome becomes a sort of collector's item for corporate and independent matchmakers all over. Issued by William J. Hudson, a lexicographer and statistician, the 11-pound, 1,700-page volume commands a price tag of $250, which is apparently willingly paid by many acquirers and matchmakers. Written, researched, published and sold by Hudson, the book includes statistics on between 700 and 800 companies that he considers to be most attractive to the corporate acquisitor. He includes in it what he calls "asset discount" or "sleeping beauty" businesses. These have assets that may be undervalued on corporate books and also have earnings potential.

According to Hudson, the big criteria in whether a company is ripe for acquisition is how its trading volume of stock compares with management ownership and the average number of shares held by each shareholder. It the latter figure is below 250 shares per stockholder, he believes, the company is an interesting candidate for an acquisition or merger.

The takeover push has spurred many corporations to set up corporate development departments manned by executives from within the organization or by outsiders with experience. In a growing number of cases the staffs appointed to spearhead merger-acquisition efforts have been beefed up to include experts on accounting, law and personnel.

The Bendix Corporation, which a few years ago had appointed a vice-president for acquisitions, decided to raise the status and priority of his activity and named him after 18 months to the new all-inclusive post of vice-president for corporate development. Bendix's goal was a ten-percent rise in annual sales, half to come from internal growth and the other half from acquisitions. Within a two-year period, the giant Detroit aviation-space-automotive parts producer acquired nine companies to meet this goal.

General Mills, the big Minneapolis food producer, which has veered sharply in the conglomerate direction, took something of a different tack. A vice-president of finance, international operations and corporate development was designated to supervise "venture teams" to explore new sources of profit. In a novel concept, the plan was to appoint "entrepreneurially minded" young men with masters' degrees in business administration who would research and locate new ventures to be created from within the concern or outside it by acquisition. After a new venture was set in motion by creation or acquisition, each team would become the nucleus of the management to operate the new enterprise.

Few major companies interested in diversification through acquisition have neglected to add the corporate development department, but these vary greatly in their scope or staff. One of the most unusual and effective operates at U.S. Industries, Inc., a conglomerate which not only has a headquarters corporate development staff headed by a vice-president, but similar departments down the line in each of its six product-service groups.

Outsiders, including Wall Street houses, the banks, the corporate development companies and the business brokers, bring likely candidates to the corporate acquisition staffs. But some of the big companies get rather huffy about maintaining these contacts or recognizing such approaches, convinced instead that they can scour the countryside as well as anyone and, since that is the case, why pay a finder's fee to an outsider?

That tendency, however, hasn't dampened the zeal of the corporate development consultant or independent broker. But assuming that companies acclimated to acquisitions can come up with their own candidates, or themselves attract likely partners, as many do, who needs a consultant firm for mergers, anyway?

There are many such fee-paid firms around and a good portion have been in business for quite a spell. Besides working to bring one company to another, the financial and corporate consultant offers the objectivity that a third party can bring to the proceedings.

But just why do negotiators need objectivity from outsiders? Why can't the managements of two firms get together, talk it out like mature, hardheaded businessmen, bring the negotations to completion and save the finder's or broker's fee?

That, I'm afraid, presupposes that businessmen can be objective, mature and sophisticated. Too many are not, especially where mergers or acquisitions are concerned. It's difficult to be lofty in viewpoint when you have either spent a lifetime building up a company or worked your way up to the top over a period of years, and, in the process, had to shoulder aside others and even to let your family life drift. So management people worry whether they will wind up as the winners or losers, that they themselves might not come out on top in the deal, that their directors and/or stockholders will object to their decisions. Probably more of a hurdle than anything else is the personal chemistry between principals and other top executives that exercises restraint or infuses the talks with genuine enthusiasm.

Consultants insist that they can act as a buffer between two strong personalities—or a strong and a weak one—in either case leading to a personality conflict that could kill a deal. The third man can then guide the personalities toward a more receptive attitude in the negotiations that could make for agreement in a deal. In many actual cases, however, the consultant more than anything else provides a technical expertise, particularly on financial, tax and legislative matters, while on the human side some have enough experience and skill to ease the personnel integration.

In case you are thinking of hanging out your merger-consultant's shingle, here, according to some of them, are the necessary steps that you would have to go through to come up with a fat fee:

You would have to draft a confidential analysis of a company to show why it is a suitable candidate for a merger or acquisition. This would include its past and present record and its potential. And don't forget to get a letter of authorization to represent it from this company.

Locating the right company to combine it with is the tough part. Why? First, there are many companies that might make just the right fit, so that a thorough canvassing is essential. Second, the trick is not to show your hand—that, is, to reveal that the concern you have analyzed is for sale, since that would tend to reduce both its salability and its bargaining power.

Then you must start traveling or get to the partner you have located, to start exploratory contacts, first talks on terms, etc. This is usually the consultant's or intermediary's function, although some companies prefer to do this sort of thing themselves from the outset.

Meetings between the two companies then follow, and this is where the consultant shows his mettle. He must possess highly sensitive antennae to spot potential deal killers before they erupt and cause everyone to walk out. I'm referring to problems of personality conflict, conflicts of interest, idiosyncratic insistence on fringe issues that could rile the other party, disagreement on terms, etc.

Get the principals to sign on the dotted line. If there is no dotted line, make sure they sign anyway.

Then you can pick up your check.

What does the check amount to? On deals involving a price of up to $10 million, the finder's fee is five percent of the first million, four percent of the second, three percent of the third, two percent of the fourth and one percent of the fifth, and scaling down on the remainder. On bigger deals that total comes to less than five percent on the total down to one percent on giant-sized deals. On some major deals it's an agreed-upon amount after a minimum.

Stockholders' meetings and even litigation are not infrequently enlivened by criticisms of finder's-fee arrangements. In one such case a special stockholders' meeting in June 1969 developed into a bit of a brouhaha. Kinney National Service, Inc., a services conglomerate, had paid Milton A. Rudin, a Hollywood lawyer, $1.5 million in finder's fees for helping Kinney to acquire for $22.5 million a 20-percent interest in the recording subsidiary of Warner Brothers–Seven Arts, Ltd. Kinney acquired the full assets of Warner–Seven Arts, but the gripe centered around the purchase of the big interest in Warner's recording business from Frank Sinatra, the entertainer.

"What services make Milton Rudin worth $1.5 million?" asked David Brown, who represented Lewis D. and John J. Gilbert, professional shareholders' representatives.

"It's most difficult to take apart portions of a deal," replied Steven J. Ross, Kinney's president. "It's the sum of the parts that counts and this is one of the best deals Kinney ever made."

Besides the finder's fee, which will be paid over a decade, Rudin became a consultant to Kinney and received 25,000 shares of its stock for $1 a share. The stock that the attorney got was worth $750,000 at the current market price. Rudin came off well; the questioning stockholder did not.

General Host Corporation took the opposite stance in connection with finder's and similar fees charged against it by two prominent Wall Street houses and a business broker. This conglomerate made no bones about its reluctance to pay a sum of between $1.8 million and $2.2 million requested by Kleiner, Bell and Company, Inc., and Allen and Company, Inc., and C. Gerald Goldsmith in connection with General Host's agreement to sell its 57-percent interest in Armour and Company to the Greyhound Corporation. General Host put it in simple language in its proxy statement calling for a special stockholders' meeting to approve its agreement with Greyhound:

> The matter of the appropriateness and amount of such fees is presently under consideration by the Company. While Allen and Company and Kleiner, Bell participated in various of the Company's negotiations with Greyhound, and may be properly entitled to some compensation in this regard, the Company is not of the opinion that fees such as those requested bear a reasonable relationship to such services as may have been performed. Any services which have been performed by Mr. Goldsmith were not performed at the Company's request. The Company is of the opinion that a fee in the nature of a broker's or "finder's fee" is not warranted in connection with the Greyhound Agreement.

Such situations are not uncommon. As the merger pace quickens, company acquisition departments are naturally eager to develop their own prospects and bring negotiations with them to fruition. Paying big finder's fees must then, at least in some measure, detract from the efforts of these staffs. Thus, a growing number of companies are becoming less available to the typical business broker and even are making the approaches of the professional corporate development consultant more difficult.

Nonetheless, both these types of matchmakers are not easily put down. The best and most active earn big incomes. Jack Sterling, of Los Angeles, for example, earns $1 million in finder's fees in a good year. Harry Samuels, a New York financial consultant, has gotten as much as $500,000. One deal involving a substantial selling company can be well worth months of effort.

Sometimes the consultant, despite what he feels is a solid, written commitment, finds he has to sue in order to obtain his fee. This type of situation occasionally involves suits by attorneys or accountants, who are not reluctant to moonlight as company finders. It's a profitable sideline activity.

Wall Street has recognized this, too, perhaps because of or in spite of the recent year-long turndown in the stock market. Merger activity has become the biggest growth area of the investment-banking field. In the 1968–1970 period it is estimated that almost 100 stock-exchange firms opened merger and acquisitions departments. Firms like Walston, Merrill Lynch, Francis I. DuPont, Smith Barney and others have been earning finder's fees of $150,-000 and $200,000 and more in addition to their other activities.

One inevitable result of this has been the raising of their fees for the matchmaking process. When it was a minor phase of their activity, the fee was usually only one percent or thereabouts. Now it falls within the one percent to five percent spread, depending on the sale price. This fee arrangement is commonly known in the corporate matchmaking trade as the "5-4-3-2-1." It has, quite understandably, attracted more than a few bright young men and even older and retired corporate executives to set up their own consultant's shops. It's definitely a new form of entrepreneurism, offering a gleaming lure for the exercise of effort and talent.

Let's examine a few of the corporate development consultants and see how they operate.

Howard R. Suslak, president of MacDonald and Company, is a nephew of Sir Isaac Wolfson, the British retailing millionaire who has also been active on the acquisition scene in the United Kingdom for many years. A heavy-set man with small, thoughtful eyes, Suslak has in the past two decades become one of the experts in the merger field. He effected such consolidations as that of General Precision Equipment Corporation and Amercon Corporation and that of Colt Industries and Elox Corporation.

Suslak took his master's degree at the Wharton School of Finance at the University of Pennsylvania, finding particular interest in a study of outstanding management consultants. His first job was that of assistant to the president of E. R. Squibb Company, the big pharmaceutical house. After a year, he became vice-president and general manager of Metacan Manufacturing Company, a Brooklyn tent-making firm. Two years later he joined the New York office of MacDonald, then a Boston-based consulting company that Suslak had first heard about at the Wharton School. He started as an assistant vice-president, then rose to vice-presi-

dent and then to general manager of all the MacDonald offices. When John M. MacDonald, an internationally known yachtsman, died in 1962, Suslak, then executive vice-president, bought control and became president.

The company, which moved its main offices to Madison Avenue in New York, had drifted into merger-making in an evolutionary way after its founding in 1919 and has concentrated on it in more recent years. It employs a number of experienced executives in a variety of specialties to help business in its acquisition efforts. No more than one client is accepted in any particular industry.

How does MacDonald earn its fees?

Suslak says there are four phases:

> One is to determine if a company that wants to make acquisitions has the necessary qualifications to make it successful in its goal. The second is to set up perimeters and guideposts of acquisition goals. Third is to submit qualified situations that would be available for acquisition by the client. And fourth is to help in the negotiation of the acquisition and assist in effecting a smooth closing.

In Suslak's experience, fitting the two presidents of the firms in a proposed deal is more vital than working out the right balance sheet. "It isn't just a matter of finance, in other words, but equally of human pyschology." His conviction is that mergers will continue on the increase because it's inherent in the corporate nature to grow. There are two routes to growth. One is internal development and the other is to buy an existing company that offers good management, products or services and market position.

"The second method," he adds, "is easier, less risky and faster."

As Suslak and I concluded our talk about his business and walked by his second-floor office, I looked up and saw all the lights ablaze. "It's a business like any other," he said, seeing my glance. "You're finished when you're done. The only problem with mergers and acquisitions is that you're rarely done."

A dozen corporate marriages in their first two years of business is the track record of two young men who operate Octagon Industries, a consulting company. Bruce Zenkel and Louis Perlmutter started the firm in July 1967, finding their second careers in the merger field. Zenkel, thirty-eight, a son-in-law of David Schwartz, founder and chairman of Jonathan Logan, Inc., had been an officer and director of that firm, one of the country's largest apparel makers. Perlmutter, thirty-five, was a lawyer formerly associated with the New York law firm of Phillips, Nizer, Benjamin, Krim and Ballon. By 1969 the partners had helped seal mergers accounting for a total purchase price of over $100 million.

Both knew a few things about acquisitions before they got together. Zenkel had been instrumental in Jonathan Logan's acquisition program, while Perlmutter had been assistant to the president of New England Industries, Inc., a diversified holding company. Two slim, handsome, well-tailored men, Zenkel and Perlmutter operate within a tight triangle of Wall Street (where the money is), Seventh Avenue (where most of their clients are) and Madison Avenue (where their offices are). But quite often they are on the run from those points to any part of the country where they think the buyers and sellers are. In January 1970 they made the firm public, offering 200,000 shares at $8 each, which were quickly bought out. Octagon is one of the few financial-corporate development firms that has gone public.

Probably the oldest and most widely known financial consulting firm specializing in mergers and acquisitions is Chicago-based W. T. Grimm and Company. Its annual merger studies, each showing big rises in the number of consolidations, are widely used and reprinted. Its founder, W. T. Grimm, has an investment-banking and financial consulting background in Chicago dating back to 1924.

Widely respected for his long tenure, Grimm has some interesting suggestions about when to sell a business. If two or more of the following conditions exist, he says, consolidation through mergers should be given active consideration: lack of diversification, uncertain future outlook, limited growth possibilities, insufficient return on investment, and personal reasons for a sale. About the last he says:

> The list of personal reasons for sale or merger is endless and at any given time a great many may overlap. From a personal standpoint, the time to consider consolidation is before a problem enlarges out of

normal proportions and while it is still possible to maintain continuity of management. It is "management" which gives a business value over and above the historic asset worth.

Another prominent financial-merger consultant, Arthur A. Burck operates in the heart of Wall Street. In the last few years he has been instrumental in completing transactions aggregating more than $200 million, including $60 million in international acquisitions.

Robert J. Burg, a Manhattan consultant, is unusual in having had personal experience in the acquisition field, experiencing the odd sensation of seeing his own business actually sold twice through successive takeovers. A native of Hungary, Burg came to the United States in 1947. He attended New York University School of Commerce, held a few jobs and then started his own business of supplying transparent polyethylene packaging. He sold the company to Spencer Chemical Company, remained as president of the subsidiary, until Spencer was acquired by Gulf Oil Company. He didn't care for the tendency of this third owner to run his company around him and departed.

Burg became a consultant about five years ago, hoping that his personal experience and general knowledge would be sufficient to help him bring buyers and sellers together. He was right. Within a few years he had put together ten mergers and acquisitions and had nine more transactions in the final stages.

He has found that a consultant is moving ahead if most of his deals are larger in scope than the previous ones. Also, he believes, a consultant can achieve standing in the field if he works only with selected clients. Burg has six of them, including conglomerates, and he spends most of his time scouring the small entrepreneurial market in an attempt to meet the buying companies' acquisitive needs.

"The constant tendency that a consultant finds," he told me, "is to become a principal, to take control of an available company, and thereby to work on capital gains. Finder's fees are, after all, only ordinary income and the tax is hefty. Each consultant has to make up his mind whether he wants to get personally and financially involved in ownership."

So much for some of the merger consultants. I should also insert here a reference to one consultant who trusts no one. He has a fine imported German tape recorder plugged into his phone so that he has an exact record of what every buyer or seller has told him, at least on the phone.

"I don't want to misinterpret or be misinterpreted," he explained. "It all goes into a log of every telephone call I have had for the last ten years. No one can tell me what I promised or didn't promise."

Now, coming full circle, we are back at the stage where we started—the case of the merger "shopping center." I visited Harlan J. Brown, head of his own consulting firm in Washington, D. C., who sponsored the wholesale company-swapping stunt in New Jersey in June 1969.

Brown, thirty-six, came into the merger field three years earlier after careers as an engineer and as a partner in an oil-drilling venture and after obtaining master's degrees in metallurgical engineering and business administration. He was drawn to merger-consulting because he learned a few interesting and vital facts about technology companies.

In his office on K Street, N.W., Brown told me:

> The technological companies are not for sale as often as you find companies in other fields. That means that companies in the technology field that are anxious to diversify have their problems attracting similar companies. But they have a great need to diversify. Product life is much shorter in the technology field. These companies have to grow to survive and they have to diversify because today's technology is tomorrow's obsolescence.

The concept of holding a "merger center" grew out of the experience of Brown and his staff in arranging acquisitions not only of the technology company but of others in varied fields.

> We researched names of companies, chief executive officers, size and assets in three states, Delaware, Pennsylvania, and New Jersey. About 3,500 companies were contacted in the fields that acquiring companies like most—electronics, leisure time, aerospace, optics, aircraft, and nuclear research and development. Many companies, as expected, didn't want to sell, but of all those telephone calls we developed 400 new acquisition prospects.

Most of these companies were small, privately held firms. We got from them the exact nature of their business, current net worth, marketing information, management, physical facilities, the acquisition outlook and the asking price range.

Brown and his people assembled all this material on the 400 companies into a large volume and sent copies to the presidents of 500 companies known to be active in acquisitions. A combination of source lists were used to draw up this mailing list. Each company included as an acquisition candidate was not identified in the book other than by code numbers.

A followup call was placed to the 500 presidents and each was requested to indicate interest in at least ten coded names. Then they were asked if they would be willing to pursue their interest in the potential sellers by participating in a merger "shopping center." At least 15 acquiring companies were sought for the center, each to contribute from $800 to $1,600 to subsidize the meeting. Actually 17 such companies were signed to contracts by Harlan Brown and his associates. They charged those companies $1,500 each as a fee for the meeting and the preparatory work done by the Brown firm, with a bonus to be paid on a successful close.

Separate suites were reserved for all company delegations. Brown's staff of 20 supervised the proceedings, working out of a communications room and juggling the participants in and around the 50 rooms involved in the "center." The half-dozen deals that resulted were considered sufficiently worthwhile to continue the project and even to expand it. "We hope to get to a point of holding one such 'center' in a different city each month of the year, not only in the U. S. but also in Canada," reported Brown.

All this may be beyond you at this point, if you are only at the stage where you are just planning to get your feet wet and make a feint at your first company. Or, if you have been in it for some time, you may feel that mergers and acquisitions are more properly conducted on a retail rather than wholesale basis. Or, perhaps you don't quite know yet if you want to be a matchmaker, but think you just might because the rewards are high and the overhead is low.

There's one way to find out—test your reaction to this actual ad which took up most of a page not long ago in *The Wall Street Journal*:

ONE HUNDRED

MILLION

DOLLARS CASH!

We have $100,000,000 cash available
for purchase of a company
with good earnings and growth potential. . . .
(All replies strictly confidential.)

14

The Never-Never and the Hardly-Ever Mergers

Saul Steinberg, who tried to take over the Chemical Bank and got clobbered instead, was out before he was in. He was young, Jewish and a conglomerator, too.

Xerox Corporation and the CIT Financial Corporation, which in 1968 might have had the biggest merger yet, were called out on just two strikes by Wall Street.

The first was the big disparity in their price/earnings multiples which financial sources had put on their stocks. Xerox's phenomenal success with copying machines had made its stock one of the bluest of blue chips, selling during premerger talks at 50 times earnings. CIT, the country's second largest finance company and four times as big as Xerox, nonetheless had not shown the same fantastic profit rise and so its shares were selling at only 30 times earnings.

The second strike against the Xerox-CIT combination was Wall Street's complete inability to understand the economic and financial benefits of the $4.2-billion merger. And when Wall

184

Street doesn't understand something, it throws up its hands, looks wildly around and lopes off in some other direction.

First National City Corporation, the holding company that owns New York's biggest bank, the First National City Bank of New York, took only three hours to call off its proposed merger in 1969 with the Chubb Corporation after the Justice Department announced that it would sue to bar the deal.

If it is true that one out of three mergers fails, winding up in a drastic reorganization or, even worse, with a divestiture of some of the company properties, it is likewise true that most proposed mergers and acquisitions never come to pass. Worse still and more traumatic to the principals, many mergers in which an agreement in principle is reached never get a chance to be born.

Why do many apparently worthwhile mergers abort?

Some of the reasons are implicit in the three aforementioned incidents—opposition generated against a "raider," Wall Street's disaffection for the dubious financial boons of a merger and reluctance to test government disfavor in the courts. But there are many other reasons, as for example:

The chemistry of the principals that was so essential in first raising the possibility of a consolidation explodes into resentment rather than harmony while the talks are still going on.

Investor reaction to the initial announcement has a negative effect on stock values, making either the buyer or the seller feel that it was all a bad idea in the first place.

Fringe benefits or additional considerations raised by either party that either adds to or reduces the purchase price can have a bombshell effect on the proceedings.

Perhaps the most important or most frequent stumbling block is the psychological effect that one party has on the other. This is a two-edged sword, cutting these ways:

—The acquiring company takes a hard, independent position, "Fine if you like our offer, fine if you don't." This is its true nature, most of the time. But quite often it is adopted to keep the price of the deal to a minimum or to gain the advantage in negotiations.

—The selling company is usually in a tender, raw state and the last thing it wants to face is a take-it-or-leave-it attitude from the buyer. So the selling principal reacts similarly, actually hurt and disappointed by the coolness, and displays his own coldness and disinterest. Result: no deal.

Another reason for the abortive negotiations is the fact that too often the talks progress so quickly and so smoothly that there is an agreement in principle before both parties have had a chance to talk things out. It's like a courtship where sex was everything, but love, nothing. The marriage just never comes off.

Again, many a promising deal is written off because one of the principals was either greedy or stingy on the purchase price. Not infrequently the difference is so small, especially when necessarily viewed over a period of years, that it is infinitesimal.

Most of these reasons pertain to the medium- and smaller-sized companies. When it comes to mergers between big companies, there are fewer reasons for the breakup but simpler ones. Usually "gut" ones.

Let's examine two of the most dramatic "unmergers" of the period and see what happened.

Steinberg *vs.* the Chemical Bank: "I don't know exactly what happened, but a good portion of American industry wondered who was safe anymore"

It will be a long time before the two-week saga of how Leasco Data Processing Equipment Corporation tried—or was forced to try—to take over Chemical Bank of New York is completely forgotten.

In one way it was a comedy of errors—with Saul Steinberg, Leasco's chairman and founder, forced into the open on what was either a latent desire to take over Chemical or an actual one; with Chemical Bank, under the direction of chairman William Renchard, so shook up with the disclosure of Steinberg's apparent aims that its directors didn't know for days whether to laugh or cry or yell for help; and such an overreaction by the Establishment that Leasco's stock dropped 25 percent in the period, Leasco's credit was threatened and pressure was put on Leasco's two investment bankers not to help the stunned Steinberg.

The flap reached to the state capital and then Washington. Frightened by the aspect of a hot-shot, school-boy financier moving to swallow up the nation's sixth largest bank, the banking community quickly gathered its forces and created a tide of opposition that found support in both the state and national capitals. Governor Nelson A. Rockefeller of New York asked for immediate legislation to protect banks in the state from being taken over. Reports indicated that Chemical Bank collected support high in the Nixon administration, in federal agencies and in Congress. A bill similar to the proposed New York statute but covering national banks was introduced in Congress on February 28, 1969, or eight days after the Leasco chairman threw in the towel, by Senator John J. Sparkman, Alabama Democrat and chairman of the Senate Banking and Currency Committee.

At least one computer-leasing competitor of Leasco's told Chemical Bank that it would withdraw its business if Steinberg's interest in the bank was formalized into a tender offer. Only one day after the Steinberg interest in Chemical Bank was disclosed, Steinberg's main investment banker, White, Weld and Company, told him that if he were serious in zeroing in on Chemical, he would have to do it without White, Weld's financial help. Lehman Brothers, another Leasco investment banker, admitted that it was pressured by commercial banks not to help Steinberg. This presented quite a problem for Lehman since it was a big borrower of bank funds for its own purposes.

The entire situation created not only the most memorable round of talk on Wall Street in some time, it also left many of its already hardened veterans with a new insight into the capability of the American business Establishment to pull together in the face of a possible raid against one of its bastions.

It also left some people on Wall Street and in other places with a bad taste in their mouths. As one leading investment banker on Wall Street told me:

> What was Bill Renchard's responsibility in the whole affair? In defeating Steinberg, he cost his own shareholders some $600 million in stock gains. . . .
> I'm not so sure that the culprits in such alleged raids as the Establish-

ment sees them are not really the heroes and the Establishment itself isn't the real villain. . . .

It's a question of morals. The ones who clothe themselves most in the American free-enterprise system are the same ones who run first to the government and yell, "Raid!" when they are threatened. But how did they get there themselves and what is the free-enterprise system at least in part but the opportunity to grow by buying other businesses?

I grant you that some of this particular comment may just be pique. Wall Street did not come off with particular valor in the Leasco-Chemical fracas, nor did anyone, for that matter, but the investment-banking community found that it had to go along for absolutely economic reasons with its arch-enemy, the commercial bankers. Courage is not, let's face it, the stuff with which the game of finance is played.

Chemical Bank refused to be drawn into a postmortem discussion of the whole matter, but Steinberg didn't mind. He said:

> Very little really happened. We here don't know the true story, only by hearsay. Everything happened because of a news break in *The New York Times*, saying that we were eyeing the Chemical Bank and it was a great shock to us.
>
> Why? Because that was not the case. You must understand the situation we were in. We had acquired Reliance Insurance, which had in its portfolio stocks of various banks, including Chemical. This meant that we naturally had a real, honest interest in banking as a cornerstone for putting together various financial services. But we had talked about putting together banking and insurance for some four, five years before that.
>
> We hadn't made any approach to Chemical up to the time the story broke. We didn't want to talk to Chemical or any other bank at that time. But when the story appeared in *The Times*, we thought that we ought to talk to the Chemical brass and tell them what our position was.

Steinberg, in this particular context, skipped over or plain omitted a few pertinent facts. One was that Leasco, knowing that an espionage system often operated in the merger field, had used code names to prevent information on acquisition plans from leaking out. "Raquel" was the name used for Reliance Insurance, a name borrowed from Raquel Welch, the movie actress, and used for Reliance because it, too, was "big and beautiful." Steinberg had a code for Chemical Bank, too, despite his disclaimer. It was "Faye" for Faye Dunaway, the Bonnie in the film *Bonnie and Clyde*. But despite all this sort of cryptography and shenanigans, Steinberg apparently let the cat slip out.

This developed in testimony before the Celler committee. Early in February 1969 Steinberg had a routine lunch with a *New York Times* reporter, a habit that many businessmen have, following a semisocial, semiprofessional practice of lunching or having drinks with reporters. During the Celler committee hearing, Steinberg was stunned when the committee general counsel showed him a document out of the files. It was a memo circulated within Chemical Bank relating almost all of Steinberg's conversation with the reporter. Steinberg told the committee that the memo accurately summarized the conversation about Leasco's intent and interest in a tie-up with Chemical.

The following week Renchard told the same committee that a *Times* reporter had called him on February 5 to check out a rumor that Leasco planned a takeover of his bank. Renchard then said that he told the reporter everything that he knew about Leasco's plans, and the following day *The Times* reported the takeover plan.

Obviously there are discrepancies here. Steinberg said that he felt bitter toward *The Times*, because what he had passed on as either off-the-record information or on the assumption that it was for background purposes wound up in an internal memo at Chemical Bank. At the same time it is a bit hard to swallow Steinberg's statement to me that he wasn't interested in acquiring Chemical Bank. He told the Celler committee that his company's practice was that "the acquisition formula was planned months in advance of the actual action or decision on the [banking] company to be acquired." And, according to inside poop, he had set his sights on either Chemical Bank or the Manufacturers Hanover Trust Company. The Franklin National Bank on Long Island had also been considered.

At any rate, let's continue with my interview with Steinberg:

> Two days later, Leasco received a hand-delivered letter from Chemical Bank, saying in effect that "we understand that you are interested in acquiring Chemical Bank. This carries serious implications for antitrust because you are already in fields that we want to get into. . . ." Our attorney, Bob Hodes, thought that the letter was really an invita-

tion to talk to them. In the meantime, we kept getting calls from all over the country, but a giant snowstorm kept us all bogged down. And the one-bank holding company legislation which would put restrictions on the type of thing we wanted to do was already in the Washington hopper and worried us.

I called Renchard and he invited us to lunch that same day, Monday, February 10.

The group was small, including besides Steinberg and Renchard such Chemical Bank people as Howard W. McCall, Jr., president, and Hulbert S. Aldrich, vice-chairman. It is not difficult to imagine the strangeness of the atmosphere—youthful, chunky Steinberg in blue blazer and slacks facing the tall austerity of the three bankers who still did not quite know whether to laugh or to be angry. The computer-leasing tycoon recalled the event in this nervous, staccato manner:

I told Renchard the *Times* article was wrong. "What do you think of the concept, anyway?" I asked. I was trying to determine if they had thought out where banking was going. "We won't do anything in a hostile way," I told him. Then I asked him, "Why don't we merge?" He replied that it couldn't be done—he couldn't become part of Leasco—the trust, responsibility and confidence in Chemical—it would be bad. They would lose officers and customers. I said, "How about Leasco becoming part of Chemical?" He said, "Would you be willing to do it?" I agreed. He said, "Who would have control of the board?" I said that these things could be worked out if we agreed on the concept. I said, "You could be the chief executive officer and we could split the board. For the time being, the emphasis in the merger would be on nonbanking but on financially related advantages, on information-related services." He asked, "What assurance do you have that we would keep you other than that you are the largest shareholder?" I said, "We would expect a commensurate voice in management if our end of it succeeds." The point then came up about the differences in the sizes of our companies. But I said that, while their net worth was close to $600 million, we were earning at the rate of $40 million, which was pretty good for our size compared to Chemical's $55–$60 million. I personally thought that the meeting had gone very well—there seemed to be some meeting ground. Renchard said he had heard a rumor that we would announce a tender bid for Chemical at our stockholders' meeting, which was scheduled the next day. I answered, "We don't go in for dramatics." I asked, "When can we meet again?" He replied that this should be done as quickly as possible—he was going around the world. We met again the next day, right after our stock-holders' meeting.

The shareholders' event was interesting as much for what it did not produce as for what it did. Under queries by stockholders, Steinberg said that Leasco had met with Chemical, but he did not announce the expected tender offer. This was widely interpreted as an indication that Leasco was beginning to feel the pressure.

"We have concluded," announced Steinberg sternly to the shareholders, "that our corporate plans and purposes would be enhanced by bringing Leasco's capabilities and assets together with those of a large bank. But the realization of so large a plan requires the exercise of careful and deliberate judgment. At the present time, we have not made a decision as to a particular bank."

Chemical's Renchard told the press the same day that he had met with Steinberg at his request, adding that "our conversation was along very general lines, in the course of which he outlined some of his objectives he has for his company. No negotiations of any kind have been initiated."

What was happening in the meantime? For one thing, Leasco's stock was moving down fast, from 140 the day the *Times* story broke to 127 the day of the annual meeting. And for another, a partner of White, Weld and Company, which had told Leasco four days earlier that after due consideration it could not go along with Steinberg on Chemical, said that Chemical would be "light-years" ahead of its competition if it could work out a deal with Leasco.

At a second luncheon with Chemical Bank, later on the day of the Leasco annual meeting, Steinberg related in the interview, there were more people "but the atmosphere was decidedly different. It seemed that they had all decided they didn't want to talk but no one said so. I finally said, 'Why don't you discuss this with your board and officers and call me?' Two days later, Renchard reached me in Philadelphia and asked, 'When can you come back for another meeting?' I said at his convenience. He said, 'Make it the following Thursday.' "

Steinberg then spent a hectic day in Washington, in which he had ten appointments, including ones with Senator John Sparkman and Congressman Wright Patman to determine how restrictive the one-bank holding company legislation might be. He left the capital, he said, feeling "somewhat depressed that the legislation would be quite restrictive and might curtail our growth and that we couldn't use the capability that we had."

At ten on the morning of February 20, the day he and his associates were to meet for the third time with the representatives of the Chemical Bank, Steinberg said that he met with Hodes in the attorney's office and drafted a press notice that Leasco had no desire to acquire the Chemical Bank or to acquire any company in a hostile manner. But he kept the release in his pocket when the luncheon started. He told me:

> There were six at the meeting. Three of them, three of us, but nothing was happening. I found them very guarded. I said, "if you're not excited—two great companies can't get together unless they are excited—then we can't get together." They seemed to sigh with relief at that.
>
> We then changed the press release to include the fact that the one-bank holding legislation was a negative factor on our plans and that without the support and enthusiasm of management, Leasco had no interest whatsoever in pressing for an affiliation with Chemical.
>
> We were never actually threatened by anyone, least of all by our own lenders. I'm certain that Chemical had the sympathy of a good portion of American industry. After all, if a fast-growing company like ours could knock over the country's sixth largest bank, who was safe?

But by then it was all over.

Northwest *vs.* Goodrich:
A Classic Counterattack, a Government Suit, a $30-Million Loss, a Public-Relations Barrage and Legislation, too.

Steinberg, though set back by a most imposing display of Establishment opposition *en masse*, still got off gently. He never even had a chance to make a formal tender offer and to take its risks. Ben W. Heineman did—for the B. F. Goodrich Company —and lost $30 million on paper for the privilege.

That was not the only experience that the president of Northwest Industries, Inc., the holding company that includes as its base the Chicago and Northwestern Railway, had during his seven-month foray to acquire control of Goodrich. That Akron-based tire-maker, whose 3.9-percent net profit on $1.1-billion sales made it the lowest-earner among the big four tire producers at the time, showed greater astuteness in beating off Northwest's threat than it had shown in years in managing its own operations.

Heineman, a confident, brusque attorney, took over ailing Chicago and Northwestern in 1956. Within a few years he had turned it around into a profitable line and then gradually started adding other concerns in the clothing, steel and chemical fields, after making a merger with the Philadelphia and Reading Corporation. The upshot of all this was the formation of Northwest Industries, which jumped in sales from $260 million in 1965 to $701 million in 1968.

Goodrich, 99 years old and the tire industry's most conservative company, had been looked upon as a target for years, although few merger-masters wanted to take on such a giant. The Tisch brothers, with a big cash position in their Loew's, Inc., had accumulated some 358,000 shares of Goodrich, apparently as an investment to be looked at eventually as the springboard for a possible acquisition.

Heineman, however, had undertaken a study of Goodrich on his own and had had a staff group do a thorough analysis of Goodrich in the fall of 1968. What the scrutiny showed was enough to spur a strong interest on Heineman's part. Unaggressive management could only have been responsible for Goodrich's lackluster performance, he reasoned. Management held only a tiny portion of the stock and most of it was widely dispersed. The ratio of equity to debt was low, always a good thing to have in your portfolio. And Goodrich was a big factor in both the tire and the chemical industries.

Deterred by an interest in another company as a possible takeover candidate, Heineman delayed any action on Goodrich until December of 1968. Then Northwest's executive committee approved the purchase of about 2.5 percent, or 350,000 shares, of Goodrich's outstanding stock. When Laurence A. Tisch, chairman of Loew's and a director of Northwest, was informed while on vacation of the proposed action, he then revealed to Heineman that Loew's itself already held a big stock position in Goodrich.

Loew's summarily stopped buying any more shares, a development that later caused Goodrich's management to claim collusion between Northwest and Loew's, a charge denied by both Heineman and Tisch.

Tisch later said that his firm was buying the stock through Lehman Brothers, whose partner John L. Weinberg, was a Goodrich director. Thus Loew's purchases of Goodrich should have been known to the tire company, Tisch insisted. Oddly enough, it was also Lehman Brothers, through another partner, who formally, but actually erroneously, felt out Northwest on a possible buying-selling deal with Goodrich. What happened was that J. Ward Keener, an austere former economics professor who had been Goodrich's president for a decade, had decided, after being warned that his company was vulnerable to a raid, to seek out help to find a preferable merger partner. Lehman then inadvertently asked the very company that had already been buying Goodrich shares for some weeks.

Heineman promptly asked to meet Keener, but this was not to happen until after Northwest announced its $1-billion tender offer. Rumors that Northwest planned such a move began to pervade Wall Street and the stock values of both Northwest and Goodrich moved up. Sensing that the time was ripe and that to wait might lead to government charges that Northwest withheld information from its shareholders, Heineman announced his offer publicly—a package of stock, warrants and debentures worth between $75 and $80 for each share of Goodrich, then worth about $55.

Keener, furious when he read of the offer in the newspapers, refused to take calls from Heineman that morning. He never fully believed, even after they finally met three days later, that Heineman had simply assumed that Lehman Brothers had posted Keener of Northwest's interest in a deal with Goodrich.

The Goodrich head then showed that he had come a long way from the economics class. He gathered a group of varied, skillful fighters against corporate raids—White and Case, a Manhattan law firm that had helped the American Broadcasting Company fend off Howard Hughes' takeover attempt, First Boston Corporation, one of the country's largest investment bankers, and three public-relations firms, including Hill and Knowlton, the biggest, which had earned its public-relations battle stars in several earlier wars for control of other companies.

But that was only the start. These are the things that the task group came up with:

Expensive advertisements were placed knocking Northwest's smaller size, its first-quarter loss and a decline in its shares so that Goodrich shareholders would get $10 less than had originally been offered. Goodrich's stock had also dropped, but this was irrelevant.

Shareholders were persuaded to stagger the terms of Goodrich's directors so that it would be just a bit harder for Heineman to get control—two years would have to elapse before he could hope to make some inroads on Goodrich's board, even if he did take over.

To set up a possible conflict-of-interest or antitrust problem, Goodrich bought for about $2.7 million a Terre Haute trucking company that competed with Northwest on certain rail routes. Then Goodrich petitioned the Interstate Commerce Commission to rule that Northwest would need ICC approval for a merger. The agency politely declined.

Goodrich issued 700,000 new shares worth about $32 million to buy a half-interest from Gulf Oil Company in a jointly owned synthetic-rubber plant, which had yet to make money. This move placed about five percent of Goodrich's stock into friendly hands and also boosted the total number of shares that Heineman would need to assume control.

A Goodrich attorney visited an old friend, Representative Wilbur Mills of Arkansas, who was the powerful chairman of the House Ways and Means Committee and passed on reports and comments about the dangers of conglomerates. Later in February 1969, Mills proposed legislation that would limit the tax deductions on debentures that were issued in tender offers.

The Ohio Division of Securities, a state agency, ruled that part of the package that Northwest offered was impossible to value and therefore could not be registered with the state securities commission. This effectively stopped Northwest from soliciting

Goodrich shareholders in the state, thus lopping off the possibility of obtaining the nine percent of the tire company's outstanding stock held in Ohio.

But the biggest, most effective blow came four months after the tender offer was made, only hours before Northwest's annual meeting in Chicago in May 1969. The Justice Department announced that it would seek to block on antitrust grounds the Northwest attempt to take over Goodrich. One could only conjecture on the timing of that announcement. But at the meeting, when a shareholder asked Heineman why he didn't give up the fight, the conglomerator snapped self-righteously, "I don't think I have ever been known as a summer soldier!"

And so the campaign mounted. During most of the Goodrich campaign, Heineman's hands—or rather mouth—were tied, squeezed shut. Federal securities laws prevent firms under registration of new securities from attempting to proselytize in favor of those shares. So Heineman had to remain silent, except, when pressed, to try to explain why the 1969 first-quarter loss occurred. He said it was due to a strike at Northwest's Lone Star Steel Company and to bad weather which had curtailed rail-line operations.

But he could still talk also about corporate control battles, at least in general terms. He said, "There are a lot of frightened, stodgy companies with frightened, stodgy managements. Conservative businessmen are running to the government saying, 'Save me, save me,' and very often it is at the expense of stockholders."

Later, however, Keener replied to this hardly indirect charge by answering a question posed by *The New York Times* on what Goodrich would do if Northwest decided to sell its shares to another acquirer:

> We would do what we did in the case of Northwest's bid, which was to evaluate what was being offered and get outside judgments as to what was in the best interests of our stockholders. . . . If we felt that any future proposal was not in the best interest of our stockholders, I'm sure we would fight it. This, of course, would be decided by our board of directors and not by the management.

In mid-August, Northwest ended its exchange offer, having failed to obtain more than 16 percent of Goodrich's outstanding shares. But investors acted as though they were disappointed. Goodrich's shares the next day dropped 2½ to close at 36¾, but Northwest's common closed at 17, off only ⅛.

It had been a hard fight, even a dirty one. Goodrich, for example, had gone to quite an extreme in its fight. Less than two weeks after Northwest had made its tender offer, Goodrich expanded its line of credit with 21 banks to $250 million and included in the agreement a proviso that the loan would be in default if there was a takeover. Also, Keener and his team were considering an additional drastic measure—to use up to $200 million of the new loan to prepay income taxes and accounts payable and contributions to pension funds. The objective of all this was very clear—to convince Heineman in advance of any successful takeover that he would have to make his own arrangements to borrow a like amount of funds.

In June, a month or so before Heineman was compelled to admit defeat, the Justice Department's antitrust case was being heard in a Chicago district court and the details of the new financing were revealed. The judge, Hubert L. Will, was shocked. He referred to the amendment regarding a loan default in the event of a takeover as a "Herman Goering cyanide pill." And he wondered something else. "Why would Goodrich voluntarily enter into an agreement," he asked, "under which it threatened to commit financial suicide in the event that this transaction is consummated? It's a shocking document. It's the worst indictment of Goodrich management of anything in this case."

But, regardless, the threat to Goodrich was over—or at least so it seemed for the time being. Eight months later, in April 1970, Heineman announced that he might yet make another bid for the "mismanaged" tire company.

Mergers Hit the Front-Page, But
Their "Unstucks" Run on Page 49

It doesn't take a genius to figure out why this happens. Just look calmly at the statistics: One out of hundreds of negotiations wind up with a tentative agreement in principle. And possibly one out of five such agreements progresses to something more conclusive.

And of them, one out of three falls below expectations and the rest of them succeed; that is, they produce the kind of successful operations and worthwhile profits that were expected of them.

So the excitement, at least from a news standpoint, is concentrated on the marriage announcement, because it seems an exciting concept and a promising new blend of corporate blood lines.

Only it doesn't work out that way at least one-third of the time. Why?

According to a veteran acquisition specialist at Merrill, Lynch, Pierce, Fenner and Smith, there are three big reasons why mergers already consummated become unstuck:

1. They are poorly conceived from the outset. They may seem to do something synergistic financially, but too many have no marketing or product "fit." In other words, "it's just a matter of someone with a high price/earnings multiple trying to get some additional earnings into their profit-and-loss statement cheaply and as quickly as possible. The Xerox–CIT proposed deal is a good example. Xerox had a multiple of 50, and by picking up a 30-times multiple, its earnings would be enhanced. But what was the marketing benefit—or the gain in product correlation? None. The same with the abortive RCA–St. Regis Paper deal. RCA, with its higher multiple, could still afford to pay a premium in order to pick up earnings. But that deal, like the Xerox–CIT one, couldn't stand up to market scrutiny and died with a whimper."

2. Lots of mergers fall apart because executives are afraid they'll lose their jobs or their clout on the executive lineup and start harpooning the merger every chance they get. In other words, it's killed or eroded internally—the least that happens in that case is that the marriage turns into a grim facsimile of what it was supposed to be.

An interesting example of this was the 1968 merger between U. S. Plywood Corporation and Champion Papers, Inc. These two companies, which had almost identical sales of $500 million each, decided that together as a $1-billion enterprise they could develop a tremendous forest-products complex. But the problem was that this merger of two too-equal companies developed a bitter competition and enmity between the two staffs, led by Gene Brewer, president of Plywood, and Karl R. Bendetson, president of Champion. The heads rolled quickly, with the Bendetson-Champion forces exerting their sway with some defections from the Plywood ranks. Brewer was eased out after being placed in an untenable position—the company's management was reorganized by Bendetson and his Champion-loaded board so that Brewer found that, though he still had a title and an office, he no longer had any job.

3. The chief or important personalities find that they just can't live together. The foregoing case is a good example, but there are many others. A danger signal usually flashes when two dynamic merger-masters or company founders combine forces. This type of guy generally functions best only when he can crack the whip. If he finds that the situation is such that he can't do so to the extent that he would like, he tends to pull out—and sometimes he tears down the temple walls on the way out.

Of course, whether it's an already consummated merger or one just being negotiated, there is no question that much depends on the people—the "gut" reaction of buyer to seller and seller to buyer. Not infrequently the buyer is nervously curious about what's in the seller's back room, in the corners of his warehouses and in the locked drawers of his safe. So he asks the seller a lot of questions, some silly, some nasty, some downgrading. The moment becomes a delicate one. For possibly the first time in his successful career the seller is being asked to unveil his innermost business life, often inseparable from his private life. Will he do so to make a deal he isn't sure of in the first place? Will he endure the ignominy of it or do what one company founder did who had a prepared list of questions thrust at him? To everyone's surprise, he suddenly rose to go, observing, "This has all been very, very interesting, I think. Don't get up. I can find my own way out."

15

The Big Blast and the
Big Scowl from Washington

That Troublesome Bunch

On a hot July day during the hottest summer that any Washington administration has ever manufactured for merger-makers, three protagonists on the capital scene were engaged in their own peculiar and strategic activities. In the beautiful, high-ceilinged room 2141 of the New Senate Building, Celler sat under a portrait of Celler and glowered. The real-life version of Emanuel Celler was more formidable than the painted one. At that stage, July 1969, he had outlived by six years Senator Estes Kefauver of Tennessee, his younger co-sponsor of the Celler-Kefauver Act, the most effective of contemporary antitrust statutes. Now the powerful chairman of the House Judiciary Committee, in his eightieth year of life and his forty-sixth as a congressman, Celler waited for the right moment to open the first public hearings in the investigation of conglomerates by the committee's antitrust subcommittee, of which he was also chairman.

A few miles away, in his office in the cavernous Justice Department, the most disliked and feared man in the entire merger arena had just returned from a trip and immediately began putting the finishing touches on his newest court suit against a conglomerate.

Richard W. McLaren, Assistant Attorney General in charge of the antitrust division, was a strapping man, blond and bluff, who in just seven months had become known as the biggest trust-buster since President Theodore Roosevelt. He had hurled five suits against three conglomerates. And he had issued some startling policy pronouncements, such as condemning the principle of reciprocity in big mergers as an illegal act and citing the "human dislocation" and "radical restructuring of the country" being perpetrated by some recent acquisition moves by Ling-Temco-Vought, Northwest Industries and ITT.

The third man was easily the least dangerous-looking. But, because of the armory of economic and demographic data that he had assembled for the use of both congressional and regulatory anti-merger probers, Willard F. Mueller, then the chief economist of the Federal Trade Commission, might well have been more of a threat to the champions of mergers than either Celler or McLaren.

At that particular moment, however, Mueller, a slight, wispy man with an easy smile and an affable way, was sitting at his desk shuffling papers. But they were hardly routine. The rumpled sheaf represented a massive FTC study which would indict big power takeovers, particularly those by conglomerates.

Celler, a grim, living monument to his restrictive legislation which had led to 225 enforcement actions in the statute's first 17 years; McLaren, the cool-eyed prosecutor who was deemed by some critics to be exceeding his own bounds and even the wishes of his superiors all the way to the White House; and Mueller, the government's smiling intellectual eminence in its fight against big mergers. Each of their moves was closely watched by the merger-acquisition community, fear-stricken and venom-filled as is was for these men who more than any others symbolized the big blast and the heavy scowl that emanated from 1968 through 1970 in Washington toward the merger movement.

This fray was marked by a vast war of words—an unending philosophical debate that eddied through many campuses, law offices and judicial chambers, foundations, business associations and media from one end of the country to the other. That debate encompassed all the major issues of antitrust law and enforcement policy, the morality of the statutes and a search into the differences between yesterday's climate, in which the major laws had been put on the books, and the contemporary environment.

Even those engaged in the debate were watching the protagonists. They knew that these would inevitably move the debate from words into direct action.

The Hearings: The Chairman Keeps His Cool But Others Get Hot

A near full house and a crowded press section waited along with Celler. They studied the subcommittee's members flanking Celler, as well as the first witnesses, particularly Charles G. Bluhdorn, who was obviously nervous but trying not to let anyone know it.

It would have been difficult for any witness not to quail under Celler's stare. Unlike the portrait overhead, in which the artist had sought to capture the Brooklyn congressman as a Solon with a paternal but judicial air, Celler in the flesh was seemingly more grizzled, more square-headed and more grim in his resolve not to let the so-called opponents of society have their way.

He began slowly. His metallic, halting speech, delivered in a low manner with a slight lisp, gave a "this-is-it" edge to his quickly expressed position of preventing the stifling of competition. As he plodded on, it was obvious that he was just what he seemed to be—an old man who had seen everything and wouldn't be fooled by anything. He said:

> In this investigation, the Antitrust Subcommittee is again concerned with the corporate merger movement and the effectiveness of the anti-

trust laws to meet the challenge of continuing concentration of economic power.

The current merger movement differs from the prior merger waves in the 1890s and in the 1920s. The current movement is lasting longer, and is of greater magnitude, than its predecessors. Moreover, the current merger movement is different because of its conglomerate character. In 1968, the Federal Trade Commission reports, conglomerate mergers accounted for 85 percent of the number and 89 percent of the assets of all recorded large acquisitions. Our free economy may be endangered by the burgeoning of more and more bigger mergers. This is one of our principal objections.

Although conglomerate mergers now dominate the merger wave and therefore are the center of attention and criticism, conglomeration is but part of a larger picture. An inexorable increase in the concentration of economic power in the American economy is our basic problem. Mergers historically have contributed to increased concentration, and conglomerate mergers, since they disregard established industry boundaries, are feared by many to presage a complete industrial restructuring.

He came to an end in his formal recitation. Looking directly at Bluhdorn and noting that Gulf and Western had made 127 acquisitions from December 30, 1957 through January 1, 1969, he smiled and said, "I am pleased to welcome Gulf and Western's representatives."

"We are happy to be invited here. Thanks for your hospitality," began Bluhdorn.

So, despite Celler's ominous opener, the House hearings started amicably enough. But it was not to last. Celler and his group put the four-man Gulf and Western team through the paces, keeping them constantly on the defensive during a harried three days. The pattern was to be followed in successive appearances of other conglomerators and their staffs through the summer and winter of 1969 and into 1970.

The first day, Celler and the subcommittee developed the fact that Gulf and Western's first big acquisition, the 1965 takeover of the New Jersey Zinc Company, was made possible by an $84-million loan through a Chase Manhattan Bank officer who was later hired by the conglomerate. The subcommittee's general counsel, Kenneth R. Harkins, had Bluhdorn confirm that Gulf and Western received the Chase loan on September 10, 1965 and on February 21, 1966 named Roy T. Abbott, Jr., senior vice-president.

Harkins read a memo that Bluhdorn had written following a meeting with Chase officials, thanking them and the bank for its loan. It read, in part, "Chase's imaginative lending would not be forgotten. Gulf and Western someday will be a $1-billion company and Chase will be on a permanent basis."

Bluhdorn agreed, in reading the memo that Harkins handed him, that it was accurate, observing, "There is such a thing as loyalty in all things, even business. They came through for us."

The second day, the subcommittee staff tightened its charge that big conglomerates such as Gulf and Western had concentrated their borrowing needs with a few lenders in the big financial centers to the detriment of small banks around the country where the conglomerates had acquired other companies. It was disclosed that in 1964 Gulf and Western had obtained a $15-million loan from five banks, led by Chase Manhattan, to replace outstanding debt with 20 banks. And, in 1965, a number of Gulf and Western subsidiaries transferred their Social Security and tax-withholding accounts from local banks to Chase Manhattan as a partial condition for Chase's remaining a large Gulf and Western lender.

David Judelson, Gulf and Western's president, denied that the firm's ambitious acquisition program had resulted in such a concentration of borrowing or other activity. Although some banking services of scattered subsidiaries had been centralized, he said, local communities had benefited from the new investment which Gulf and Western put into its acquisitions. Celler displayed impatience with the conglomerate management's constant recitation of its success stories, admonishing the Bluhdorn team to reply to simple questions with a "simple yes or no."

On the third day, Celler's lack of enthusiasm showed again. Bluhdorn had launched into a warm discourse on the qualities of conglomerates. "The day you take the incentive away from young companies and people who want to build, that day the balance-of-payments problem is going to be magnified 1,000 percent." He added, "We have never hesitated to work 20 hours a day." Gulf and Western's executives thrive on Chock Full o' Nuts lunches, he continued, in contrast to European businessmen, who take a leisurely two- and three-hour meal.

Celler stared at him intently. Then he said that the subcommittee had started its hearing with no preconceived ideas, but now Gulf and Western's 100 acquisitions reminded him of the scores of mistresses maintained by Don Giovanni in the famous Mozart opera. "I cannot help but make comparison between Gulf and Western and Don Giovanni," Celler said. "We're a little bit concerned about that."

The final day of Gulf and Western's appearance in room 2141 was marked by several other developments. The company disclosed that Chase Manhattan and some 25 other banks involved in the conglomerate's financing receive inside information on its acquisition plans as part of its normal business relationship with them. The information passed on to these banks is given to them before it is made public or even made available to the Securities and Exchange Commission. The subcommittee pointed out, however, that stock prices of companies involved in acquisitions with Gulf and Western had skyrocketed, offering the prospect of quick profits to "insiders."

The Celler team also established the close relationship that existed between Chase Manhattan and Gulf and Western and reported that the bank had a "broker" service in which Chase Manhattan introduced Gulf and Western to companies seeking to be acquired. The bank also maintained a survey service, the subcommittee brought out, in which Chase compiled for Gulf and Western fact sheets of public information on companies or industries in which the conglomerate demonstrated an interest.

In November 1969 Celler tussled with Harold Geneen, chairman of the International Telephone and Telegraph Corporation, biggest of the conglomerates to appear before the subcommittee. Geneen quickly took the initiative by proposing that federal regulators expand their efforts to protect investors in conglomerates. He suggested that the SEC should organize a new division to "protect" investors against the terms that some conglomerates have offered in taking over other concerns. The SEC, under current law, only has authority to ensure that there is full disclosure in stock offerings. During the height of the conglomerate trend, SEC officials expressed fears that the traditional disclosure policy was inadequate, but no specific remedies were offered.

If Geneen's suggestion had validity, Celler wasn't admitting it or, for that matter, acknowledging it. Instead, he and his colleagues pushed ahead with a line of questioning that attempted to document ITT's fast growth by takeover. The loquacious Geneen, never without a few thousand well-selected words of enthusiastic appreciation for his and his company's efforts, responded with a lengthy defense of the conglomerate concept. Far from stifling competition, he declared, ITT and other conglomerates stimulated competition in the industries which they entered by acquisition.

Responded Celler, "You almost make me think that ITT has wings." He went on to say that he "emphatically disagreed" with Geneen's contention that ITT's mergers had increased competition. Instead, charged Celler, competition was actually reduced by the disappearance of acquired companies as individual enterprises. "You remind me of the elephant who cried, 'Every man for himself,' as he danced among the chickens," the congressman said.

Hardly halfway through the investigation of conglomerates, in which he was seeking to determine if additional legislation was needed against them, Celler was then already willing to say publicly that new legal teeth were necessary. He had heard enough.

The Chief Antitruster. ("Reasonable to the Point of Distraction")

They were saying in Washington in those days—with some apparent justification—that McLaren, the controversial antitrust chief, and Mueller, the chief economist of the FTC, had an interesting little routine going between them. In the midafternoon when things let up a bit, McLaren would call Mueller and ask him: "What can we do to stir things up again on the antitrust front?"

Mueller's eyes would light up and his wiry body would quiver as he replied, "Well, let's see now. . . ."

As a man on a hot seat, McLaren only a year after he had been in office was being linked with another Washington rumor. It was that any head of the Justice Department's antitrust division has only a limited amount of time and political license to survive. Each was appointed by the various administrations for a sincere purpose. But once the trust-buster started taking off on violators and the complaints, letters, wires and phone calls accumulated at the White House, new names to fill his post were pulled out of a hat in Justice and were seriously discussed at the White House.

In McLaren's case there seemed to be even more reason than usual to foresee this imminent possibility. McLaren was a Chicago lawyer and Republican who had specialized in merger and antitrust matters throughout his career. His standing in the field was shown by the fact that he had been head of the anti-trust-law section of the American Bar Association. Within one year in the agency he had moved quickly to the top of the list as the big bad boy of the merger-antitrust field. He had quickly zeroed in on conglomerates and so was generally accused of being pro-Establishment and anti-the new breed. Although he disclaimed being against bigness, he latched on to the concept of the Celler-Kefauver amendment by charging that it applied because bigness does lessen competition indirectly by fostering reciprocity. Bigness, he also charged, curbs the potential competition even if a merger company entered the field by starting its own concern rather than through acquisition and by expanding the concentration of industrial might to the detriment of new entrants. It was what Madison Avenue lovingly calls "a bold new concept," and it worked—mostly.

McLaren obviously carried on as he did because he was really convinced that the merger mill was running out of control. The lawsuits he generated against the conglomerates gave second thoughts to other big merger-makers and caused them to pull in their horns. The conglomerators and Wall Street in particular made no effort to disguise their dislike. But the Establishment companies loved him, especially, claimed his critics, those which probably would have been or thought they would have been subjects of takeover attempts by the conglomerates.

The aggressive legal approach, especially the concept of linking the three indirect offshoots of big mergers, ran into some real flak in the district courts. In Chicago a judge declined to give McLaren an injunction against Northwest Industries' attempt to take over B. F. Goodrich, an effort that came to naught anyway. And a New Haven judge also refused him temporary injunctions against ITT's designs on Hartford Fire Insurance and the Grinnell Corporation.

The Establishment had its own rude awakening, especially after many old-line companies had concluded that McLaren and even his boss, Attorney General Mitchell, were dedicated to defending them from corporate invaders. In mid-1969 Mitchell came out with a statement that the administration would probably start lawsuits to bar any merger among the 200 largest manufacturers or similar companies or any acquisition by one of them of a leading company in any concentrated industry.

During all this, McLaren became the subject of some nasty innuendo. This included charges that he was exhibiting some anti-Semitism and partisanship since many conglomerates were being run by Jews and Democrats, as opposed to the Establishment, which had non-Jews and Republicans in many of the choice posts.

This smear campaign also enveloped Mitchell and President Nixon. Expanding on the partisanship allegation *vis à vis* Mitchell, the whispered charges were that in the past antitrust activity was pushed by liberals, but the Nixon administration picked up the antitrust ball not against the Establishment (Republicans naturally), but against the conglomerates (Democrats naturally), and summarily blamed the real antitrust abuses on them.

But McLaren may well have been more than his superiors bargained for. When I spoke to a number of government people in Washington, several observed that McLaren had exceeded in energy and zeal both the degree and the scope of antitrust action that both Mitchell and the President had wanted. McLaren's frequent explanation of his action as a "reasonable approach to implementing the laws" drew one official's comment that "he's so reasonable that he drives you to the point of distraction—and worse."

I saw McLaren late on a summer day, but he responded calmly and in detail to all my questions. He denied emphatically charges of government-Establishment collusion. When I mentioned the Leasco–Chemical Bank fracas in particular, he denied that the antitrust division had been involved in any way. "As far as favoring the Establishment," he said, "I take it the charges refer to our moving against Northwest's attempt to acquire Goodrich or L-T-V's acquisition of Jones and Laughlin. There's absolutely no basis to the charges. Our interest is not who gets in control but to avoid a lessening of competition when two giants get together."

On partisanship he observed, "It's been said that we're against some leading Democrats who are the top officers of conglomerates. The fact is that often I don't know who the officers of these companies are or what their politics is. We have a simple statutory responsibility and that is what we are trying to carry out."

Are conglomerates a threat to the economy and to competition generally? He replied, "I don't think you can generalize on that question. We have a vigorous national economy in which some of our Establishment giants are conglomerates. They know that they can't grow much further by acquiring other big companies. A well-managed, diversified manufacturing company is a good thing in terms of labor and continuance of jobs. I'm not against its making acquisitions, either. Sometimes this offers a fine incentive when a family business can't solve its problems other than through selling its ownership to another company. We certainly don't want to kill that—but what we don't want are large companies merging with large companies if it will tend to lessen competition and form a monopoly."

McLaren added, however, that the pattern in the country has been waves of merger movements created by executives "trying to keep busy. . . . It's become a kind of game—a competition among executives to make mergers and acquisitions and outdo each other."

Concluding, he said, "We have something over a $900-billion plus economy. Only $100 billion of it is regulated, but $800 billion is in the unregulated sector. That imposes quite a responsibility on government. . . . Frankly I think that this division ought to be called 'The Pro-Competition Division' rather than the 'Antitrust Division.' "

Economist in a Hurry

In an interview with Willard Mueller, sweeping statements come out of him so casually, seemingly with no harm intended, that it takes a while to get the real import of what he is saying. Then you understand why some of the merger-masters would like to hang him in effigy, maybe even for real.

He told me:

> The real question here is centralization, not size or growth. About two-thirds of our country's entire manufacturing is vested in 200 companies. In 1941 the same percentage was in the hands of 1,000 firms. It is inevitable that the present share of the 200 will grow even more, unless they are checked. So, you see, it is the encroachment of economic centralization, not size alone that concerns us.

He conceded that a great debate was being waged on the issue. Some insisted that concentration was being created by technological imperatives which made a growing share in the hands of fewer and fewer companies an irrevocable fact of life. But others such as he ("and 90 percent of all the economists") believe that technology isn't the cause of increasing concentration but a striving for "absolute size." The antidote to "absolute size" is the maintenance of competition in the marketplace; the result of not curbing "absolute size" is ever-growing concentration.

Competition already has some natural forces working in its behalf, he went on. These include the growth of the country's markets, the continuing development of technology which requires many large companies, but the markets are so large that they can sustain them, and the propensity of many companies to grow into areas where profit opportunities exist.

> Size by itself is no great threat to competition if it is, in the form of a big company, competing with other big companies.
>
> But take the consumer-goods area, where concentration is most prevalent. Bigness works to establish concentration. Real economies are created by large-scale companies—big advertising, big manufacturing, big distribution, in general the ability of big companies to deploy their

resources strategically. This is the case in autos, food, cereal, detergents, electrical appliances, apparel—any consumer commodity where advertising is important. This giantism of resources and of ownership allows such companies to clobber their competition. You see an advertising warfare that runs rampant. You find companies asking and getting discriminatory discounts on TV advertising. . . . There should be more restraints on all these things that create centralization in certain industries.

Mueller, who earned a Ph.D. in economics in 1955 from Vanderbilt University, was for nine years one of the government's secret weapons on mapping antitrust strategy. During the litigation carried on by the Justice Department again ITT and Northwest Industries, he was one of the government's chief witnesses. He was also responsible for the FTC's January 1967 decision to call for premerger notification by acquisition-minded companies. McLaren and Mueller quickly found a close rapport in the ten months that their official government careers coincided.

"He [McLaren] and I agreed on a sort of basic philosophy," Mueller said. "It was that the harm that a too-tough policy would do would be to stop the trend of big mergers for a couple of years. But if we said we don't know enough yet, then the consequences could be disastrous because the results would be irreversible."

All this was preceded and preempted in importance by the November 1969 release of the FTC's monumental staff study on the economic effects of conglomerate mergers. A month earlier, Mueller had left the agency to return to the faculty of the University of Wisconsin. But when the 700-page report came out after 17 months of preparation under his direction, he returned briefly to Washington. He presented the findings at a hearing before the Senate Antitrust and Monopoly Subcommittee, which had requested the FTC to undertake the study.

The report concluded that the recent wave of mergers among American companies was concentrating business decision-making in a "few vast corporations." The trend threatened to create what the study alleged amounted to "closed-circuit markets" from which small and medium-sized companies would be excluded. It proposed that more detailed financial reports be required from large, diversified companies and that the laws be tightened on interlocking directorates.

But the report contained a surprise—a goodie for the conglomerate community: The conglomerates, contrary to popular belief, did not dominate the merger wave of the 1960s. The report said:

> During 1961–1968, the most active acquiring corporations made acquisitions totaling $20 billion, or almost 60 percent of all acquisitions of the top 200 during the period. Only 11 of these 25 were among the so-called new conglomerates, and even some of these were not, strictly speaking, new companies, for example, the International Telephone and Telegraph Corporation. Eight of the most active acquirers were petroleum companies and six others covered a variety of industries.

When I asked Mueller whether he considered the entire matter of economic concentration through mergers a "really urgent matter," he said that he knew that as an economist he was being criticized for his haste in wanting new action or legislation. He said:

> The problem is, I guess, that the economist often thinks of himself as a scientist, and that like a scientist he doesn't know all because that would bring him to some precipitous conclusions that might be harmful. Well, I don't feel that way at all. "Agnosticism" in a crisis is dangerous. It's like trying to figure out how many angels fit on the head of a pin when you should be calling out the troops.

The Great Antitrust Debate, Bitter, Frustrating, Endl-e—s——s

Naturally, with an issue as controversial as a rampant merger trend, quite a cacophony arose on its merits and demerits and on whether new legal protection was needed. Law, it seems, is subject not just to individual interpretation. In the case of business consolidations, the attitude toward the law is also subservient to the prejudices and even the life-style of those who carry it out or of those who wish to expand or limit its application.

The debate also reached to the White House, where a strong political influence was injected by at least two recent administrations, shaping the philosophy in which enforcement was carried out. If it is true that antitrust policy needs enough political constituency, there is little doubt that Presidents Johnson and Nixon provided more than a trickle of it from 1600 Pennsylvania Avenue.

In 1967, when the conglomerate issue first began to heat up, President Johnson ordered a study by a task force on antitrust laws. But, instead of emerging ten months later with the expected violent opposition against conglomerates, the blue-ribbon panel headed by Dean Phil C. Neal of the University of Chicago rendered a report critical of the attack on conglomerates being generated by the new administration.

Johnson had consigned the Neal report to a closed file probably because he already sensed the spreading disaffection of the electorate and concluded that politically the report would have been inopportune. It would probably have been permanently withheld except for James Ling, already selected by McLaren as his first target for a test case. At a public forum Ling told the new antitrust chief that he understood there was a "still secret" study that "would exonerate the conglomerate movement from any monopolistic tendencies." When, demanded Ling, staring pugnaciously at his audience, would that report be issued? Later the same day in May 1969, the Justice Department released copies of it to the press minus any comment of its own.

In the report the Neal group warned that an attack on the conglomerates through the existing Clayton Act could only be a "contrived interpretation." And then, spurning the Clayton Act, which McLaren was zealously employing to swat away at the conglomerates, the lawyers and educators suggested Congress write a new law barring any company with more than $250,000 in assets from taking over any leader in a concentrated industry, especially where four concerns held more than 50 percent of the market.

Going that far, the Neal panel decided to go whole hog. It urged an attack on oligopolies with new legislation that would ultimately break up big companies in the highly concentrated auto, steel, computer, flat-glass, tobacco and organic-chemical industries. Such a law would give the courts the right to declare that an oligopoly existed in an industry where four companies had at least 70 percent of the market.

These and some of the other recommendations were not new, having already been suggested by some of McLaren's Democratic predecessors. But McLaren, certainly aggressive on his own hook, found the panel's recommendations too stringent.

Strangely enough, the issuance of the Neal report on May 21, 1969 was predated by another study by a task force appointed by President Nixon. This was another blue-ribbon panel, headed by Professor George J. Stigler of the University of Chicago, and it, too, was promptly ignored by the administration that appointed it. Why? Was it a question of "Ask a task group to look into a tough problem and you will probably get a lot more than you bargained for"? It's difficult not to believe this, based on the Stigler group's findings.

Knocking current administration policy and slapping at Mitchell's and McLaren's offensive against the conglomerates, this report recommended that the President ensure that "competition" should be the goal of antitrust and all regulatory policy and that regulatory commissions abandon minimum rate controls in order to permit free entry to industry. And to "enhance the effectiveness of the antitrust division," the group urged Mitchell and McLaren to insist that every antitrust suit "make good economic sense."

Bringing cheer to the conglomerators, the Stigler report "strongly" recommended that the Justice Department "decline to undertake a program of action against conglomerate mergers and conglomerate enterprises, pending a conference to gather information and opinion on the economic effects of the conglomerate phenomenon." And the panel snapped further at the Mitchell-McLaren effort with a blunt admonition: "More broadly, we urge the Department to resist the natural temptation to utilize the antitrust laws to combat social problems not related to the competitive functioning of markets."

And then the Stigler group took on the Neal panel. This rhubarb settled on the earlier group's recommendations for curbs on oligopolies. The Stigler team insisted that it couldn't endorse "proposals whether by new legislation or new interpretation of existing law to deconcentrate highly concentrated industries by dissolving their leading firms." But an "unremitting scrutiny" of oligopolistic industries was urged and in particular a probe under the Sherman Act on pricing of a highly noncompetitive nature.

Unquestionably, the Stigler report's critical nature stung Mitchell, although he never acknowledged it one way or another. But not long after, the Attorney General emerged with his dramatic "top 200" pronouncement. He said that the Justice Department "may well oppose" any merger among the country's top 200 producers or companies of comparable size in other segments of the economy and would probably also act on any merger by a top-200 manufacturer with any leading producer in a concentrated industry.

So, in one bold step, President Nixon's old law partner combined a number of moves. He dispelled the spreading rumor that the administration was displeased with McLaren's aggressiveness. He cast aside the previous administration's emphasis on economic data as a basis for judging mergers and threw back the Stigler committee's stress on this point without specifically knocking the Nixon-requested study.

As expected, the Mitchell announcement proved to be a bombshell, unloosing a wave of rhetoric. *The New York Times* hailed the administration's bravery in the face of criticism but doubted that the new curbs would increase price competition. *The Wall Street Journal* saw the Mitchell action as a "sterile view of antitrust," and suggested that the statutes be reexamined. *Business Week* said that new laws were needed to replace those drafted before the dawn of the modern conglomerate. And *Fortune* magazine flailed away at the new proof of the administration's "reactionary bias" on mergers.

And so it went, the decibels increasing along with the displays of hot emotion and professed cold logic. Donald F. Turner, an antitrust division chief under President Johnson, told a Senate hearing that reciprocal dealings as a basis for suits against the conglomerates had no legal basis but should be dealt with by directly attacking the reciprocal activities. Representative Wilbur Mills, Democrat of Arkansas and Congress's top tax man, was blasted by the conglomerates when he proposed tax reforms curbing use of debentures.

McLaren and Mitchell kept stepping up their offensive. The

antitrust chief declared that joint ventures, in which two companies combine to enter a new market, could be a violation of antitrust law. Mitchell asked Congress to increase the fine for criminal antitrust violations from $50,000 to $500,000 as a means of catching up with inflation. But the merger-masters could hardly laugh for gnashing their teeth.

Two other issues, raised by Congress and the country's accounting profession, stirred up yet new waves of verbiage as well as disenchantment among merger-minded companies. One was proposed legislation aimed at curbing one-bank holding companies, or corporations that control not only a commercial bank but also one or more nonbanking companies. Congress asked for administration-backed legislation that would stiffen federal banking laws that already prohibit banks from directly engaging in most nonbanking activities. The congressional proposal would clearly have a profound effect on the banking community. About 900 holding companies already had something like 45 percent of all bank deposits and eight of the country's ten largest banks have already either reorganized as one-bank holding companies or announced that they would do so.

The other issue—the accounting fraternity's proposal to limit pooling-of-interest deals to those mergers affected by an exchange of common stock for common stock—led to perhaps the loudest, most acrimonious brouhaha of all. The industry's Accounting Principles Board also proposed the pooling-of-interest concept could only be used when one of the merging companies was no more than nine times as large as the other.

After long delays marked by bitter opposition and internal dissension, the industry group voted in favor of the curb in the former case but not in the latter. It was a modified victory for the merger-makers, many of whom tend to exploit the pooling-of-interest accounting method by treating their combined companies' financial figures as if they had always been combined in a sort of "instant-earnings game."

That particular battle, like those involving other key issues in the merger field, is not yet over. The mushroom cloud of words that overhangs it all will last for years and is, despite the current vociferousness, in probably yet an early stage of formation. Eventual Supreme Court decisions are inevitable on the modern-day application of laws put on the books in simpler days. And new laws are also certain to be passed soon which will create new rules by which to play the merger game.

16

The Shape of the Future

Changeless Change

The CEO ("chief executive officer" to you, but otherwise the Charley, Ernie and Ollie types who startled the business community with their aggrandizing sweep of all in sight) poses at a mirror. He studies his reflection, but he does not quite see it. Instead, he sees a shadowy figure detach itself from the solid one and float toward him as if in recognition.

Who the hell is it? he wonders irritably. And then he knows.

It is himself, not as he is but as he was, five, ten, 15 years ago. Events, it comes to him, change; people really don't. But people make events and so by some odd equation nothing changes. He hasn't. He is still himself, the one he knows well and loves well.

So it is that the merger movement, apparently changing so rapidly, is beginning to resemble itself more and more. It is passing temporarily from the entrepreneurial to the custodial on its way to becoming once again entrepreneurial, not intra- or even necessarily inter-industry, but rather trans-industry in relation to function, not product. As it was. No changes are more profound than the transformation back to the pre-change state.

But the experts, the pundits, the consultants who spend endless hours studying and worrying about the takeover tumult know what's happening to Charley, Ernie and Ollie and what they stand for.

Says a highly qualified merger expert:

> The forces that created a fertile atmosphere for mergers, despite the changes, still exist. Acquisitions are a tool, like a computer, and can be used correctly or incorrectly, but their use will have to mature as the acquirers will have to mature, and then things will begin to take on logical proportions and the long-term effectiveness of the acquisition syndrome will really be felt.

Says another expert:

> True, there was no patron saint in the country's merger trend, but neither was it a monolithic event but something that developed, changed and was influenced by some of the major personalities. Each man delivered some of his own stamp.
>
> But with all that, the creative conglomerator will break his back if all he does is build and not take care of his custodial needs, like "Automatic" Sprinkler and, at least partially, Litton Industries, too, which lost some of its best custodial people because they were so good that they had no challenges left and so they took off.

A third expert asserts:

> Many of the merger-builders of the fifties and sixties were bright, opportunistic, quick-thinking, part salesman, part philosopher, part psychologist and part rabbi-priest. They had to be all of these because they gave the world to you, charismatic types of guys, mercurial, first up and then down. They're changing because they have to—like they always have to change. . . .
>
> Anything that is immediately significant looks like it is permanent, but it isn't. Basic human situations always remain. Mergers will boom in the next ten years not because of ups and downs in the stock market, but because a man of forty to fifty-five who has a successful private business is no longer going to be interested in maintaining it as a family business and he wants to cash in on it while he's still alive. The son doesn't want it—and the son-in-law isn't so sure, either. They

would rather argue about it. Meantime, the old man has to decide what to do or just shut down.

The Deals, the Big and the Little

What happened to the big deal? Its day is mostly over, at least for a while. Perhaps the cycle has run out, but it is not certain that the cycle won't start again. Bigness by consolidation has been threatened at least three other times following excesses in the last century of the type we have seen in the 1960s. But bigness is so much a part of the American marrow that it is difficult to predict flatly that the big merger deal is really through.

Richard W. McLaren, the government's chief antitruster, reported the lower trend of big-scale mergers with some apparent glee to the Senate antitrust subcommittee early in 1970: major mergers declined about 7 percent, or from 1,800 in 1968 to 1,700 in 1969. "This is the first recent year in which we observe even a leveling off, much less a measurable decrease," he said.

Four chief reasons were responsible for the decline in big mergers, he said, citing tight money, a general drop in the stock market, debate over tax reform during most of 1969 and a "tough" stand by the Justice Department.

Then, characteristically, he added that, while there was no immediate need for quick merger legislation, not only would the Justice Department plan to keep up its pressure but conglomerate mergers would also remain under intensive study by Congress and government agencies. The "emergency" created by mushrooming mergers and acquisitions appeared to have ended.

While everything appears against the big deal at the moment—the continuing government antitrust push, a new, much more wary attitude by the financial community and considerable disaffection among the millions of private investors—the likelihood is that the climate will change in the not too distant future. Subtle but definite adjustments now taking place in American industry may require new thinking by all three currently disenchanted groups. That change in attitude back to the more open one toward big mergers that earmarked most of the 1960s will be almost vital to save a number of big companies from severe loss of market position, bankruptcy and even extinction.

These include technology companies, which have been hard hit by changes and declines in government contracts in the last two years. The merger of the computer facilities of both General Electric Company and Honeywell, Inc., in May 1970 is a case in point. It was simply an attempt by GE to prop up a long-troubled computer division by combining it with a more successful computer manufacturer. Similar moves can be expected not only in the computer industry but in aircraft, electronics, nuclear, chemicals and other technology fields.

Other dynamic factors cry out for free enterprise, economy size.

In the service fields—retailing, travel services, medical services, food franchising, transportation and financial services—economies and efficiency are vitally linked to big-scale enterprises. This is no longer a matter of debate but a widely accepted concept. Thus, as the spectrum of services grows to cope with rising population, income, taste, as well as the explosion of leisure-time needs, it is inevitable that consolidations of large proportions will follow. And the proponents of such mergers will be able to marshall telling arguments in support of their moves.

But the principle of efficiencies and economies related to scale is one which government has sought to combat in both pragmatic and even theoretical terms. Obviously, both the legal seesaw and the antitrust debate are due for prolonged exercise.

In the meantime, if a hiatus has appeared for big mergers, much the opposite unfolds for mergers of medium- and small-sized companies.

"We are coming into a very big market for mergers of family businesses," says Korbin Day, vice-president for acquisitions of Goldman Sachs and Company, the prominent investment bankers. He said:

> These companies with sales of from $5 million to $20 million a year are being run mostly by founders who are getting along in years, or by second-generation men, either of whom is faced with a problem of standing still, growing or giving up the business. There are literally thousands of such companies.
>
> Many are grappling with the decision of future continuation and future growth. Most are too tiny to go public, because their stock issue would be small and not likely to attract a large group of investors. Their direction has to be a merger or acquisition by a larger firm or

the probability is that unless new family members come into the business, the company will have to liquidate.

If you view this problem from the standpoint of the number of such firms and the socioeconomic ramifications of the alternatives, it isn't difficult to see that it's important for our economy to have an environment for this type of activity. Take it away and you would have a tremendous waste of human and economic assets.

Most merger specialists, bankers and others who study the field support this position and predict that the incidence of mergers of this type will continue to mount in the 1970s, regardless or in spite of the already evident decline of big mergers.

Deconglomeration, the Newer Note

What's the current definition of a conglomerator? Wall Street, in the flush of its big disenchantment with the species, comes up with this one: A conglomerator is a guy who comes in in the morning, sorts quickly through all the deals that have come in the mail, ignores those which his subordinates have tagged "Good business prospect" or "Good financial deal for the company" and considers only those which he can personally label "Greatest short-term financial deal for me." Everything else goes into the wastebasket.

Of course, the definition is unkind and even has the bitterness of sour grapes. But it shows, at least at this writing, how financial people have come to regard the most characteristic, or the most prototypical, of the conglomerators.

What are the prospects for new merger deals involving conglomerates? Short-term, not good for big deals; long-term, very limited or questionable. Short-term, the conglomerates no longer possess the financial tools, have little or no debt capacity, their stock values are low and investors are vexed. Long-term, all these problems may have eased but chances are that, while the government eye will be a bit softened, it will still be sufficiently directed at them to deter all but the least objectionable big mergers.

In the meantime, what?

The conglomerate group will probably undergo a deconglomeration, a wave of spinoffs over the next few years, of either less desirable divisions and subsidiaries or even of desirable ones. The goal will be two-pronged. One will be to provide the "currency" or the funds to do other things, to pay off heavy debt or to finance internal needs or to pay for new, smaller acquisitions.

The other objective will be to function within the government's "top 200" limitation on inter-giant mergers. The Justice Department, as a matter of fact, probably would prefer to see a good flurry of deconglomeration in the interests of loosening up the competitive climate, as well as to remove some of the super-giantism from the big conglomerates themselves.

Many in the financial community are convinced that spinoffs and deconglomeration will represent the new game not of mergers, but of "demergers." In principle, at least, it was underscored by the Justice Department's agreement with Ling-Temco-Vought in that company's acquisition of Jones and Laughlin, which it "paid for" by deciding to spin off two of its own largest subsidiaries. However, the impetus behind spinoffs will come more from the need to find a new access to cash and better earnings in the face of the stony attitude of both Wall Street and the banks.

Rating the Potential of the Merger-Masters

Observes Martin E. Kantor, executive vice-president of D. H. Blair and Company:

> The adventurous, aggressive entrepreneur was the catalyst—all successful conglomerates are headed by one of these, but until the vehicle of the catalytic adventurer develops effectively into the custodial phase, it hasn't got long-term sustaining powers.
>
> But these men have an inherent antipathy for the custodial way of thinking. Their sales pitch is just the reverse, but they can't sit still long enough to let anything take root. Some, though, are changing, as a result of a confluence of factors and pressures. The more sophisticated of these entrepreneurs know that their ability to adopt a custodial approach is essential for the viability of their companies. The large custodial company has to attract creative people—it's very important to provide an opportunity for these entrepreneurs to move their companies into the enlightened management structure of the

custodial company. So it's vital that the merger pipeline not be obstructed by the government—too much is at stake.

If the ability to shift from virtually unlimited swashbuckling, finally curbed by counterpressure, to a period of skillful consolidation represents the true measure of survival among the conglomerators, which ones are most likely to make it—the men and the companies?

Some of the most astute observers of the takeover scene were asked to evaluate the survival prospects of the big guns among the merger-makers. I submit the list, fully aware of the risks of constantly changing factors which might sweep away most of its contents. A modicum of human kindness and tolerance toward these obviously tenuous analyses, if you don't mind.

Charles B. Thornton, Litton Industries—A pioneer in the formation of the conglomerate that was "scientifically managed," and successful in attracting the cream of young Harvard graduate-school men. But the problem of creating incentive for everyone (the top tier, all division heads and closest associates) proved self-defeating. Thornton lost many good men who should have stayed, who tasted the fruits of great responsibility without the opportunity to make major decisions. In addition, Thornton and Roy Ash, his number-two man, ultimately showed the characteristic conglomerator's failure to maintain proper communications with subsidiaries so that earnings control lagged. Thornton's high rating slipped badly in 1969 and 1970, when earnings sagged, along with the departure of many key men to found or administrate other conglomerates. "The illusion of 'Tex' Thornton's invincibility and allure to the bright young man has slipped away," said a a prominent Wall Streeter. Survival ratio: 75 percent the man, 85 percent the company.

James J. Ling, Ling-Temco-Vought—A "guy who always reached just beyond his grasp and usually managed to succeed." Ling's ship almost broke on the reef known as Jones and Laughlin. He borrowed so heavily to buy Jones and Laughlin and then found that the reef was so extensive under the water's surface that it broke not just the prow but also the entire ship. Pressure by the First National Bank of Dallas and the Bank of

America for Ling to move over and co-administrate with a Dallas banker was obviously the result of fear that L-T-V's mountainous debt, plus Jones and Laughlin's misfortunes, represented major troubles. Once the conglomerate group's brightest boy, Ling now has a potential which one merger expert tartly called "a sometime thing." Survival ratio: 60 percent the man, 65 percent the company.

Charles G. Bluhdorn, Gulf and Western Industries—One of the busiest players of the merger game who went at it "too heavily" at times, Bluhdorn is one of the most controversial subjects among the evaluators. "He's been as successful as anyone could be who's been completely opportunistically inclined, looking at mergers as a financial game and at his own role from an ego standpoint." But earnings erosion and some question about major divisional performance have cast a certain measure of doubt over his successful future. Survival ratio: 80 percent the man, 85 percent the company.

Harold S. Geneen, ITT—This consummate conglomerator rates highest in the field, few experts registering any serious qualms about the man or the company's future. For everyone who fears the oligopolistic tendencies of business as personified in Geneen's maneuvers, there are at least as many who admire his ability to install custodial controls. The successful acquisition of Hartford Fire Insurance and the Grinnell Corporation are seen as capstones on his pedestal. If the man has a hard hand with people and a penchant for crowding his own throne, these, in the light of his accomplishments, are considered as idiosyncracies of the type with which an egocentric potentate indulges himself. Survival ratio: 90 percent the man, 95 percent the company.

Meshulam Riklis, Rapid-American Corporation—Much heaped with criticism in earlier years and even ridiculed for his European characteristics, Riklis has come into a bright climate of favor and even enthusiasm. "Courage" and "common sense," offsetting a natural theatricalism, are used to describe his behavior during 1969 and 1970, particularly because of ability to stand pat in the face of opposition to his merger with Schenley

Industries and during the period when he decided consolidation was wisest. "He worked up from being just a financial manipulator to being an operator, with custodial leanings, of a financial empire." Whether he has provided enough management potential, however, remains an unanswered question. Survival ratio: 90 percent the man and the company.

Saul Steinberg, Leasco Data—Youngest of the major conglomerators, the bright young would-be acquirer of Chemical Bank and the successful purchaser of Reliance Insurance and Pergamon Press undoubtedly has a great future. This is especially so if he uses his experiences of the recent past with Wall Street and the Establishment to mature and grow. Survival ratio: 85 percent the man, 90 percent the company.

And now a group of capsule analyses: *Ralph E. Ablon*, Ogden Corporation—Generally considered one of the ablest and most practical of multi-industry builders, Ablon has shown an ability to consolidate his position after a series of important and well-founded mergers. Survival rate: 90 percent the man, 95 percent the company. *Nick Salgo*, Bangor-Punta—Well-regarded but subject to some concern, particularly after a dissipating court experience with Chris-Craft Industries on a fight to obtain Piper Corporation. Likened to Bluhdorn for arrant opportunism, he is credited with having the potential for effective custodial behavior. Survival rate: 85 percent the man, 90 percent the company. *Ben W. Heineman*, Northwest Industries—An unusual combination of lawyer and freebooter, he has an ability to weld and sustain a diverse group of companies from railroads to apparel producers, despite his abortive attempt to take over B. F. Goodrich. This entitles him to a high rating for the future. Survival rate: 90 percent the man, 95 percent the company. *The Tisches, Laurence and Robert*, Loew's Inc.—Smart and yet lean in their approach, the two builders of a hotel, movie theater, real-estate and tobacco empire are considered to have a golden future, mainly because of their close attention to business and their well-planned acquisitions. Survival rate: 95 percent the men and the company.

So much for ten of the top merger-masters. How accurate are the appraisals of their prospects? Ah, only time will tell, it always does.

High-Trend Industries for Mergers

The rampant merger movement, slowed down at least for the foreseeable future in its largest-scale examples, is headed for a big breakout in three major areas.

These are the technological, highly volatile fields where a decline in budgetary expenditures by both the government and the private sector has forced a decline in output and market; the greatly fragmented industries, where the family-oriented management has either failed to keep up with the new business techniques or where growth through affiliation with a larger company is almost tantamount to survival; and the marketing or service industry, where mergers and acquisitions represent a vital link to greater efficiency, economy and the ability to cope with a rapidly expanding market.

With that as a springboard, the following list of high-trend industries and their components for mergers in the 1970s has been assembled from a consensus of merger authorities, consultants and financial sources.

Technology industries—computers, electronics, aircraft, chemicals.

Small-entrepreneurial industries—Apparel, furniture and home furnishings, construction and real estate.

Service-oriented fields—Clinical laboratories, hospitals, medical services, insurance agencies, financial services, advertising and public-relations agencies, employment agencies and accounting services.

Distribution—Retailers, particularly discount stores and chains, supermarkets, restaurants and mass-feeding services, appliance chains, publishers and printing concerns, and cosmetics and toilet-goods producers.

What's the common denominator for all this potential merging?

The twin one of survival and growth, as it has always been at the pounding heart of the American business saga.

The Establishment Will Never Be the Same

Perhaps the strangest element of all in the contemporary merger climate has been the shifting attitudes about the excesses and the boons of the conglomerates. As with every dramatic, controversial issue, emotion flooded in to replace the measured analysis, followed by a new period of introspection and a return of enthusiastic approval. The upshot was that the consensus ultimately gave the subject of the hot issue a better rating at the height of its pursuits.

So the conglomerates may be due for an eventual, and not too far distant, reappraisal which will result in a new climate of favor for them. Will it be on the same high level as when they were earning enviable returns and making shareholders wealthy, especially those who knew when to buy and especially when to sell? Probably not.

But there was a completely different side to it, too, and I would like to tune you in to a conversation I had recently with a number of executives of one of America's most prestigious investment-banking houses. We were discussing the future of the merger movement, particularly that of the congloms.

Partner A said:

> I think that there has been a very healthy outcome to the conglomerate activity. We spent a good deal of both 1968 and 1969 and part of 1970 sitting down with every one of our clients who feared raids by the conglomerates. We found that the fervor which this created among these managements made them very conscious of their exposed position and put them on guard, perhaps permanently, that they didn't own their companies and therefore didn't have a proprietary right to remain in office. If the entrenched management couldn't prove in a raid that it had done a good job of management for the shareholders, why shouldn't they be turned out? I think the lesson has stuck.

Partner B added:

> What the conglomerates have done is to have sounded the death knell for the old style of management. I mean those production-oriented managements who thought more about how to accommodate

their equipment than how to use it to increase their company's market share. No longer will they be able to ask themselves, "Can I sell what my machines can make?" Now it's got to be, "What can I sell and how do you make it?"

But if the conglomerates have indeed put the Establishment companies on their guard, a fact that few will dispute, they have also shown them an ability to manage from a central core or headquarters that is lean and tight—perhaps too lean and tight. The principle, however, of controlling $2-billion companies with no more than a corps staff of 200 has not been lost on the older, more conservative company. Perhaps it hasn't yet produced a much-needed pruning of executive staffs, but it will probably guide many of the established companies in their future organizational efforts.

What the conglomerates have also done is to demonstrate the value of decentralization for the sake of establishing individual profit centers. Even the conglomerates' excesses and failures have not removed the appeal of granting incentives and of delegating profit-making responsibility to division heads. The trend among both conglomerates and Establishment firms may even go one step further into fully separating the lines of authority and beefing up incentive by setting up divisions and subsidiaries as joint venture or partnership-in-profit with management.

A Final Word or Two About Charley, Ernie and Ollie—and a Fast Beer with Some Others

Our dynamic friends Charley, Ernie and Ollie are hardly only members of the conglomerates. They're among the established companies, too, and were highly visible even a few years ago when there was scarcely a CEO who dared to get up at an annual shareholder's meeting and not mention, seemingly in passing, "I might say, too, that we're negotiating for an acquisition. Of course, that's all I can tell you about it at this time."

Both the conglomerates and the Establishment companies will find their big-merger efforts circumscribed so that they will have to quell their appetites and seek toehold acquisitions rather than a large share of any new market that they enter.

Smaller companies will find themselves courted by Charley, Ernie and Ollie and the prospect will be a pleasant one for them, although the CEOs may approach such acquisitions with noticeable disdain, as if finding the taste of lesser exploits bitter, even disappointing.

Does this mean that the smaller entrepreneur should be on his guard, vigilant against unequitable terms and unfair considerations? Yes—but not just because of the attitude of the big acquirers, but because caution, attention and vigilance should always be an important part of the behavior of any businessman preparing to sell his business and thus to take the "heel" of another man. The plain fact is, you see, that Charley, Ernie and Ollie are having a bit of a rough time right now and are somewhat more ornery than usual.

And that possibly brings us back to a fast beer with a few older friends.

Remember Tom Smersh, the bemused, bewildered junior executive; Harris, his troubled boss; and Bruno, the impatient head of a conglomerate? Quite a while back I mentioned that we might, if it seemed appropriate, return to these men with their merger-caused neuroses.

So drink up, Smersh, Harris and Bruno. Now that you've faced all those pile drivers and have not been exactly pulverized by them, I salute you, men. Mergers may be a new management tool, an important competitive force, an instrument at least as valuable as the computer, and may even represent the newest form of research and development.

But mergers are made by men, don't forget, and not the reverse. And man, even in this difficult world of ours, ought to be able to cope with what another man has done.

Can't you? Can't we? If not, we had better learn. Because mergers, like death, birth, taxes and love, will be around a long, long time. Any doubts?

Glossary of
Business and Financial Terms

ARBITRAGE—The tricky business of taking advantage of different prices in different markets for the same stocks or bonds. The transaction is designed to net a higher price. For example, you might decide to be an international trader by buying ATT common shares in Philadelphia and then immediately selling them in Dusseldorf. If there is a spread between the markets, you've got a profit.

BEAR—Mostly an unpopular type who expects lower prices, or who sells shares in the hope of repurchasing them at a lower price. But to give him his due, he also helps to create lower prices.

BOND—An interest-bearing certificate issued by the government or a corporation or various authorities promising to pay the holder a specified sum on a fixed maturity date.

BULL—More liked than the bear, someone who believes that prices are due to increase, or who buys in anticipation of higher prices.

CALL—More financial than religious, it's a demand for money owed, or a contract giving the holder the right to buy securities or commodities at a fixed price for a stipulated time. It is also a procedure used by most commodity exchanges to open the day's trading, an attendant "calling" out each delivery month as members make bids and offers.

CAPITAL STOCK—Not stock in Washington, D.C., but common stock when it is the company's issued stock.

CARTEL—A rough bunch, or a group of producers or other businessmen who try to control sales, output, or prices for their mutual benefit, each one cutting the pie.

COMMERCIAL PAPER—Sometimes called "the third currency," after the green stuff and stocks and bonds, these are short-term unsecured notes issued by bankers or businesses with top financial ratings. In effect, they are IOUs issued and callable at specified dates.

COMMON STOCK—Common because it is so widespread, it is one of the stocks which represent the ownership in a corporation. Occasionally it is issued in several classes, but voting power mostly remains in only one class. Common stock takes a lesser priority than other securities in its claim to profits or payment.

CONVERTIBLE BOND—A bond that can be converted into or exchanged for stock, under certain conditions, most of the time of the same company or occasionally of affiliates.

CURRENT ASSETS—These are the assets on hand, or available on the date specified in the annual report, or which will be owned soon. What are they? Cash on hand or in the bank, short-term investments, accounts receivable and on-hand inventories of materials or products.

CURRENT LIABILITIES—Debts payable within a year. Mainly, these consist of debts of fixed repayment that fall due within the following year, sinking fund or amortization obligations on bank, short-term borrowings and debt and accounts payable.

DEBENTURE—An interest-bearing bond issued, most often without collateral, by a corporation.

DEPRECIATION—The income-tax payer's boon, it is an allowance given for wear or tear or obsolescence.

DISCOUNT RATE—An up or down proposition, this is the rate that member banks pay on loans from the Federal Reserve System. The interest rate is discounted in advance.

DISPOSABLE PERSONAL INCOME—The income, such as it is, which remains after personal tax deductions and non-tax payments to the government.

FLOOR TRADER—A stock-exchange member on the floor of the exchange who buys and sells for his own account, and also may be a broker.

FUNDED DEBT—Usually long-term debt, in the form of bonds, which is repaid according to a schedule.

GROSS NATIONAL PRODUCT (GNP)—The most frequently used measure of the economy's growth, the GNP represents the market value of goods and services produced by the economy.

HEDGING—Just what it means in everyday language, the offsetting of one type of risk for another.

ISSUE—A given block of securities, or a corporation's securities.

JUNIOR SECURITIES (or BONDS)—Those which hold a lesser priority on dividends or on property in case of a bankruptcy.

LEVERAGE—Using some asset or activity as a means of accomplishing another purpose.

LIEN—A claim against property, such as a mortgage, which can be taken over by the lien holder in the event of default.

MANIPULATION IN THE STOCK MARKET—Watch out for this practice of artificially influencing the market to yield misleading prices or quotations that are not set by normal supply and demand. The Securities Exchange Act of 1934 prohibits traders from circulating rumors or adopting tactics to create activity or the illusion of activity in a stock.

MARGIN—The important matter of money deposited with a stockbroker to protect trades already made or to be made. This also represents the difference between the market value of collateral and the amount that a bank will lend against the collateral.

NATIONAL BANK—A banking institution which operates under a government charter and is compelled to belong to the Federal Reserve System.

ODD LOTS—Not strange groups of people, but less than the usual unit of trading, which is considered to be 100 shares.

OVER-THE-COUNTER (STOCK MARKET)—A market which is outside the registered exchanges. OTC (as it is known) broker-dealers also can act as brokers, but mostly they act as principals, meaning that they buy or sell to the investor for their own accounts.

PARTNERSHIP—A company owned by two or more people who have legal responsibility for the liabilities of the business, unless it is a limited partnership with limited responsibility.

PREFERRED STOCK—Stock, usually of a nonvoting nature, which has priority over common shares to obtain a fixed dividend and has preference over common stock in the event of bankruptcy or liquidation.

REDISCOUNT RATE—This is the interest rate at which the Federal Reserve System lends to member banks.

SERIAL BONDS—Bonds payable in installments based on a series of fixed maturities. Used frequently in state and municipal financing, the bonds' serial-payment procedure allows a systematic reduction in the principal of the loan.

SHORTING THE MARKET—Another tricky business, in which an investor sells securities or commodities that he doesn't own so that he can buy them later at a lower price. As a stock-market investor, he must borrow stock to sell, while, if he is a commodity trader, he contracts to deliver at a future date.

SPECIALIST—A broker or broker member who may execute orders in stocks either for himself or for other brokers as an agent. He "maintains" a market in specific stocks assigned to him.

SPLITTING THE STOCK (STOCK SPLIT)—This is the interesting process of exchanging the number of outstanding shares of a corporation for a larger number of shares, but with a proportionate reduction of the par (or stated value) of the shares. The "reverse split" is just that—reducing the outstanding number of shares.

STOCK DIVIDEND—Ordinarily a means of conserving cash, this is the issuance of partial or whole shares of stock in payment of a dividend on the shares of the same or of some other class of stock. A stock split is also a stock dividend.

TENDERING or TENDERS—The submission of bids to purchase a security, or the process of delivering a commodity to be sold at a future time.

TREASURY STOCK—Stock that a corporation has issued but which it has repurchased and now holds in its "treasury."

WORKING CAPITAL—The state of current funds, obtained by subtracting current liabilities from current assets. A "working deficit" represents the excess of current liabilities over current assets.

THIS BOOK WAS SET IN

BASKERVILLE AND FORTUNE TYPES BY

MARYLAND LINOTYPE COMPOSITION CO.

IT WAS PRINTED BY

HALLIDAY LITHOGRAPH CORPORATION

AND BOUND BY THE HADDON CRAFTSMEN.

DESIGNED BY JOEL SCHICK

ILLUSTRATIONS BY RICHARD ROSENBLUM